COOPERATIVE
LEARNING

UNIVERSITY OF NEW HAVEN

W9-BBU-735

COOPERATIVE LEARNING
Theory, Research, and Practice

Robert E. Slavin

Center for Research on Elementary and Middle Schools
The Johns Hopkins University

UNIVERSITY OF NEW HAVEN

Prentice Hall, Englewood Cliffs, New Jersey 07632

Library of Congress Cataloging-in-Publication Data

SLAVIN, ROBERT E.
    Cooperative learning : theory, research, and practice / Robert E.
Slavin.
        p.   cm.
    Includes bibliographical references.
    ISBN 0-13-172594-7
    1. Group work in education.   2. Team learning approach in
education.   3. Group work in education—Evaluation.   I. Title.
LB1032.S543 1990
371.1′48—dc20   89-38793
                                                     CIP

Editorial/production supervision
   and interior design: Mary Anne Shahidi
Cover design: Amy Rosen
Manufacturing buyer: Peter Havens/Bob Anderson

 © 1990 by Prentice-Hall, Inc.
A Division of Simon & Schuster
Englewood Cliffs, New Jersey 07632

All rights reserved. No part of this book may be
reproduced, in any form or by any means,
without permission in writing from the publisher.

Printed in the United States of America
10 9 8 7 6 5 4 3 2

ISBN 0-13-172594-7

Prentice-Hall International (UK) Limited, *London*
Prentice-Hall of Australia Pty. Limited, *Sydney*
Prentice-Hall Canada, Inc., *Toronto*
Prentice-Hall Hispanoamericana, S.A., *Mexico*
Prentice-Hall of India Private Limited, *New Delhi*
Prentice-Hall of Japan, Inc., *Tokyo*
Simon & Schuster Asia Pte. Ltd., *Singapore*
Editora Prentice-Hall do Brasil, Ltda., *Rio de Janeiro*

For Nancy

Contents

Preface

Cooperative learning has always had a place in instructional methodology. Most teachers have at one time or another used discussion groups, project groups, lab groups, or peer tutoring. However, since the early 1970s there has developed a set of principles and methods intended for use over extended periods as major elements of classroom organization and instruction. Long a subject of brief laboratory experiments in psychology, cooperative learning has in the 1970s and 1980s been examined in longer-term classroom studies involving every major school subject and grade level. Evidence has mounted documenting the effectiveness of cooperative learning strategies for a wide array of outcomes, from enhanced achievement to improved intergroup relations and acceptance of mainstreamed classmates to self-esteem and positive attitudes toward school. As a result, use of cooperative learning methods has mushroomed in recent years at all levels of schooling. No one knows how many teachers currently make regular use of cooperative methods, but the numbers are certainly in the hundreds of thousands.

Cooperative learning is expanding not only in classroom use but also as an important topic in undergraduate and graduate education courses. This book is primarily intended for such courses. There are many books on research on cooperative learning, and many practical manuals for teachers. These are listed in the resource section of Chapter 8. Yet up to now there has been no one book that presents theory, research, and practical guides for cooperative learning in a form designed for use in education courses. This book is intended to fill this gap. It focuses on the ideas underlying the various approaches to cooperative learning, presents up-to-date reviews of research on practical applications of cooperative learning in elementary and secondary classrooms, and provides detailed guides to some of the most widely used and extensively researched methods.

One attraction of cooperative learning is that it lends itself so well to simulations. It is only logical to use cooperative learning methods to teach about cooperative learning. An *Instructor's Guide* available from Prentice-Hall presents suggestions and materials for teaching the content of this book using a variety of cooperative learning methods. Having students experience at least one of these simulations is extremely important; we remember far more about things we personally experience than about things we only hear or read about.

This book was written with the assistance of funding from the Office of Educational Research and Improvement, U.S. Department of Education (Grant No. OERI-G-86-0006). However, any opinions expressed are my own and do not necessarily reflect OERI positions or policy.

Lastly, I would like to thank the following reviewers for their helpful comments: Jean A. Trout, University of Northern Iowa; Susan Prescott, California State University-Dominguez Hills; and Joseph L. McCaleb, University of Maryland.

COOPERATIVE LEARNING

ONE

An Introduction to Cooperative Learning

"Class," said Ms. James, "who remembers what part of speech words such as 'it,' 'you,' and 'he' belong to?"

Twenty hands shoot up in Ms. James's fifth-grade class. Another ten students try to make themselves small in hopes that Ms. James won't call on them. She calls on Eddie.

"Proverb?"

The class laughs. Ms. James says, "No, that's not quite right." The students (other than Eddie, who is trying to sink into the floor in embarrassment) raise their hands again. Some of them are halfway out of their seats, calling "Me! Me!" in their eagerness. Finally, Ms. James calls on a student. "Elizabeth, can you help Eddie?"

Think about the scene being played out in Ms. James's class, a common sequence of events at every level of schooling, in every subject, in all sorts of schools. Whether or not she is conscious of it, Ms. James has set up a competition between the students. The students want to earn her approval, and they can do this only at the expense of their classmates. When Eddie fails, most of the class is glad: students who know the answer now have a second chance to show it, while others know that they are not alone in their ignorance. The most telling part of the vignette is when Ms. James asks if Elizabeth can "help" Eddie. Does Eddie perceive Elizabeth's correct answer as help? Does Elizabeth? Of course not.

What is wrong with the competitive situation Ms. James has established? If properly structured, competition can be a healthy, effective means of motivating individuals to perform. However, competition in the classroom is typically less positive. Consider what is going on below the surface in Ms. James's class. Most of the class is hoping that Eddie (and also Elizabeth) will fail. Their failure makes their classmates look good in comparison, and makes it easier for others to succeed. Because of this, students will eventually begin to express norms or values opposed to doing too well academically. Students who try too hard are "teacher's pets," "nerds," "grinds," and so on. Students are put in a bind: their teachers reward high achievement, but their peer group rewards mediocrity. As students enter adolescence, the peer group becomes all-important, and most students accept their peers' belief that doing more than what is needed to get by is for suckers.

Research clearly shows that academic success is not what gets students accepted by their peers, especially in middle and high school.

Typical classroom competition can be detrimental for another reason. Recall the ten students who tried to make themselves invisible when Ms. James asked her question. For most low achievers a competitive situation is a poor motivator; for some it is almost constant psychological torture. Students enter any class with widely divergent skills and knowledge. Low-achieving students may lack the prerequisites to learn new material. For example, students who never learned to subtract well may have difficulty learning long division. For this and other reasons, success is difficult for many students, but comes easily for others. Success is defined on a relative basis in the competitive classroom. Even if low achievers learn a great deal, they are still at the bottom of the class if their classmates learn even more. Day in, day out, low achievers get negative feedback on their academic efforts. After a while, they learn that academic success is not in their grasp, so they choose other avenues in which they may develop a positive self-image. Many of these avenues lead to antisocial, delinquent behavior.

How can teachers avoid the problems associated with classroom competition? How can students help one another learn and encourage one another to succeed academically?

Think back to Ms. James's class. What if Eddie and Elizabeth and two other students had been asked to work together as a team to learn parts of speech, and the teams were rewarded on the basis of the learning of all team members? Now the only way for Eddie and Elizabeth to succeed is if they make certain that they have learned the material and that their teammates have done so. Eddie and Elizabeth are now motivated to help and encourage each other to learn. Perhaps most important, they are rooting for each other to succeed, not to fail.

This is the essence of *cooperative learning* (Slavin, 1983a,b). In cooperative learning methods, students work together in four-member teams to master material initially presented by the teacher. For example, in a method called Student Teams–Achievement Divisions, or STAD (Slavin, 1986a), a teacher might present a lesson on map reading, then give students time to work with maps and to answer questions about them in their teams. The teams are heterogeneous—made up of high, average, and low achievers, boys and girls, and students of different ethnic groups. After having a chance to study in their teams, students take individual quizzes on map reading. The students' quiz scores are added up. All teams whose average scores meet a high criterion receive special recognition, such as fancy certificates or posting of their team picture in the classroom.

The idea behind this form of cooperative learning is that if students want to succeed as a team, they will encourage their teammates to excel and will help them to do so. Often, students can do an outstanding job of explaining difficult ideas to one another by translating the teacher's language into kid language.

Of course, cooperative learning methods are not new. Teachers have used them for many years in the form of laboratory groups, project groups, discussion groups, and so on. However, recent research in the United States and other countries has created systematic and practical cooperative learning methods intended for use as the main element of classroom organization, has documented the effects of these methods, and has applied them to the teaching of a broad range of curricula. These methods are now being used extensively in every conceivable subject, at grade levels from kindergarten through college, and in all kinds of schools throughout the world.

COOPERATIVE LEARNING METHODS

Social psychological research on cooperation dates back to the 1920s (see Slavin, 1977a), but research on specific applications of cooperative learning to the classroom did not begin until the early 1970s. At that time, four independent groups of researchers began to develop and research cooperative learning methods in classroom settings. At present, researchers all over the world are studying practical applications of cooperative learning principles, and many cooperative learning methods are available. Some of the most extensively researched and widely used cooperative learning methods are introduced in this chapter, and these and other methods are described in more detail later in this book.

Student Team Learning

Student Team Learning methods are cooperative learning techniques developed and researched at Johns Hopkins University. More than half of all studies of practical cooperative learning methods involve these methods.

All cooperative learning methods share the idea that students work together to learn and are responsible for their teammates' learning as well as their own. In addition to the idea of cooperative work, Student Team Learning methods emphasize the use of team goals and team success, which can be achieved only if all members of the team learn the objectives being taught. That is, in Student Team Learning the students' tasks are not to *do* something as a team but to *learn* something as a team.

Three concepts are central to all Student Team Learning methods—team rewards, individual accountability, and equal opportunities for success. Teams may earn certificates or other *team rewards* if they achieve above a designated criterion. Teams do not compete to earn scarce rewards; all (or none) of the teams may achieve the criterion in a given week. *Individual accountability* means that the team's success depends on the individual learning of all team members. Accountability focuses the activity of the team members on tutoring one another and making sure that everyone on the team is ready for a quiz or any other assessment that students take without teammate help. *Equal opportunities for success* means that students contribute to their teams by improving on their own past performance. This ensures that high, average, and low achievers are equally challenged to do their best, and that the contributions of all team members will be valued.

Research on cooperative learning methods (summarized in Chapter 2) has indicated that team rewards and individual accountability are essential for basic skills achievement (Slavin, 1983a,b, 1989). It is not enough to simply tell students to work together; they must have a reason to take one another's achievement seriously. Further, research indicates that if students are rewarded for doing better than they have in the past, they will be more motivated to achieve than if they are rewarded for doing better than others, because rewards for improvement make success neither too difficult nor too easy for students to achieve (Slavin, 1980a).

Four principal Student Team Learning methods have been extensively developed and researched. Two are general cooperative learning methods adaptable to most subjects and grade levels—Student Teams–Achievement Divisions, or STAD, and Teams–Games–Tournament, or TGT. The remaining two are comprehensive curricula designed for particular subjects in grades 3–6—Team Assisted Individualization (TAI)* for mathematics and Cooperative Integrated Reading and Composition (CIRC) for reading and writing. All four methods incorporate team rewards, individual accountability, and equal opportunities for success, but in different ways.

Student Teams–Achievement Divisions. As we have seen, in STAD (Slavin, 1978a, 1986a), students are assigned to four-member learning teams that are mixed in performance level, sex, and ethnicity. The teacher presents a lesson, and then students work within their teams to make sure that all team members have mastered the lesson. Finally, all students take individual quizzes on the material, at which time they may not help one another.

---

*TAI was originally developed and researched under the name Team Assisted Individualization (see Slavin, Leavey, and Madden, 1986), but is published under the name Team Accelerated Instruction.

Students' quiz scores are compared with their own past averages, and points are awarded based on the degree to which students meet or exceed their earlier performance. These points are then summed to form team scores, and teams that meet certain criteria may earn certificates or other rewards. The whole cycle of activities, from teacher presentation to team practice to quiz, usually takes three to five class periods.

STAD has been used in every imaginable subject, from mathematics to language arts to social studies, and from grade two through college. It is most appropriate for teaching well-defined objectives with single right answers, such as mathematical computations and applications, language usage and mechanics, geography and map skills, and science facts and concepts.

The main idea behind Student Teams–Achievement Divisions is to motivate students to encourage and help one another to master skills presented by the teacher. If students want their team to earn *team rewards,* they must help their teammates to learn the material. They must encourage their teammates to do their best, expressing norms that learning is important, valuable, and fun. Students work together after the teacher's lesson. They may work in pairs and compare answers, discuss any discrepancies, and help each other with any roadblocks. They may discuss approaches to solving problems, or they may quiz each other on the content they are studying. They teach their teammates and assess their strengths and weaknesses to help them succeed on the quizzes.

Although students study together, they may not help each other with quizzes. Every student must know the material. This *individual accountability* motivates students to do a good job tutoring and explaining to each other, as the only way for a team to succeed is if all team members have mastered the information or skills being taught. Because team scores are based on students' improvement over their own past records (*equal opportunities for success*), all students have the chance to be a team "star" in a given week, either by scoring well above their past record or by getting a perfect paper, which always produces a maximum score regardless of a student's past average. A detailed guide to the use of STAD appears in Chapter 4.

Teams–Games–Tournaments. TGT (DeVries and Slavin, 1978; Slavin, 1986a) was the first of the Johns Hopkins cooperative learning methods. It uses the same teacher presentations and teamwork that STAD does, but replaces the quizzes with weekly tournaments in which students compete with members of other teams to contribute points to their team scores. Students compete at three-person "tournament tables" against others with similar past records in mathematics. A "bumping" procedure, which consists of changing students' table assignments weekly based on their performance in each tournament, keeps the competition fair. The winner at each tournament table brings six points to his or her team, regardless of which table it is; this means that low achievers (competing with other low achievers) and high achievers (competing with other high achievers) have *equal opportunities for success.* As in STAD, high-performing teams earn certificates or other forms of *team rewards.*

TGT has many of the same dynamics as STAD, but adds a dimension of excitement contributed by the use of games. Teammates help one another prepare for the games by studying worksheets and explaining problems to one another. But when students are competing their teammates cannot help them, ensuring *individual accountability.* A detailed guide to TGT appears in Chapter 4.

Team Assisted Individualization. TAI (Slavin, Leavey, and Madden, 1986) shares with STAD and TGT the use of four-member mixed-ability learning teams and certificates for high-performing teams. But where STAD and TGT use a single pace of instruction for the class, TAI combines cooperative learning with individualized instruction. Also, where STAD and TGT apply to most subjects and grade levels, TAI is specifically designed to teach mathematics to students in grades 3–6 (or older students not ready for a full algebra course).

In TAI, students enter an individualized sequence according to a placement test and then proceed at their own rates. In general, team members work on different units. Teammates check each other's work against answer sheets and help one another with any problems. Final unit tests are taken without teammate help and are scored by student monitors. Each week, teachers total the number of units completed by all team members and give certificates or other *team rewards* to teams that exceed a criterion score based on the number of final tests passed, with extra points for perfect papers and completed homework.

Because students take responsibility for checking each other's work and managing the flow of materials, the teacher can spend most of the class time presenting lessons to small groups of students drawn from the various teams who are working at the same point in the mathematics sequence. For example, the teacher might call up a decimals group, present a lesson on decimals, and then send the students back to their teams to work on decimal problems. Then the teacher might call the fractions group, and so on.

TAI has many of the motivational dynamics of STAD and TGT. Students encourage and help one another to succeed because they want their teams to succeed. *Individual accountability* is assured because the only score that counts is the final test score, and students take final tests without teammate help. Students have *equal opportunities for success* because all have been placed according to their level of prior knowledge; it is as easy (or difficult) for a low achiever to complete three subtraction units in a week as it is for a higher-achieving classmate to complete three long-division units.

Unlike STAD and TGT, TAI depends on a specific set of instructional materials. These materials cover concepts from addition to pre-algebra. Although designed for use in grades 3–6, they have been used for primary instruction in grades 2–8 and as remedial instruction in secondary schools. The TAI materials include lesson guides that suggest methods of introducing specific mathematical concepts through demonstrations, manipulatives, and examples. The curricular emphasis in TAI is on rapid, firm conceptual mastery of algorithms and on applications of mathematical ideas to the solution of real-life problems. TAI is described further in Chapter 5.

Cooperative Integrated Reading and Composition. This newest of the Student Team Learning methods is a comprehensive program for teaching reading and writing in the upper elementary grades (Madden, Slavin, and Stevens, 1986; Stevens, Madden, Slavin, and Farnish, 1987). In CIRC, teachers use basal readers and reading groups, much as they would in traditional reading programs. Students are assigned to teams composed of pairs of students from different reading groups. While the teacher is working with one reading group, students in the other groups are working in their pairs on a series of cognitively engaging activities, including reading to each other, predicting how stories will end, summarizing stories to each other, writing responses to stories, and practicing spelling, decoding, and vocabulary. Students work in teams to understand the main idea and master other comprehension skills. During language arts periods, students write drafts, revise and edit one another's work, and prepare to "publish" team books.

In most CIRC activities, students follow a sequence of teacher instruction, team practice, team preassessments, and quiz. Students do not take the quiz until their teammates have determined that they are ready. *Team rewards* are certificates given to teams based on the average performance of all team members on all reading and writing activities. Because students work on materials appropriate to their reading levels, they have *equal opportunities for success*. Students' contributions to their teams are based on their quiz scores and their final independently written compositions, which ensures *individual accountability*. CIRC is described more fully in Chapter 5.

A Day in the Life of Sara Cooper

To see what goes on in Student Team Learning classes, let's follow a hypothetical student through a day as she experiences three of the Student Team Learning methods—STAD, CIRC, and TAI.

Sara Cooper is an average fifth grader at Hooperville Elementary School. The principal and teachers at Hooperville Elementary have decided to make cooperative learning the centerpiece of an effort to improve their school, so teachers throughout the school are using a variety of Student Team Learning methods. Sara's teacher, Ms. Jackson, has decided to use STAD to teach spelling, CIRC in reading and writing/language arts, and TAI in mathematics.

Sara is on the same team for all three Student Team Learning methods. Her team, the Masterminds, has four students—Sara, Luis, John, and Tamika. These students sit as a team, with their desks pulled together, throughout the day.

STAD. The first subject today is spelling. Yesterday Ms. Jackson taught the whole class a lesson on forming possessives. As today's period begins, the students in all the teams work together to practice the new skill. Ms. Jackson distributes worksheets and worksheet answers to the teams, and announces that students will have thirty minutes to study before taking a quiz.

The worksheets consist of thirty phrases, such as "the hair of the dog," which students are to restate using possessives ("the dog's hair"). Within the Masterminds team, Sara and Luis have decided to work as a pair, while John and Tamika work together.

The first item is "the book of the boy." Luis says, "That's easy. You just put an 'apostrophe s' after 'boy'. Sara agrees, and writes "the boy's book" on the worksheet. Luis checks the answer sheet, which is face down on his desk, and confirms that they were right.

Sara and Luis have a problem with the next item: "the horns of the cars." Sara starts, "Isn't that just 'the car's horns'?"

Luis thinks for a moment. "No, it's more than one car," he says. "It's plural, so you put the apostrophe after the 's.'"

"I guess you're right," says Sara. "So it would be 'the cars' horns.'" Luis writes the answer on the worksheet and Sara checks the answer sheet to confirm they were right.

The next item stumps both partners: "The toys of the children." Luis suggests that since *children* is plural, they should add *s'* to make *the childrens' toys.* But Sara recalls that Ms. Jackson warned them about plurals that do not end in *s.* They ask John and Tamika for help.

Tamika says, "We just got up to that one ourselves. Ms. Jackson said you add 'apostrophe s.'"

Luis still thinks he's right. "'Cars' was plural, so why should 'childrens' ' be any different?"

"Because the apostrophe always goes right after the main word," John explains. "Then you add an 's' if there isn't already one there. That's why it's got to be 'children's,' because the main word is 'children.'"

"I think you're right," admits Luis.

They check the answer sheet and see that *the children's toys* is correct.

Adapted from Slavin, 1986a.

Ms. Jackson, who has been listening in on the team's discussion, comes over to compliment the team on how well they are working together. "You're all doing a great job of explaining to each other," she says. "Keep it up, and you'll be a Superteam in spelling this week!"

At the end of thirty minutes, most of the teams have completed the worksheets and Ms. Jackson asks the students to stop work and move their desks apart. She then hands out a ten-item quiz, which the students do on their own. When everyone has finished, Ms. Jackson has students exchange papers with nonteammates, reads off the answers, and has students mark the papers and return them to their owners.

"Wow!" says Sara after the students have all passed their papers up to Ms. Jackson to be rechecked. "We all got nine or ten right. I'm sure we'll be a Superteam this week!"

CIRC. The next period is reading. Sara and Tamika are in one reading group, the Rockets, while John and Luis are in another, the Stars. The class is starting new stories in their basal readers. Ms. Jackson calls up the Stars for their reading group lesson. John and Luis take their chairs to the reading group area. Sara and Tamika stay at their desks; they have an Assignment Record Form, which tells them everything they need to do in their teams over the course of the week. While they are waiting for the Rockets to be called, they work together on vocabulary exercises relating to their new story. Meanwhile, Ms. Jackson is introducing the new story to the Stars—setting a purpose for reading, introducing new vocabulary words, and having students predict what the story might be about, based on the title, headings, vocabulary words, and pictures. When Ms. Jackson has completed the lesson, the Stars return to their team areas and the Rockets are called for their lesson.

When the students return to their teams, they read half of their story silently, and then read the same half aloud to their partners, alternating paragraphs. The students read in soft voices so only their partners can hear them. When students make errors, their partners give them the correct word.

After Ms. Jackson has seen all the reading groups, she circulates among the teams to listen to students read. She hasn't heard John for a while, so she spends some time listening to him reading with Luis, and praises both students for doing a good job of helping each other.

When they complete their reading of the first half of the stories, the partners work together on a Treasure Hunt activity. The "treasures" are the elements always present in a narrative—characters, setting, problems to be solved, and solutions to problems. The partners jointly identify the characters, settings, and problems, and then discuss how they think the problems will be resolved. Sara and Tamika have just read the first half of "The Emperor's New Clothes," by Hans Christian Andersen. They had no trouble identifying the main character (the Emperor) or the setting (his castle and the surrounding kingdom). However, they were puzzled by one of the Treasure Hunt questions: "What was it about the emperor that kept him from catching on to the weavers' trick?"

"I guess he didn't want anyone to know he wasn't fit to be the emperor," Tamika says.

"Yeah, but why didn't he just throw them out? He's the emperor!"

"I think you're right—we have to figure out why he believed the weavers in the first place," replies Tamika. "Let's look at the beginning of the story again to see what he was like."

"He spent all his time and money on clothes and didn't care about anything else," says Sara. "I'll bet he was so greedy and liked clothes so much that it was easy for the weavers to fool him."

"Especially when his minister said he could see the cloth," adds Tamika.

Sara and Tamika write their answers to the question and continue to the end of the first section of the Treasure Hunt. As always, the final question involves a prediction: "How do you think the story will turn out? Will the weavers get away with their trick or will the emperor catch on?"

"He won't catch on," states Sara. "He's too stuck-up and he's afraid people will think he's not fit to be emperor."

"But maybe someone's going to tell him he doesn't have clothes on," says Tamika.

"I don't think so," Sara replies. "Anyone who says they don't see the cloth could get into trouble."

"*Somebody* has to say something. Maybe it will be a kid or some weirdo who doesn't know he's not supposed to laugh."

Sara and Tamika agree to disagree about their predictions. Sara writes and justifies her prediction and Tamika does the same.

Tomorrow Ms. Jackson will discuss students' predictions and Treasure Hunts in the reading groups. Later in the week, the students will complete their reading and Treasure Hunts and then take tests on the story content, vocabulary words, and oral reading, and write a follow-up paragraph on some aspect of the story. Finally, they will receive a special reading comprehension lesson and practice reading comprehension skills in their teams. All of these activities will count toward their teams' success in reading, and teams that meet high criteria will earn certificates. The Masterminds usually earn Goodteam or Greatteam certificates, but this week they have resolved to put in extra effort to earn a Superteam certificate, the highest honor of all.

After reading comes writing/language arts period. The students are in the writer's workshop part of the program, in which they write on topics of their choice, revise and edit their compositions with the help of teammates and the teacher, and finally share their compositions with the class and publish them in team and/or class books. Today, Ms. Jackson begins with a ten-minute mini-lesson to the whole class on "*and* disease," the tendency many students have to write long, boring sentences linked by many *ands*. Following the mini-lesson, the students begin working on their compositions. Sara is just completing the first draft of a composition on the time her cat, Tinky, had kittens in a drawer. Her teammates are working on their own compositions, and are at various points in the plan–draft–revise–edit–publish sequence.

Early in the period, Sara finishes her draft. "Okay guys," she says to her teammates, "I'm ready to read my composition." She reads it through.

"I like it," says Luis when Sara finishes. "Especially the part when you couldn't find Tinky and you ran all over the house."

"I don't understand why you couldn't find Tinky," John frowns.

"Well," says Sara, "she was supposed to be in a special box with old clothes in it, but she wasn't there."

"You went to all this trouble to make a special place for Tinky to have her babies and then she goes and has them in a drawer!" says Tamika. "You should say something about that special place in your story."

"That's a good idea," says Sara. "I think I know just where to put it, too."

"You started the story with how you got Tinky at the animal shelter," says John. "But then the rest of the story is about having kittens. What's the animal shelter got to do with the rest of the story?"

"Hmm . . . not much, I guess. . ."

"Maybe you should tell us at the beginning that the story is about having kittens," says Luis.

"I know!" says Sara. "I'll start it with, 'The big day had come at last!' Then I can talk about how we got everything ready for Tinky to have kittens."

"Great idea!" says Tamika. "That would grab the reader's interest better!"

"Thanks, guys," says Sara. "I'll try this out and read you my next draft later."

While the Masterminds are helping Sara with her composition, Ms. Jackson is meeting with students on other teams to review their work and suggest changes. In some cases, when she sees a particular problem that is holding a student back, she explains skills or concepts. For example, John is writing a composition about a big, mean, ugly, one-eyed, hairy monster, but he is shaky about where to put commas in a series. Later in the period, Ms. Jackson will spend five minutes with John going over this skill in the context of his own composition. If Ms. Jackson sees several students with similar problems, she will make a note to devote a mini-lesson to that skill for the class as a whole.

TAI. After lunch and recess, it's time for TAI math. At the beginning of the period, Ms. Jackson announces who the monitors will be for the day. The students get out their Student Books and start working where they left off the previous day. Tamika is working on ratio and percent, Sara and Luis on decimals, and John on advanced fractions. When all students have started to work, Ms. Jackson calls up the advanced fractions group for a lesson; the rest of the students keep working in their team areas.

Sara is starting a unit on decimal inequalities. After reading a guide-page, which reviews the concepts Ms. Jackson presented the previous day to the decimals group, Sara tries the first four problems in Skill Practice 1:

1. .600 ? .006   2. .080 ? .08
3. .009 ? .09   4. .10 ? .010

Sara copies the problems on notebook paper, replacing the question mark with $=$, $<$, or $>$. Then she asks Tamika to check her work. Sara's book has the answers in the back, and she has the place marked with a bookmark. Tamika quickly checks Sara's answers and tells her they're all correct.

Sara moves to Skill Practice 2 and tries the first four problems:

1. .69 ? .70   2. .124 ? .012
3. 4.01 ? 4.10   4. .017 ? .160

Sara replaces the ? with $>$ or $<$. She has Tamika check her work. This time she missed problem 4.

"What's wrong?" Sara asks Tamika. "Seventeen is more than sixteen, so .017 is more than .160."

"Look at where the decimal point is," says Tamika. "Is seventeen thousandths more than one hundred sixty thousandths?"

"I guess not," Sara admits. "So I have to look at the decimal point first before I look at the numbers. I'll try it on the next four."

Sara works problems 5–8 in Skill Practice 2, and this time Tamika tells her they're all correct. Sara then passes Skill Practice 3 and goes on to the formative test. In the meantime, Ms. Jackson has finished her lesson to the advanced-fractions group and has called up Tamika's group (ratio and percent) for a lesson on time, rate, and distance problems using ratios. When Sara finishes her formative test, John checks it and signs at the bottom of her paper to indicate that she's ready for the unit test. Sara shows her signed paper to the student monitor, and he gives her the unit test, which she takes at a special testing table at the back of the class. When she finishes, she returns the test to the monitor and he checks it against an answer book. "Congratulations!" he says. "You got fourteen out of fifteen right. Go put your score up on your team summary sheet!"

Sara does so, and sees that her team is making good progress and might make Superteam in math by the end of the week. She goes back to the Masterminds to tell them the good news.

At the end of the day, Sara reflects on how much fun school has become since Hooperville Elementary began using Student Team Learning. "We still get to learn from the teacher, but we also get to learn from each other," she thinks. "I sure am glad Ms. Jackson lets us work in teams!"

Other Cooperative Learning Methods

Jigsaw. Jigsaw was designed by Elliott Aronson and his colleagues (1978). Students are assigned to six-member teams to work on academic material that has been broken down into sections. For example, a biography might be divided into early life, first accomplishments, major setbacks, later life, and impact on history. Each team member reads his or her section. Next, members of different teams who have studied the same sections meet in "expert groups" to discuss their sections. Then the students return to their teams and take turns teaching their teammates about their sections. Since the only way students can learn sections other than their own is to listen carefully to their teammates, they are motivated to support and show interest in one another's work.

A modification of Jigsaw has been developed at Johns Hopkins University as part of the Student Team Learning program; it is called Jigsaw II (Slavin, 1986a). In this method, students work in four- or five-member teams, as in TGT and STAD. Instead of each student being assigned a separate section, all students read a common narrative, such as a book chapter, a short story, or a biography. Each student receives a topic on which to become an expert. Students with the same topics meet in expert groups to discuss them, then return to their teams to teach what they have learned to their teammates. Then students take individual quizzes, which result in team scores based on the improvement-score system of STAD. Teams that meet preset standards may earn certificates. Detailed descriptions of Jigsaw, Jigsaw II, and other Jigsaw variations appear in Chapter 6.

Group Investigation. Group Investigation, developed by Shlomo Sharan at the University of Tel-Aviv, is a general classroom-organization plan in which students work in small groups using cooperative inquiry, group discussion, and cooperative planning and projects (Sharan and Sharan, 1976). In this method, students form their own two-to-six-member groups. The groups choose topics from a unit being studied by the entire class, break these topics into individual tasks, and carry out the activities necessary to prepare group reports. Each group then presents or displays its findings to the entire class. Group Investigation and a similar method, Co-op Co-op, are described further in Chapter 6.

Learning Together. David and Roger Johnson at the University of Minnesota developed the Learning Together model of cooperative learning (Johnson and Johnson,

Table 1–1 Typology of Major Cooperative Learning Methods

Method	Group Goals	Individual Accountability	Equal Opportunities for Success	Team Competition	Task Specialization	Adaptation to Individuals
Student Team Learning Methods						
Student Teams–Achievement Divisions	yes	yes	yes (improvement points)	sometimes	no	no
Teams–Games–Tournament	yes	yes	yes (tournament system)	yes	no	no
Team Assisted Individualization	yes	yes	yes (individualized)	no	no	yes
Cooperative Integrated Reading and Composition	yes	yes	yes (by subgroup)	no	no	yes
Learning Together	yes	sometimes	no	no	no	no
Jigsaw	no	yes (task specialization)	no	no	yes	no
Jigsaw II	yes	yes (task specialization)	yes (improvement points)	no	yes	no
Group Investigation	no	yes (task specialization)	no	no	yes	no
Traditional Group Work	no	no	no	no	no	no

1986). The methods they have researched involve students working in four- or five-member heterogeneous groups on assignment sheets. The groups hand in a single sheet, and receive praise and rewards based on the group product. For more on these methods, see Chapter 7.

A TYPOLOGY OF COOPERATIVE LEARNING

Cooperative learning methods differ in many ways, but they can be categorized according to the following six principal characteristics. Table 1–1 summarizes the characteristics of the most widely researched methods plus traditional group-work methods.

1. *Group Goals.* Most cooperative learning methods use some form of group goals. In the Student Team Learning methods, these may be certificates or other recognition given to teams that meet a preset criterion; in the Johnsons' methods, group grades are often given.

2. *Individual Accountability.* This is achieved in two ways. One is to have group scores be the sum or average of individual quiz scores or other assessments, as in the Student Team Learning models. The other is task specialization, whereby each student is given a unique responsibility for part of the group task (see below).

3. *Equal Opportunities for Success.* A characteristic unique to the Student Team Learning methods is the use of scoring methods that ensure all students an equal opportunity to contribute to their teams. These methods consist of improvement points (STAD), competition with equals (TGT), or adaptation of tasks to individual performance levels (TAI and CIRC).

4. *Team Competition.* Early studies of STAD and TGT used competition between teams as a means of motivating students to cooperate within teams.

5. *Task Specialization.* A key element of Jigsaw, Group Investigation, and other task-specialization methods is the assignment of a unique subtask to each group member.

6. *Adaptation to Individual Needs.* Most cooperative learning methods use group-paced instruction, but two—TAI and CIRC—adapt instruction to students' individual needs.

The following chapters present theories and research linking each of these characteristics to student achievement and other outcomes.

TWO

Cooperative Learning and Student Achievement

The principal reason that schools are built is to provide students with the knowledge, concepts, skills, and understandings needed for survival in our society. The most important outcome of cooperative learning, and the one that has been most extensively researched, is enhanced achievement. If properly structured, cooperative learning methods can significantly accelerate the learning of all children. This chapter reviews research on the achievement effects of applications of cooperative learning in elementary and secondary schools.

WHAT MAKES GROUP WORK WORK?

Why should students who work in cooperative groups learn more than those in traditionally organized classes? Researchers investigating this question have suggested a wide range of theoretical models to explain the superiority of cooperative learning (see Slavin, in press). The theories fall into two major categories, *motivational* and *cognitive*.

Motivational Theories

Motivational perspectives on cooperative learning focus primarily on the reward or goal structures under which students operate (see Slavin, 1977a, 1983a). Deutsch (1949) identified three goal structures: cooperative, where each individual's goal-oriented efforts contribute to others' goal attainment; competitive, where each individual's goal-oriented efforts frustrate others' goal attainment; and individualistic, where individuals' goal-oriented efforts have no consequences for others' goal attainment. From a motivational perspective (such as those of Johnson et al., 1981, and Slavin, 1983a), cooperative goal structures create a situation in which the only way group members can attain their own personal goals is if the group is successful. Therefore, to meet their personal goals, group

This chapter is adapted from Slavin, 1989.

members must help their group mates to do whatever helps the group to succeed, and, perhaps more important, encourage their group mates to exert maximum effort. In other words, rewarding groups based on group performance (or the sum of individual performances) creates an interpersonal reward structure in which group members will give or withhold social reinforcers (such as praise and encouragement) in response to groupmates' task-related efforts (see Slavin, 1983a).

The critique of traditional classroom organization made by motivational theorists is that the competitive grading and informal reward system of the classroom create peer norms that oppose academic efforts (see Coleman, 1961). Since one student's success decreases the chances that others will succeed, students are likely to express norms that high achievement is for "nerds" or teachers' pets. Such work-restriction norms are familiar in industry, where the "rate buster" is scorned by fellow workers (Vroom, 1969). But when students work together toward a common goal, as they do when a cooperative reward structure is in place, their learning efforts help their groupmates succeed. Students therefore encourage one another's learning, reinforce one another's academic efforts, and express norms favoring academic achievement.

Several studies have found that when students work together to accomplish a group goal, they come to express norms in favor of doing whatever is necessary for the group to succeed (Deutsch, 1949; Thomas, 1957). In a cooperative classroom, a student who tries hard, attends class regularly, and helps others to learn is praised and encouraged by groupmates, much in contrast with the situation in a traditional class. For example, Hulten and DeVries (1976), Madden and Slavin (1983a), and Slavin (1978b) all found that students in cooperative learning classes felt that their classmates wanted them to learn. In cooperative groups, learning becomes an activity that gets students ahead in their peer group. Slavin (1975) and Slavin, DeVries, and Hulten (1975) found that students in cooperative groups who gained in achievement improved their social status in the classroom, whereas in traditional classes such students lost status. These changes in the social consequences of academic success can be very important. Coleman (1961) found that bright students in high schools in which academic achievement helped a student to be accepted by the "leading crowd" turned their efforts more toward learning than bright students in schools in which athletic or social achievement was considered more important. And Brookover, Beady, Flood, Schweitzer, and Wisenbaker (1979) found that students' support for academic goals was the most important predictor of their achievement (controlling for ability and social class).

Clearly, cooperative goals create proacademic norms among students, and proacademic norms have important effects on student achievement.

Cognitive Theories

Whereas motivational theories of cooperative learning emphasize the degree to which cooperative goals change students' incentives to do academic work, cognitive theories emphasize the effects of working together in itself (whether or not the groups are trying to achieve a group goal). There are several different cognitive theories, which fall into two major categories: developmental theories and cognitive elaboration theories.

Developmental Theories. The fundamental assumption of the developmental theories is that interaction among children around appropriate tasks increases their mastery of critical concepts (Damon, 1984; Murray, 1982). Vygotsky (1978, p. 86) defines the zone of proximal development as "the distance between the actual developmental level as determined by independent problem solving and the level of potential development as determined through problem solving under adult guidance *or in collaboration with more capable peers*" (emphasis added). In his view, collaborative activity among children promotes growth because children of similar ages are likely to be operating within one another's proximal zones of development, modeling in the collaborating group behaviors more advanced than those they could perform as individuals. Vygotsky (1978, p. 47) describes the influence of collaborative activity on learning as follows: ''Functions are first formed in the collective in the form of relations among children and then become mental functions for the individual. . . . Research shows that reflection is spawned from argument.''

Similarly, Piaget (1926) held that social-arbitrary knowledge—language, values, rules, morality, and symbol systems (such as reading and math)—can be learned only in interactions with others. Research in the Piagetian tradition has focused on *conservation*, the ability to recognize that certain characteristics of objects remain the same when others change. For example, a child who has not yet learned the conservation principle will watch an experimenter pour a liquid from a wide jar into a tall, narrow one and say that the tall jar contains more liquid, or will believe that a ball of clay has a different weight when it is flattened. Most children attain the principal of conservation between the ages of five and seven.

There is a great deal of support for the idea that peer interaction can help nonconservers become conservers. Many studies have shown that when conservers and nonconservers of about the same age work collaboratively on tasks requiring conservation, the nonconservers generally develop and maintain conservation concepts (Bell, Grossen, and Perret-Clermont, 1985; Murray, 1982; Perret-Clermont, 1980). In fact, a few studies (for example, Ames and Murray, 1982; Mugny and Doise, 1978) have found that *both* members of pairs of disagreeing nonconservers who had to come to consensus on conservation problems gained in conservation. The importance of peers operating in one another's proximal zones of development was demonstrated by Kuhn (1972), who found that a small difference in cognitive level between a child and a social model was more conducive to cognitive growth than a larger difference.

On the basis of these and other findings, many Piagetians (such as Damon, 1984; Murray, 1982; Wadsworth, 1984) have called for an increased use of cooperative ac-

---

TEACHERS ON TEACHING

Research shows that the success of cooperative learning methods depends on the degree to which students give one another elaborated explanations of critical concepts. How do you help students to give one another complete explanations rather than just sharing answers?

The best way to teach students to give complete explanations rather than just sharing answers is to be a model for this behavior yourself. I tell my students over and over again that teachers, good ones, lead their students to discover the answers for themselves. Good teachers have countless ways to explain a skill. If one approach doesn't work, then a teacher simply chooses another way to explain how to find the answer. My students all know that they need to ask for further explanations when they are confused. They know that their teacher is willing and eager to reexplain.

When the students get into their STAD groups, they are taught the importance of giving complete explanations, of "leading" their members to the answers. They are told to use the same methods that their teacher uses with them (model the teacher). The students know how vital it is for the student to understand how to discover the answer. The students get where they don't ask for the answers (they have the answers available anytime they choose to look at them). They ask *why* such and such is the answer.

Jacquie Alberti,
Language Arts Teacher
Norman C. Toole Middle School
N. Charleston, SC

tivities in schools. They argue that interaction among students on learning tasks will lead *in itself* to improved student achievement. Students will learn from one another because in their discussions of the content, cognitive conflicts will arise, inadequate reasoning will be exposed, and higher-quality understandings will emerge.

Cognitive Elaboration Theories. What we might call the cognitive elaboration perspective is quite different from the developmental viewpoint. Research in cognitive psychology has found that if information is to be retained in memory and related to information already in memory, the learner must engage in some sort of cognitive restructuring, or elaboration, of the material (Wittrock, 1978). For example, writing a summary or outline of a lecture is a better study aid than simply taking notes, because the summary or outline requires the student to reorganize the material and sort out what is important in it (Brown, Bransford, Ferrara, and Campione, 1983; Hidi and Anderson, 1986).

One of the most effective means of elaboration is explaining the material to someone else. Research on peer tutoring has long found achievement benefits for the tutor as well as the tutee (Devin-Sheehan, Feldman, and Allen, 1976). More recently, Donald Dansereau and his colleagues have found in a series of studies that college students working on structured ''cooperative scripts'' can learn technical material or procedures far better than can students working alone (Dansereau, 1985). In this method, students take roles as recaller and listener. They read a section of text, and then the recaller summarizes the information while the listener corrects any errors, fills in any omitted material, and thinks of ways both students can remember the main ideas. On the next section, the students switch roles. Dansereau (1988) has found that while both recaller and listener learned more than did students working alone, the recaller learned more. This mirrors both the peer-tutoring findings and the findings of Noreen Webb (1985), who discovered that the students who gained the most from cooperative activities were those who provided elaborated explanations to others. In this research as well as in Dansereau's, students who received elaborated explanations learned more than those who worked alone, but not as much as those who served as explainers.

Pitfall of Cooperative Learning

While both the motivational and the cognitive theories support the achievement benefits of cooperative learning, there is one important pitfall that must be avoided if cooperative learning is to be instructionally effective. If not properly constructed, cooperative learning methods can allow for the ''free-rider'' effect, in which some group members do all or most of the work (and learning) while others go along for the ride. The free-rider effect is most likely to occur when the group has a single task, as when they are asked to hand in a single report, complete a single worksheet, or produce one project. Such assignments can also create a situation in which students who are perceived to be less skillful are ignored by other group members. For example, if a group's assignment is to solve a complex math problem, the ideas or contributions of students believed to be poor at math could be ignored or brushed off, and there is little incentive for the more active participants in the problem-solving activity to take time to explain what they are doing to the less active group members.

This problem, which we might call ''diffusion of responsibility'' (Slavin, 1983a), can be detrimental to the achievement effects of cooperative learning. Diffusion of responsibility can be eliminated in cooperative learning in two principal ways. One is to make each group member responsible for a unique part of the group's task, as in Jigsaw, Group Investigation, and related methods. The danger of task specialization, however, is that students may learn a great deal about the portion of the task they worked on themselves but not about the rest of the content.

The second means of eliminating diffusion of responsibility is to have students be individually accountable for their learning. For example, in the Student Team Learning methods (Slavin, 1986a), groups are rewarded based on the sum of their members' individual quiz scores or other individual performances. In this way, the group's task is to make sure that everyone has learned the content. No one can be a free rider, and it would be foolish for a group to ignore any of its members.

CLASSROOM RESEARCH ON THE ACHIEVEMENT EFFECTS OF COOPERATIVE LEARNING

There is a strong theoretical basis for predicting that cooperative learning methods that use group goals and individual accountability will increase student achievement. Even so, it is critical that cooperative methods be assessed in actual classrooms over realistic time periods to determine if they have an impact on measures of school achievement. Fortunately, cooperative learning is one of the most extensively evaluated of all instructional innovations. The remainder of this chapter reviews the research on practical applications of cooperative learning methods in elementary and secondary schools.

Review Methods

This research review uses an abbreviated form of best-evidence synthesis (Slavin, 1986b). The literature-search procedures, statistical methods, and study-inclusion criteria are essentially identical to those used in an earlier review of research on group-based mastery learning (Slavin, 1987a). The study-inclusion criteria were slightly adapted to the characteristics of the cooperative learning literature. They were as follows.

Germaneness Criteria

To be included in this review, studies had to evaluate forms of cooperative learning in which small groups of elementary or secondary students worked together to learn. Studies of peer tutoring, in which one student teaches another, were excluded.

Methodological Criteria

1. Studies had to compare cooperative learning with control groups studying the same material. This excluded a few studies that used time-series designs (for instance, Lew, Mesch, Johnson, and Johnson, 1986; Hamblin, Hathaway, and Wodarski, 1971), and a few comparisons within studies in which control groups were not studying the same materials as experimental groups (for example, Vedder, 1985). In a few studies (such as Johnson, Johnson, and Scott, 1978), cooperative learning students could help one another on the test used as the outcome measure while individualistic or competitive students could not. Comparisons involving these ''congruent tests'' or ''daily achievement'' were excluded (see Slavin, 1984a, for more on this).

    2. Evidence had to be given that experimental and control groups were initially equivalent. Studies had to either use random assignment of students to conditions or present evidence that classes were initially within 50 percent of a standard deviation of one another and used statistical controls for pretest differences. This excluded a few studies with large pretest differences (Ziegler, 1981; Okebukola, 1986c; Oishi, Slavin, and Madden, 1983).

    3. Study duration had to be at least four weeks (twenty hours). This caused by far the largest number of exclusions. For example, of seventeen achievement studies that used control groups at the elementary or secondary level cited by Johnson and Johnson (1985) in a review of their own work, only one (just barely) met the four-week requirement. The median duration of all seventeen studies was ten days. Such brief studies are useful for theory building, but are too short to serve as evidence of the likely achievement

effects of cooperative learning as a principal mode of classroom instruction. Studies of such limited duration are often also quite artificial; in the case of the Johnsons' studies, none of the treatment groups received any instruction. This means that in the cooperative groups, students at least had a chance to receive explanations from groupmates, while students in the individualistic and competitive control groups were left to try to figure out worksheets on their own with limited teacher assistance.

4. Achievement measures had to assess objectives taught in experimental as well as control classes. If experimental and control classes were not studying precisely the same materials, then standardized tests had to be used to assess objectives pursued by all classes.

Computation of Effect Sizes and Medians

This research review uses effect size as the measure of the impact of cooperative learning on student achievement. An *effect size* is the proportion of a standard deviation by which an experimental group exceeds a control group (see Glass, McGaw, and Smith, 1981). An effect size of +1.0, for example, would be the equivalent of an experimental-control difference of 100 points on the SAT Verbal or Quantitative scales, two stanines, or fifteen IQ points. With the exception of one-to-one tutoring, few educational interventions produce effect sizes this large; effect sizes of +.25 are generally considered educationally significant. Effect sizes provide a convenient measure of program impact, but for any given study they should be interpreted cautiously, for they can be greatly influenced by study characteristics.

Summary of Research

Research on the achievement effects of cooperative learning methods is summarized in Tables 2–1 to 2–7. A total of sixty studies met the inclusion requirements. Since studies that compared multiple cooperative learning methods are listed more than once, the tables list sixty-eight comparisons of cooperative learning and control methods. Effect sizes could be computed for fifty-one of the comparisons. Effects in the remaining seventeen are characterized in the tables as significantly positive (+), no significant differences (0), or significantly negative (−).

Overall, the effects of cooperative learning on achievement are clearly positive: forty-nine of the sixty-eight comparisons were positive (72 percent); only eight (12 percent) favored control groups. However, a look across Tables 2–1 to 2–7 also reveals that the different cooperative learning methods vary widely in achievement effects.

Table 2–8 summarizes the outcomes of cooperative learning studies according to several criteria. The first column lists the percentage of effect sizes in each category of studies above the overall median of +.195. For this column, studies coded as (+) were counted as above the median and those coded as (0) or (−) were counted as below the median. The second column lists the percentage of studies falling at or above the median (+.21) when only studies from which effect sizes could be computed are included. The third column lists the median effect size for these studies, and the median effect sizes on standardized achievement measures are listed in the fourth column.

Table 2–8 shows that the methods that emphasize group goals and individual accountability, in particular the Student Team Learning methods (STAD, TGT, TAI, and CIRC), are consistently more effective for increasing student achievement than are other forms of cooperative learning. Comparisons within several studies generally support the same differences. In two studies done in Nigeria, Peter Okebukola compared alternative forms of cooperative learning in secondary science classes. In one (Okebukola, 1986a) a form of STAD was found to be significantly more effective than the Johnsons' Learning Together methods (ES = +1.28). In another, TGT, STAD, Jigsaw, and Learning Together were compared with individual competition and control treatments (Okebukola,

Table 2–1 Student Teams–Achievement Division

Article	Grades	Location	Sample Size	Duration (weeks)	Design	Subjects	Effect Size by Subgroup/Measure	ES Standardized	ES Total
Slavin (1980c)	4	Hagerstown, MD	424	12	STAD classes compared with matched controls.	Language Arts	Hoyum-Sanders	+.18	+.18
Madden and Slavin (1983b)	3,4,6	Baltimore, MD	183	7	Teachers taught 1 STAD, 1 focused-instruction class, randomly assigned.	Math	Nonhandicapped +.12 Handicapped +.18	+.13	+.13
Slavin and Karweit (1981)	4–5	Hagerstown, MD	486 (17 classes)	16	Cooperative learning classes used STAD in language arts, TGT in math, Jigsaw in social studies. Compared with matched controls.	Language Arts	CTBS Language Mechanics +.12 CTBS Language Expression +.12	+.12	+.12
Stevens, Slavin, Farnish, and Madden (1988)	3–4	Harrisburg, PA	30 classes	4	Classes randomly assigned to STAD, control.	Reading Comprehension	Main Ideas +.24 Inferences +.11	+.18	+.18
Slavin (1978b)	7	Frederick, MD	205 (8 classes)	10	Teachers taught 1 STAD, 1 focused-instruction class, randomly assigned.	Language Arts		(0)	(0)
Slavin (1977c)	7	Baltimore, MD	62 (2 classes)	10	Teachers taught 1 STAD, 1 focused-instruction class, randomly assigned.	Language Arts	Blacks + Whites 0 Hoyum-Sanders +.76 Experimenter-Made Test +.36	+.76	+.56
Slavin (1979)	7–8	Baltimore, MD	424	12	Teachers taught 1 STAD, 1 focused-instruction class, randomly assigned.	Language Arts	Hoyum-Sanders	(0)	(0)
Slavin and Oickle (1981)	6–8	Rural MD	230	12	Teachers taught 1 STAD, 1 focused-instruction class, randomly assigned.	Language Arts	Hoyum-Sanders: Blacks +.72 Whites +.14	+.33	+.33
Slavin and Karweit (1984)	9	Philadelphia, Low ach.	588	30	Teachers randomly assigned to STAD, mastery learning, combined and control.	General Math	CTBS: STAD vs. control +.19 STAD + ML vs. control +.23	+.21	+.21
Tomblin and Davis (1985)	4–6	San Diego, CA	509 (8 classes)	8	Classes randomly assigned to STAD, untreated control.	Spelling		+.07	+.07
Frantz (1979)	4–5	Rural VA	48	6	Classes randomly assigned to STAD, control.	Reading		+.27	+.27

(continued)

Table 2–1 Student Teams–Achievement Division (Continued)

Article	Grades	Location	Sample Size	Duration (weeks)	Design	Subjects	Effect Size by Subgroup/Measure	ES Standardized	ES Total
Kagan, Zahn, Widaman, Schwarzwald, and Tyrell (1985)	2–6	Riverside, CA	600 (25 classes)	6	Student teachers randomly assigned to STAD, TGT, untreated control.	Spelling			(0)
Perrault (1982): Study 1	7	Suburban MD	88 (4 classes)	6	Teacher taught 2 STAD, 2 control classes, randomly assigned.	Drafting	Achievement Test +.28 Drawing +.81		+.55
Study 2	7	Suburban MD	48 (4 classes)	6	Teacher taught 2 STAD, 2 control classes, randomly assigned.	Drafting	Achievement Test +.53 Drawing (0)		+.26
Sherman and Thomas (1986)	10	Ohio	38 (2 classes)	5	Classes randomly assigned to STAD, individualistic.	General Math			+1.20
Allen and Van Sickle (1984)	9	Rural GA	51 (2 classes)	6	Teacher taught 1 STAD, 1 control class, randomly assigned.	Geography			+.94
Sharan et al. (1984)	7	Israel	Eng: 470 Lit: 538	16	Teachers randomly assigned to STAD, Group Investigation, or control.	English as a second language English literature	+.14 −.08		+.03
Mevarech (1985a)	5	Israel	134	15	Students randomly assigned to STAD, ML, combined, and control.	Math	STAD vs. control +.19 STAD + ML vs. control +.28		+.24
Mevarech (1985b)	9	Israel	113	18	Students randomly assigned to combination of STAD and mastery learning or to mastery learning.	Consumer Math			+1.04
Okebukola (1985)	8	Nigeria	358	6	Student teachers randomly assigned to STAD, TGT, Jigsaw, LT, competitive, or control.	Science	STAD vs. control +2.52 STAD vs. competitive +1.79		+2.15
Okebukola (1986a)	7	Nigeria	99	24	Students randomly assigned to STAD, LT, competitive, control, all taught by same teacher.	Science	STAD vs. control +5.14 STAD vs competitive +2.72		+3.93

From Slavin, 1989.

Key: (+) Significant effect favoring cooperative learning.
(0) No significant difference.

Table 2–2 Team–Games–Tournament

Article	Grades	Location	Sample Size	Duration (weeks)	Design	Subjects	Effect Size by Subgroup/Measure	ES Standardized	ES Total
DeVries and Mescon (1975)	3	Syracuse, NY	60 (2 classes)	6	Students randomly assigned to TGT or control classes.	Language Arts	Hoyum-Sanders +.19 Experimenter-made test +.57	+.19	+.38
DeVries, Mescon, and Shackman (1975a)	3	Syracuse, NY	53 (2 classes)	5	Students randomly assigned to TGT or control classes.	Verbal Analogies	Gates-McGinitie +.60 Experimenter-made tests +.85	+.60	+.73
DeVries, Mescon, and Shackman (1975b)	3	Syracuse, NY	54 (2 classes)	6	Students randomly assigned to TGT or control classes.	Language Arts	Hoyum-Sanders +.64 Experimenter-made tests +.80	+.64	+.72
Edwards, DeVries, and Snyder (1972)	7	Baltimore, MD	96 (4 classes)	9	Classes randomly assigned to TGT or control all taught by same teacher.	Math	Stanford: +.50 GE Experimenter-made tests: (+)	(+)	(+)
Edwards and DeVries (1972)	7	Baltimore, MD	117 (4 classes)	4	Students randomly assigned to TGT or control classes.	Math			(0)
Edwards and DeVries (1974)	7	Baltimore, MD	128 (4 classes)	12	Students randomly assigned to TGT or control classes.	Math (+) Social Studies (0)			(+)
DeVries, Edwards, and Wells (1974)	10–12	Suburban FL	191 (6 classes)	12	Classes randomly assigned to TGT, control.	American History			+.29

(continued)

Table 2-2 Team–Games–Tournament (Continued)

Article	Grades	Location	Sample Size	Duration (weeks)	Design	Subjects	Effect Size by Subgroup/Measure	ES Standardized	ES Total
Hulten and DeVries (1976)	7	Suburban MD	299	10	Classes randomly assigned to TGT, control.	Math	Stanford	+.33	+.33
DeVries, Lucasse, and Shackman (1980)	7–8	Grand Rapids, MI	1742	10	Teachers randomly assigned to TGT or individualized instruction.	Language Arts	Hoyum-Sanders (0) Experimenter-made tests (+)	(0)	(+)
Slavin and Karweit (1981)	4–5	Hagerstown, MD	465 (17 classes)	16	Coop learning classes used TGT in math, STAD in language arts, Jigsaw in social studies. Compared with matched controls.	Math	CTBS: Math computations .00 Math concepts .10	–.05	–.05
Kagan, Zahn, Widaman, Schwarzwald, and Tyrell (1985)	2–6	Riverside, CA	600 (25 classes)	6	Student teachers randomly assigned to STAD, TGT, or control.	Spelling			(0)
Okebukola (1985)	8	Nigeria	359	6	Student teachers randomly assigned to TGT, STAD, Jigsaw, LT, competitive, or control.	Science	TGT vs. control +2.41 TGT vs. competitive +1.69	+2.05	+2.05

From Slavin, 1989.
Key: (+) Significant effect favoring cooperative learning.
(0) No significant difference.

Table 2–3 Team Assisted Individualization and Cooperative Integrated Reading and Composition

Article	Grades	Location	Sample Size	Duration (weeks)	Design	Subjects	Effect Size by Submeasure/Measure	ES Standardized	ES Total
Team Assisted Individualization									
Slavin, Leavey, and Madden (1984):									
Study 1	3–5	Suburban MD	506	8	Schools randomly assigned to TAI, control.	Math	CTBS Computations	+.09	+.09
Study 2	4–6	Suburban MD	320	10	TAI classes compared with matched control.	Math	CTBS Computations	+.11	+.11
Slavin, Madden, and Leavey (1984):									
Experiment 1	3–5	Suburban MD	1371	24	TAI classes compared with matched control.	Math	CTBS Computations +.18 CTBS Concepts +.10	+.14	+.14
	4–6	Wilmington, DE	212	18	Classes randomly assigned to TAI, control.	Math	CTBS Computations +.77 CTBS Concepts .00	+.39	+.39
Experiment 2	3–5	Hagerstown, MD	220	16	Classes randomly assigned to TAI, control.	Math	CTBS Computations +.58 CTBS Concepts +.04	+.31	+.31
Cooperative Integrated Reading and Composition									
Stevens, Madden, Slavin, and Farnish (1987):									
Study 1	3–4	Suburban MD	461	12	CIRC classes matched with control.	Reading	CAT Reading Comprehension +.19 CAT Reading Vocabulary +.18	+.20	+.21
						Language	CAT Language Expression +.24 CAT Language Mechanics +.12		
						Spelling	CAT Spelling +.29		
						Writing	Writing Samples +.25		
Study 2	3–4	Suburban MD	450	24	CIRC classes matched with control.	Reading	CAT Reading Comprehension +.35 CAT Reading Vocabulary +.12 Durrell IRI's +.60	+.33	+.32
						Language	CAT Language Expression +.29 CAT Language Mechanics +.30		
						Writing	Writing Samples +.23		

From Slavin, 1989.

23

Table 2–4 Learning Together (Johnsons' Methods)

Article	Grades	Location	Sample Size	Duration (weeks)	Design	Subjects	Effect Size by Subgroup/Measure	ES Total
Learning Together Models Lacking Individual Accountability								
Johnson, Johnson, and Scott (1978)	5–6	Minnesota, High ach.	30	10	Students randomly assigned to LT or individual instruction.	Math	Posttests −7.1 Retention −.81 (2 months)	−.71
Johnson, Johnson, Scott, and Ramolae (1985)	5–6	Suburban MN	154	4	Students randomly assigned to LT or individualistic. No teacher instruction.	Science		.00
Robertson (1982)	2–3	Suburban NJ	166	6	Teachers randomly assigned to LT, individualistic/competitive, control.	Math	LT vs. individualistic/competitive −.02 LT vs. control +.16	+.07
Okebukola (1985)	8	Nigeria	356	6	Student teachers randomly assigned to LT, STAD, TGT, Jigsaw, competitive, control.	Science	LT vs. control +.43 LT vs. competitive −.30	+.37
Okebukola (1986a)	7	Nigeria	97	24	Students randomly assigned to LT, STAD, competitive, or control, all taught by same teacher.	Science	LT vs. control +3.43 LT vs. competitive +1.20	+2.32
Okebukola (1984)	9	Nigeria	720	11	Student teachers randomly assigned to LT, competitive, control.	Biology	LT vs. control +.27 LT vs. competitive −.89	−.31
Okebukola (1986b)	9	Nigeria	493	6	Student teachers randomly assigned to LT or competitive.	Biology	Prefer cooperative +1.85 Prefer competitive −1.97	−.06
Learning Together Models with Individual Accountability								
Humphreys, Johnson, and Johnson (1982)	9	Suburban MN	44	6	Compared LT, competitive, individualistic, controlling for pretests. Grades in LT based on group averages. No teacher instruction.	Physical Science	Posttest (+) Retention (+) (1 week)	(+)
Yager, Johnson, Johnson, and Snider (1986)	3	Suburban MN	88	5	Students randomly assigned to LT or individualistic grades in LT based on group averages. No teacher instruction.	Transportation	Posttest (+) Retention (+)	(+)

From Slavin, 1989.
Key: (+) Significant effect favoring cooperative learning.

Table 2-5 Jigsaw

Article	Grades	Location	Sample Size	Duration (weeks)	Design	Subjects	Effect Size by Subgroup/Measure	ES Standardized	ES Total
Gonzales (1981)	3-4	Hollister, CA (bilingual)	99	20	Bilingual Jigsaw classes compared with matched controls.	Reading Language Arts Math	CAT Reading CAT Language CAT Math	(0) (0) (0)	(0)
Moskowitz, Malvin, Schaeffer, and Schaps (1983)	5-6	Suburban CA	261	24	Schools randomly assigned to Jigsaw, control.	Reading Math	Stanford Reading Stanford Math	(0) (0)	(0)
Moskowitz, Malvin, Schaeffer, and Schaps (1985)	5	Suburban CA	480	30	Jigsaw classes compared with matched controls.	Reading Math	Stanford Reading Stanford Math	(0) (-)	(-)
Tomblin and Davis (1985)	Jr. High	San Diego, CA	90	8	Classes randomly assigned to Jigsaw, control.	English			-.51
Lazarowitz, Baird, Hertz-Lazarowitz, and Jenkins (1985)	10-12	Suburban UT	113 (4 classes)	6	Jigsaw classes compared with matched individual instruction.	Biology			(0)
Hertz-Lazarowitz, Sapir, and Sharan (1981)	8	Israel	68	5	Same teacher taught matched Jigsaw, GI, control classes.	Arabic language and culture			+.22
Rich, Amir, and Slavin (1986)	7	Israel	339 (9 classes)	12	Classes randomly assigned to Jigsaw, control.	Literature -.32 History +.04			-.14
Okebukola (1985)	8	Nigeria	359	6	Student teachers randomly assigned to Jigsaw, STAD, TGT, LT, competitive, control.	Science	Jigsaw vs. control +1.41 Jigsaw vs. competitive +.87		+1.14

From Slavin, 1989.

Key: (+) Significant effect favoring cooperative learning.
(0) No significant difference.
(-) Significant effect favoring control group.

Table 2–6 Group Investigation and Related Methods

Article	Grades	Location	Sample Size	Duration (weeks)	Design	Subjects	Effect Size by Subgroup/ Measure	ES Standardized	ES Total
Sharan et al. (1984)	7	Israel	English: 504 Literature: 465	18	Teachers randomly assigned to GI, STAD, or control.	English as a second language Literature		+.10 +.14	+.12
Hertz-Lazarowitz, Sapir, and Sharan (1981)	8	Israel	67	5	Same teachers taught matched Jigsaw, GI, control classes.	Arabic language and culture			.00
Sharan and Shachar (1988)	8	Israel (private school)	351 (11 classes)	18	Classes randomly assigned to GI, control.	Geography +1.41 History +1.45			+1.43
Sherman and Zimmerman (1986)	10	Ohio	46 (2 classes)	7	Compared GI and matched competitive class taught by same teacher.	Biology			−.15
Talmage, Pascarella, and Ford (1984)	2–6	Elgin, IL	493	1 year	Teachers using a form of GI compared with matched controls.	Reading	SAT Reading +.18 SAT Language Arts +.11	+.14	+.14

From Slavin, 1989.

Table 2–7   Other Cooperative Learning Methods

Article	Grades	Location	Sample Size	Duration (weeks)	Design	Subjects	Effect Size by Subgroup/Measure	ES Standardized	ES Total
Methods Lacking Group Goals and Individual Accountability									
L. Johnson (1985)	4–5	Suburban Houston, TX	859 (51 classes)	27	Teachers trained in Marilyn Burns "Groups of Four" method compared to matched controls.	Math	Romberg-Wearne: Comprehension –.08 Application +.01 Problem Solving +.22	+.04	+.04
Johnson and Waxman (1985)	8	Houston, TX	150	1 year	Teachers trained in Marilyn Burns "Groups of Four" method compared with matched controls.	Math	SAT Problem Solving: High Achievement (0) Moderate Achievement (0) Low Achievement (+)	(0)	(0)
Van Oudenhoven, Van Berkum, and Swenkoopmans (1987)	3	Netherlands	218 (14 classes)	12	Classes randomly assigned to pair learning with individual feedback, pair learning with shared feedback, or control.	Spelling	Pairs with individual feedback: (+) Pairs with shared feedback: (+)		(+)
Van Oudenhoven, Wiersma, and Van Yperen (1987)	3	Netherlands	261	15	Classes randomly assigned to pair learning, individual learning with feedback from classmate, or individual learning with no feedback.	Spelling	High Average Achievement (0) Low Achievement (+)		(+)
Vedder (1985)	4	Netherlands	191	4	Classes randomly assigned to pair learning or individual learning.	Geometry	Posttests +.06 Follow-up +.05 (3 weeks)		+.06
Methods with Group Goals but No Individual Accountability									
Artzt (1983)	9–11	Suburban New York	304	20	Teachers taught experimental and control classes. Cooperative groups in competition based on one group worksheet.	Math			+.13

From Slavin, 1989.
Key: (+) Significant effect favoring cooperative learning.
       (0) No significant difference.

Table 2–8   Breakdown of Effect Sizes by Characterisitcs of Methods

	Percentage at or Above Median, All Studies	Percentage at or Above Median, ES Known	Median, ES Known	Median, Standardized Tests
All studies	50 (68)	50 (51)	+.21	
Student Team Learning methods:				
STAD	57 (21)	67 (18)	+.265	+.21
TGT	75 (12)	86 (7)	+.38	+.33
TAI/CIRC	57 (7)	57 (7)	+.21	+.20
All STL	63 (40)	69 (32)	+.30	+.21
Learning Together	44 (9)	29 (7)	.00	
Jigsaw	25 (8)	50 (4)	+.04	
Group Investigation	20 (5)	20 (5)	+.12	
Other	33 (6)	0 (3)	+.06	
Group goals and individual accountability	65 (43)	69 (32)	+.30	+.21
Group goals only	25 (8)	25 (8)	+.035	
Individual accountability only (task specialization)	23 (13)	33 (9)	+.12	
No group goals or individual accountability	25 (4)	0 (2)	+.05	

From Slavin, 1989.

Note: Numbers in parentheses are total numbers of studies in each category.

1985). Both STAD (ES = +1.72) and TGT (ES = +1.60) were found to be substantially more effective than Learning Together and Jigsaw (ES = +1.09, and +.98, respectively). On the other hand, an Israeli study comparing Group Investigation and STAD in teaching literature and English as a second language found no significant differences (Sharan et al., 1984).

Overall the Student Team Learning methods had a median effect size of +.30; on average, students experiencing these methods attained scores that would be at the sixty-second percentile on the control group's distribution. On standardized tests—typically a much more stringent criterion of treatment effects because of their lack of overlap with any particular curriculum—the median effect size for all Student Team Learning methods was +.21.

The median effect sizes presented in Table 2–8 may underestimate the effects of a few of the cooperative learning methods. First, it is important to note that the studies of TAI and CIRC used *only* standardized tests, except for the writing samples used in CIRC. Since standardized tests usually produce smaller effect-size estimates than do criterion-referenced or experimenter-made tests, this makes the effects for TAI and CIRC appear smaller than they actually are. One interesting indication of this is that on computations measures, TAI students gained an average of twice as many grade equivalents as control students across all studies (see Slavin, 1985a); CIRC gains had a similar ratio to control-group gains in reading comprehension, reading vocabulary, language expression, language mechanics, and spelling (Stevens, Madden, Slavin, and Farnish, 1987).

The median effect size of .00 for Learning Together also requires explanation. This estimate is probably accurate for forms of Learning Together lacking individual accountability, in which students are "praised and rewarded" on the basis of a single group worksheet. However, the situation may be different for forms of Learning Together that do incorporate group goals and individual accountability by grading students on the basis of the average of all group members' individual quiz scores. Two studies that used a

TEACHERS ON TEACHING

Many teachers who use cooperative learning have a particular success story—a child who was turned around, a new perspective on teaching, markedly improved grades or test scores. If you have such a success story, please briefly tell it.

Using STAD and TGT has brought about a significant increase in my students' test scores. There are other successes too, but this increase in test scores excites me the most. Test scores didn't increase at first. Only after students started working together as a real team did they score better on tests. In the last five tests dealing with punctuation, I have not had any students score below 85. Before I started using STAD, I had these same students score from 50s to 95s on similar tests.

I started to get nervous about all the high grades. Were my tests hard enough? Had my students devised some ingenious plan for cheating? Wasn't I supposed to have a certain number of students fail? These were the questions that plagued me. I honestly believe that cooperative learning does improve test scores. To test the retention level of students, I periodically gave tests on previously tested material and the results were still high. I have now concluded that research is right! Test scores improve when cooperative learning is used in the classroom.

Jacquie Alberti,
Language Arts Teacher
Norman C. Toole Middle School,
N. Charleston, SC

reward structure of this kind found significantly positive effects on student achievement (Humphreys, Johnson, and Johnson, 1982; Yager, Johnson, Johnson, and Snider, 1986), and a third study of eighteen days' duration (Yager, Johnson, and Johnson, 1985) found similar effects. Unfortunately, none of the three studies presented data from which effect sizes could be estimated. These three studies suggest that the Learning Together model can be instructionally effective if it uses group goals and individual accountability. On the other hand, these studies are highly artificial experiments. In all three, teachers did not present lessons to students but only helped individuals with worksheets. This arrangement creates a possible bias against the individualistic and competitive control students, who have no resources other than their worksheets to help them learn.

Finally, the effect-size estimate for Group Investigation may be too low. The Sharan and Shachar (1988) study, which found by far the largest achievement effects of Group Investigation, was very well designed and executed; even though it is only one study, its effects cannot be discounted.

Group Goals and Individual Accountability

One problem in the cooperative learning literature is that theoretically important *factors* are often confounded with particular *methods*. For example, two of the factors identified in previous reviews as critical for positive achievement effects are group goals and individual accountability. Most of the studies that used specific group goals and individual accountability are Student Team Learning studies, and therefore also used equal-opportunity scoring systems, prepared instructional materials, and, in the case of most of the TGT and STAD studies, team competition. However, in addition to the evidence supporting the instructional effectiveness of the Student Team Learning methods, there is evidence supporting the importance of group goals and individual accountability. As noted earlier, the Learning Together studies that used group goals and individual accountability appear to have been markedly more successful than those that did not; setting aside the

TEACHERS ON TEACHING

Individual accountability has been found to be a critical feature of cooperative learning. How do you help students see that every team member must individually know the material? How do you keep students from coasting along rather than working to help others and to learn the material themselves?

From the beginning we explain to the students that in order for a group or team to be successful, members must contribute and work toward completing their assignments. Explanation of the concept usually needs to be followed with a strong motivational component to ensure task completion at a successful level. For the secondary student a three-tiered system of rewards (individual, team, and class) has proven especially effective for increasing individual productivity and successful groups. Offering recognition for individual efforts while at the same time encouraging intrateam and interteam success builds a powerful motivational dynamic which fosters success and excellence.

Motivation seems to be one of the essential components of ensuring individual performance and thus improving individual accountability. If the team members are enthused about becoming a superteam, they will assist, encourage, and evaluate one another's performances. If individuals on the team are motivated to achieve the team goals, they will do their best to fulfill their responsibilities and contribute to the team.

Not all students have the skills to understand how to interact individually with various processes involved in group work. In TAI we have implemented a structured system of rotating individual roles with weekly self- and group- evaluation monitoring. Knowing their duties as "coach," "supervisor," "go-getter," and "recorder" gives the team members a conceptual framework and a focus that each has an important individual function but all are necessary to effectively work as a group.

Lynne Mainzer,
Special Education Teacher
Francis Scott Key High School,
Union Bridge, MD

Nigerian studies, these are the only studies that found significantly positive achievement effects for Learning Together. Two of the Nigerian studies (Okebukola, 1985, 1986a) found effects favoring a form of Learning Together without individual accountability, but two others (Okebukola, 1984, 1986b) found an opposite trend.

A three-week study in West Germany by Huber, Bogatzki, and Winter (1982) specifically compared a form of STAD with traditional group work lacking group rewards or individual accountability. The former was found to produce higher mathematics achievement (ES = +.23). In a study of TAI math, Cavanagh (1984) found that students who received group recognition based on the number of units accurately completed by all group members both learned more (ES = +.24) and completed more units (ES = +.25) than did students who received individual recognition only. On the other hand, a Dutch study of pair learning in spelling found no achievement differences between a condition in which students received individual feedback only and one in which they received shared feedback, which might be considered a group goal (Van Oudenhoven, Van Berkum, and Swen-Koopmans, 1987).

The failure to find significant achievement effects in year-long studies of such traditional group-work methods as Marilyn Burns's (1981) "Groups of Four" program (Johnson, 1985; Johnson and Waxman, 1985) further suggests the necessity of group goals and individual accountability. Traditional group work, in which students are encouraged to work together but are given little structure and few incentives to do so, has been repeatedly found to have small or nonexistent effects on student learning.

Table 2–8 breaks down the results of the cooperative learning studies according to their use of group goals and individual accountability. As the foregoing discussion suggests, studies of methods that incorporate group goals and individual accountability found considerably more positive instructional effects than did other studies. The reason for the importance of group goals and individual accountability is that there must be some incentive for students to help one another learn. In traditional group work, students are encouraged to work together but have no stake in one another's success. Under this condition, students do not necessarily provide one another the elaborated explanations that are essential for the achievement effects of cooperative learning (see Slavin, 1987b; Webb, 1985). Similarly, when there are group goals but no individual accountability, as in most of the Learning Together studies, the group's goal is to complete a single worksheet or solve a single set of problems. In this circumstance, stopping and explaining concepts to group members who are having problems may waste time and interfere with the group's success; the students who are perceived to be the most able may simply do the work with little input from others.

Task Specialization

One interesting difference not shown in Table 2–8 is a difference between the two major task specialization methods, Group Investigation and Jigsaw. In both, students are given responsibility for one unique portion of the group's overall learning task. Yet in another respect the two methods are quite different. In the original form of Jigsaw, the principal team activity involves students taking turns reporting to one another on the topics they studied; in the absence of group goals, there is little incentive for students to help one another learn. In contrast, interaction among groupmates in Group Investigation is constant, and the group works together to prepare a report to the rest of the class. Since the group report is evaluated by the teacher, Group Investigation could be considered to use a form of group goals and individual accountability.

Except for the Okebukola (1985) study, positive achievement effects of Jigsaw have not been found. In one particularly well designed study done in Israel, Jigsaw students learned significantly less than control students in literature (Rich, Amir, and Slavin, 1986). In contrast, the two longest and best-designed studies of Group Investigation, by Sharan and colleagues (1984) and Sharan and Shachar (1988), both found significant positive effects, as did an earlier study of three weeks' duration (Sharan, Hertz-Lazarowitz, and Ackerman, 1980).

Other than comparisons among methods and across the factors of group goals and individual accountability, few other factors clearly differentiated more and less successful studies. There was a tendency for different methods to be differentially effective at different grade levels: STAD and TGT were the most successful methods at the secondary level; TAI, CIRC, and TGT were the most successful in elementary schools (TAI and CIRC are used only in elementary schools). There were no consistent patterns according to study duration, sample size, or experimental design.

Effect sizes were greatest for Student Team Learning methods in science, but this was due entirely to the Okebukola studies, which tended to find extraordinarily large effects. Research examining effects separately for high, average, and low achievers has tended to find equal effects for all students (see Slavin, 1983a).

Conclusion

As with earlier reviews by Slavin (1980c, 1983a,b), Davidson (1985), and Newmann and Thompson (1987), the review summarized in this chapter concludes that cooperative

TEACHERS ON TEACHING

When they first hear about it, many teachers and parents are concerned that cooperative learning may hold back the progress of high achievers, although research usually finds that such students do achieve more in cooperative than in traditional classes. Have you seen benefits of cooperative learning for your most able students? What kinds of specific strategies do you use to meet the needs of high achievers when you use cooperative learning?

I have discovered that my high achievers are more challenged through cooperative learning methods. Because of their responsibility and commitment to their teammates' learning, they are required to look at problems from many angles. One of the greatest advantages of cooperative learning is the increase in high-er-level thinking skills of my high achievers. Simply solving a problem or answering a question is now only the beginning for them. They break concepts down into smaller components, looking for various alternatives in finding solutions. This is all done within the practice, discussion, and reteach in their team study times.

Debra Kauffman,
Fifth Grade Teacher
Taylor Elementary School,
Columbia, PA

I have definitely seen benefits of cooperative learning for the most able students. Very often students who do well academically are weak in social skills. Cooperative learning helps these students learn important interpersonal skills along with the academics. Many of the most able students are shy and withdrawn and are considered to be "nerds" by the other students. Cooperative learning helps students to learn and accept differences and to appreciate that everyone has something valuable to contribute to the group.

Some of the strategies used in my classroom to meet the needs of the high achiever are the same ones we have always used to meet the needs of the more able student.

1. Peer tutoring: high achiever helping a less able student with a specific lesson or concept.
2. Providing extra books on the subject or topic the group is studying. Let students share this information with the group.
3. Field trips and resource people.
4. Enrichment exercises that extend specific lessons.

Georgiann Ash,
Fifth–Sixth Grade Teacher
George C. Weimer Elementary
School, St. Albans, WV

learning methods can be an effective means of increasing student achievement, but only if they incorporate group goals and individual accountability. Among the methods that use group goals and individual accountability (principally Student Team Learning methods), the median effect size is about $+.30$ for all measures and $+.21$ for standardized measures. These are moderate but important effects, particularly since they can be achieved in practice at very little cost and since cooperative learning also has positive effects on such outcomes as race relations (Slavin, 1985b), acceptance of mainstreamed academically handicapped students (Madden and Slavin, 1983a; Johnson and Johnson, 1980), self-concept, and other social variables (Slavin, 1983a). Effects of cooperative learning on these variables are discussed in Chapter 3.

Much research remains to be done if we are to further understand the effects of cooperative learning and to apply cooperative learning principles to new objectives and settings. But the research reviewed in this chapter clearly shows that under certain well-defined circumstances, cooperative learning can be an effective form of classroom organization for accelerating student achievement.

THREE

Cooperative Learning and Outcomes Other Than Achievement

Cooperative learning is a social method. It involves students working together as equals to accomplish something of importance to all of them. Cooperative learning is also fun, and it engages students in active rather than passive learning. For these reasons, it is logical to expect that cooperative learning would have positive effects on social, motivational, and attitudinal outcomes as well as on achievement. Many researchers have studied such noncognitive outcomes, and have indeed found evidence that cooperative learning can have impacts on a broad range of variables. This chapter discusses theory and research relating to some of the most extensively studied of the noncognitive outcomes of cooperative learning.

INTERGROUP RELATIONS

Since midcentury, school desegregation has been one of the most important and controversial social issues on the American scene. Ever since the 1954 *Brown vs. Board of Education* decision, it has been assumed that desegregation would improve relations between students of different ethnic backgrounds. Yet all too often, desegregated schools are not really integrated schools: in most schools, black, white, and Hispanic students remain much more likely to have friends of their own ethnic background than to make many cross-ethnic choices (Gerard and Miller, 1975). Although school desegregation does have a positive effect on racial toleration (Scott and McPartland, 1982), ethnicity is still a major barrier to friendship and respect in many desegregated schools.

Desegregation must be seen as an opportunity for improvement of intergroup relations, not as a solution in itself. Stuart Cook (1979) participated in the deliberations that led to the famous Social Science Statement ("Effects of Segregation," 1953) which played a part in the *Brown vs. Board of Education* decision. He has pointed out that in the early 1950s social scientists knew that school desegregation must be accompanied by changes in school practices if it were to have positive effects on relations between black and white students.

Gordon Allport, one of the signers of the Social Science Statement, was particularly influential. In *The Nature of Prejudice* (1954), Allport made explicit the importance of interracial contact. He cited research evidence that superficial contact could impair race relations, as could competitive contact and contact between individuals of markedly different status. However, he also cited evidence that when individuals of different racial or ethnic groups worked to achieve common goals, when they had opportunities to get to know one another as individuals, and when they worked with one another on an equal footing, they became friends and did not continue to hold prejudices against one another. Allport's contact theory of intergroup relations, based on these findings, has dominated social science inquiry in race relations for four decades. His own summary of the essentials of contact theory is as follows:

Prejudice . . . may be reduced by equal status contact between majority and minority groups in the pursuit of common goals. The effect is greatly enhanced if this contact is sanctioned by institutional supports . . . and if it is of a sort that leads to the perception of common interests and common humanity between members of the two groups. (Allport, 1954, p. 281)

Traditional school organization hardly fulfills the conditions outlined by Allport. Interaction between students of different ethnic groups is typically competitive and superficial. Black, Anglo, Hispanic, and other groups compete for grades, for teacher approval, for places on the student council and the cheerleading squad. Students have little chance for in-depth contact. In the classroom—the one setting in which students of different races or ethnic backgrounds are likely to at least be sitting side by side— traditional instructional methods permit little contact between students that is not superficial. Otherwise, since black, Anglo, and Hispanic students usually ride different buses to different neighborhoods, participate in different activities, and go to different social functions, opportunities for positive intergroup interaction are limited. One major exception is sports: sports teams in integrated schools are almost always integrated. Sports teams create conditions of cooperation and nonsuperficial contact among team members, and research has shown that students who participate in sports in desegregated high schools are much more likely to have friends outside of their own race group and to have positive racial attitudes than are students who do not (Slavin and Madden, 1979).

Cooperative learning is an ideal solution to the problem of providing students of different ethnic groups with opportunities for nonsuperficial, cooperative interactions. Cooperative learning methods specifically use the strength of the desegregated school— the presence of students of different races or ethnic backgrounds—to enhance intergroup relations. In these methods, cooperation between students is emphasized by the classroom rewards and tasks and by the teacher, who tries to communicate an "all for one, one for all" attitude. Also, Student Team Learning methods are structured so that each student has a chance to make a substantial contribution to the team; teammates are equal, at least in the sense of role equality specified by Allport (1954). Cooperative learning provides daily opportunities for intense interpersonal contact between students of different races. When the teacher assigns students of different ethnic groups to work together, he or she communicates unequivocal support for the idea that interracial or interethnic interaction is officially sanctioned. Even though race or race relations per se need never be mentioned (and rarely are) during cooperative learning experiences, it is difficult for a student to believe that the teacher favors racial separation when he or she has assigned the class to multi-ethnic teams.

Thus, at least in theory, cooperative learning methods satisfy the conditions outlined in the Social Science Statement and by Allport (1954) for positive effects of desegregation on race relations—interracial cooperation; equal status roles for students of different races; contact across racial lines that permits students to learn about one another as individuals; and the communication of unequivocal teacher support for interracial contact.

Research on Cooperative Learning and Intergroup Relations

The cooperative methods that have been evaluated for effects on intergroup relations are a subset of those studied for achievement effects, with the addition of a method used by Weigel, Wiser, and Cook (1975). As in Chapter 2, experiments of four weeks' duration or more that were conducted in elementary or secondary classrooms and used appropriate research methods and analyses to rule out obvious bias are highlighted in this chapter. Most of the studies used sociometric (e.g., "Who are your friends in this class?"), peer-rating, or behavior-observation measures to measure intergroup relations.

Several studies used such sociometric questions as "Who have you helped in this class?" Because only students in the cooperative learning classes are likely to have helped their classmates, this and related measures are biased toward the cooperative learning treatments, and so the results of these measures are not presented in this chapter. Also, observations of cross-racial interaction during the treatment classes—another measure of implementation rather than outcome—are excluded.

The experimental evidence from studies of cooperative learning has generally supported the conclusions of the Social Science Statement and of Allport (1954). With only a few exceptions, this research has demonstrated that when the conditions outlined by Allport are met in the classroom, students are more likely to have friends outside of their own race groups than they would in traditional classrooms.

STAD. The evidence linking STAD to gains in cross-racial friendships is strong. In two studies, Slavin (1977c, 1979) found that students who had experienced STAD for ten to twelve weeks gained more in cross-racial friendships than did control students. Slavin and Oickle (1981) found significant gains in white friendships with blacks as a consequence of STAD, but found no differences in black friendships with whites. Kagan, Zahn, Widaman, Schwarzwald, and Tyrell (1985) found that STAD (and TGT) reversed a trend toward ethnic polarization of friendship choices among Anglo, Hispanic, and black students. Sharan and associates (1984) found positive effects of STAD on ethnic attitudes of both Middle Eastern and European Jews in Israeli schools. However, a study by Tomblin and Davis (1985) found no significant effects of STAD on intergroup relations.

Slavin's (1979) study included a follow-up into the next academic year, in which students who had been in the experimental and control classes were asked to list their friends. Students in the control group listed an average of less than one friend of another race, or 9.8 percent of all of their friendship choices; those in the experimental group named an average of 2.4 friends outside their own race, or 37.9 percent of their friendship choices. The STAD research covered grades 2–8 and took place in schools ranging from 13 percent to 61 percent minority.

TGT. DeVries, Edwards, and Slavin (1978) summarized data analyses from four studies of TGT in desegregated schools. In three of these, students in classes that used TGT gained significantly more friends outside their own racial group than did control students. In one, no differences were found. The samples involved in these studies varied in grade level (seven to twelve) and in percentage of minority students (10 percent to 51 percent). In addition, Kagan and colleagues (1985) found positive effects of TGT on friendship choices among black, Mexican-American, and Anglo students.

TAI. Two studies have assessed the effects of TAI on intergroup relations. Oishi, Slavin, and Madden (1983) found positive effects of TAI on cross-racial nominations on two sociometric scales, "Who are your friends in this class?" and "Whom would you rather *not* sit at a table with?" No effects were found on cross-racial ratings of classmates as "nice" or "smart," but TAI students made significantly fewer cross-racial ratings of "not nice" and "not smart" than did control students. In a similar study, Oishi (1983) found significantly positive effects of TAI on cross-racial ratings of smart and on reductions in ratings of not nice. The effect on "smart" ratings was due primarily to increases in whites' ratings of black classmates.

Jigsaw. The effects of the original Jigsaw method on intergroup relations are less consistent than those of STAD, TGT, or TAI. Blaney, Stephan, Rosenfield, Aronson, and Sikes (1977) did find that students in desegregated classes using Jigsaw preferred their Jigsaw groupmates to their classmates in general. However, since students' groupmates and their other classmates were about the same in ethnic composition, this cannot be seen as a measure of intergroup relations. No differences between the experimental and control groups in interethnic friendship choices were reported.

Gonzales (1979), using a method similar to Jigsaw, found that Anglo and Asian-American students had better attitudes toward Mexican-American classmates in the Jigsaw groups than in control groups, but he found no differences in attitudes of students toward Anglo or Asian-American classmates. In a subsequent study, Gonzales (1981) found no differences between Jigsaw and control bilingual classes in attitudes of students toward Mexican-Americans, blacks, or Anglos. Tomblin and Davis (1985) and Rich, Amir, and Slavin (1986) also found nonsignificant effects of Jigsaw on intergroup relations.

The most positive effects of a Jigsaw-related intervention were found in a study by Ziegler (1981) of Jigsaw II in classes composed of recent European and West Indian immigrants and Anglo-Canadians in Toronto. She found substantially more cross-ethnic friendships in the Jigsaw II classes than in control classes, both on an immediate posttest and on a ten-week follow-up. These effects were for both "casual friendships" ("Who in this class have you called on the telephone in the last two weeks?") and "close friendships" ("Who in this class have you spent time with after school in the last two weeks?")

Learning Together. Two studies, both lasting only three weeks, have investigated the effects of the Johnsons' methods on intergroup relations. Cooper, Johnson, Johnson, and Wilderson (1980) found greater friendship across racial lines in a cooperative treatment than in an individualized method in which students were not permitted to interact. However, there were no differences in cross-racial friendships between the cooperative condition and a competitive condition in which students competed with equals (as in the TGT tournaments). Johnson and Johnson (1981a) found more cross-racial interaction in cooperative than in individualized classes during free time.

Group Investigation. In a study in Israeli junior high schools, Sharan and associates (1984) compared Group Investigation, STAD, and traditional instruction in terms of effects on relationships between Jews of Middle Eastern and European backgrounds. They found that students who experienced Group Investigation and STAD had much more positive ethnic attitudes than students in traditional classes. There were no differences between Group Investigation and STAD on this variable.

Weigel et al. Method. One of the largest and longest studies of cooperative learning was conducted by Weigel, Wiser, and Cook (1975) in tri-ethnic (Mexican-American, Anglo, black) classrooms. They evaluated a method in which students in multi-ethnic teams engaged in a variety of cooperative activities in several subjects, winning prizes based on team performance. They reported that their method had positive effects on white students' attitudes toward Mexican-Americans, but not on white–black, black–white, black–Hispanic, Hispanic–black, or Hispanic–white attitudes. They also found that cooperative learning reduced teachers' reports of interethnic conflict.

The effects of cooperative learning methods are not entirely consistent, but sixteen of the nineteen studies reviewed here demonstrated that when the conditions of contact theory are fulfilled, some aspect of friendship between students of different ethnic backgrounds improves.

How Close Are the New Cross-Ethnic Friendships? It is not surprising that friendships across racial or ethnic boundaries are rare, compared with friendships within these groups. Black, Hispanic, and Anglo students typically live in different neighborhoods, ride different buses, and prefer different activities. Secondary school students of different ethnic groups often come from different elementary schools. Socioeconomic and achievement differences further separate students. These factors work against friendship formation even when race is not a factor (see Lott and Lott, 1965). Racial differences accentuate students' tendencies to form homogeneous peer groups, and sometimes result in overt prejudice and interracial hostility.

Given the many forces operating against the formation of cross-racial friendships, it would seem that if cooperative learning influences these friendships, it would create relatively weak relationships rather than strong ones. On first thought, it seems unlikely that a few weeks of cooperative learning would build strong interracial relationships between students in the classroom at the possible expense of prior same-race relationships.

A detailed analysis of the Slavin (1979) STAD study by Hansell and Slavin (1981) investigated this hypothesis. Their sample included 424 seventh- and eighth-grade students in twelve inner-city language arts classrooms. Classes were randomly assigned to cooperative learning (STAD) or control treatments for a ten-week program. Students were asked on both pre- and posttests, "Who are your best friends in this class? Name as many as you wish." Choices were defined as "close" if they were among the first six made by students, and "distant" if they ranked seventh or later.

The results showed that the positive effects of STAD on cross-racial choices were due primarily to increases in *strong* friendship choices. Reciprocated and close choices, both made and received, increased more in STAD than in control classes. Thus, contrary to what might have been expected, this study showed positive effects of cooperative learning on close, reciprocated friendship choices—the kind of friendships that should be most difficult to influence.

ACCEPTANCE OF MAINSTREAMED ACADEMICALLY HANDICAPPED STUDENTS

In the 1940s and 1950s, educators concerned with providing the best possible education for children with learning problems advocated the development of special programs for these children that removed them from regular classrooms. Part of the impetus behind this policy was that these children were rejected by and isolated from other children in their classes because of their academic incompetence, and that this experience was harmful to their social development and self-concept (Johnson, 1950; Shattuck, 1946). It was felt that removing the child from this hostile environment was essential to fostering emotional and social development, as well as academic growth.

However, disappointing results of research on the academic and social outcomes of special-class placement as well as concerns over the negative effects of segregating a child from normal-progress peers and other normal experiences that form a vital part of education (Dunn, 1968) promoted the development of the current policy of *mainstreaming*. Within this system, now mandated by the federal government under Public Law 94-142, children with mild academic handicaps who need special education are placed in the "least restrictive environment" possible. By *mild academic handicaps* is meant academic performance that is significantly behind that of normal-progress students (usually at least two grade levels behind). Students with such handicaps are usually described as learning-disabled or educable mentally retarded. These children are often placed in regular classes for the largest part of their school day, and given supportive educational services by a special teacher. Usually this requires that students go to resource rooms for an hour or more a day to receive more individualized instruction.

Now that the academically handicapped child has often been placed back in the regular classroom, research has again demonstrated poor relationships between special and regular-class children. Students classified as learning-disabled, who are of normal intelligence but not performing up to grade-level expectations, have been found to be less well accepted and more frequently rejected on sociometric instruments than were their normal-progress peers (Bruininks, 1978; Bryan, 1974, 1976; Scranton and Ryckman, 1979; Siperstein, Bopp, and Bak, 1978). Similar results have been found in studies of mainstreamed educable mentally retarded students (Bruininks, Rynders, and Gross, 1974; Goodman, Gottlieb, and Harrison, 1972; Iano, Ayers, Heller, McGettigan, and Walker, 1974; Rucker, Howe, and Snider, 1969). If mainstreaming is to fulfill its potential to socially integrate handicapped children, something more than the usual instructional methods is needed.

As in the case of intergroup relations, cooperative learning is an obvious solution. There is good reason to believe that the structure of the traditional classroom contributes to the expression of negative affect toward low-performing students. Students in almost all classrooms compete with one another for acceptable grades and other rewards (Johnson and Johnson, 1974; Slavin, 1977a). Only a few—those who do *better* than the others—will receive A's. The academically handicapped special child, who is inevitably on the "losing" end of the competition more frequently than on the "winning" side, is no doubt an appropriate target for expression of the negative feelings found to be generated in competitive situations (Ames, Ames, and Felker, 1977). The deprecating comments common in competitive situations (Stendler, Damrin, and Haines, 1951) fall upon the special child more frequently than on more academically competent children. If the classroom is changed so that cooperation rather than competition is emphasized and so that academically handicapped students can make a meaningful contribution to the success of a cooperative group, acceptance of such students seems likely to increase.

Research on Cooperative Learning and Mainstreaming

Procedures for summarizing research on cross-handicap relations are the same as those used for intergroup relations. Two principal types of measures have been used to study the effects of cooperative learning on cross-handicap relations: sociometric and observational. Many studies used sociometric friendship measures, such as "Who are your friends in this class?" and a few used sociometric rejection measures, such as "If you were going to be working on a project with other children, there might be some children you would *not* want to have in your group. Please name these children if there are any." Only the Learning Together studies used observational measures of cross-handicap interaction. In general, they provided a ten-minute free period at the end of class in which the frequency of cross-handicap interactions in experimental and control classes was observed. This measure of interaction does not necessarily have meaning outside of the classroom because students may simply stay in their heterogeneous groups during the free time. Nevertheless, these studies are important in that the researchers actually observed cross-handicap interaction instead of depending only on paper-and-pencil sociometric measures. Many studies have reported such measures as "Who has helped you in this class?" and in-class observations of interaction between academically handicapped and normal-progress students. Since cross-handicap interactions are mandated by the cooperative treatments, these findings are not presented as outcomes of the treatments.

One study of STAD (Madden and Slavin, 1983a) has been conducted in mainstreamed classes. In this study, academically handicapped students received many fewer rejection choices in the STAD groups than in control groups. However, there were no differences on a sociometric "friends" measure.

TAI was specifically developed (under funding from the U.S. Office of Special Education) to solve the problems of the mainstreamed classroom. Its combination of cooperative learning with individualized instruction allows academically handicapped students to contribute substantially to their team's success (by doing well at their own level). As a consequence, the effects of TAI on acceptance of the academically handicapped have been particularly strong (Slavin, 1984b). Positive effects have been found in two studies both for friendships with academically handicapped students and for reducing rejections of these students. Further, marked improvements were seen in teacher ratings of the academically handicapped students' behavior. On four scales—classroom behavior, self-confidence, friendship behavior, and negative peer behavior—academically handicapped students in the TAI classes were rated as having many fewer problems than their counterparts in the control classes. In fact, by the time of the posttest, academically handicapped students in the TAI classes were rated as equal in behavior problems to normal-progress students in the control classes, even though they were rated much worse than these students on the pretests.

The largest number of cooperative learning studies involving mainstreaming of academically handicapped students evaluated the effects of the Learning Together model on cross-handicap relations. These studies are very similar to one another. They all used random assignment of students, very small sample sizes (the largest sample is fifty-nine students), and very brief durations (three to four weeks). They all used the same cooperative treatment, in which students work in small, heterogeneous groups to produce a single worksheet, and are praised and rewarded as a group.

The results of the Learning Together studies on acceptance of academically and emotionally handicapped students are mixed but generally positive. Cooper, Johnson, Johnson, and Wilderson (1980) found significantly more friendship choices of academically or emotionally handicapped students in a cooperative condition than in an individualistic one, but there were no differences between the cooperative condition and a competitive one. Armstrong, Johnson, and Balow (1981) found no differences between cooperative and individualistic treatments on sociometric measures. They did find positive effects on two peer-rating scales in which students rated one another from smart to dumb and from valuable to worthless, but there was no separate analysis of ratings of the academically handicapped students.

One of the four studies that measured cross-handicap interaction during free time found significantly positive effects for the cooperative treatment (Johnson and Johnson, 1981), and one study (Johnson and Johnson, 1982) found marginally significant positive effects. The remaining two studies (Johnson and Johnson, 1981b; Johnson and Johnson, 1983) found no differences. The Johnson and Johnson (1981b) study used a measure in which students were assigned to new groups and asked to play a structured game; the researchers wished to determine whether a tendency toward cross-handicap interaction would transfer to a new setting and task. No differences were found, although the trend favored the cooperative treatments.

Finally, Johnson and Johnson (1981b) found more cross-handicap acceptance as work partners among students in a cooperative condition than among students in an individualistic one, but they did not state whether they found positive effects both for acceptance of handicapped students by their peers and for acceptance of nonhandicapped students by handicapped classmates.

The earliest and largest of the cooperative learning field experiments to study the effects of cooperation in heterogeneous groups on acceptance of academically handicapped students was conducted by Ballard, Corman, Gottlieb, and Kaufman (1977). In this study, thirty-seven classes in grades three to five were randomly assigned to cooperative or control conditions (twenty-five experimental, twelve control). One educable mentally retarded student was in each class. In the cooperative class, students were assigned to four-to-six member heterogeneous groups; one group in each class contained the EMR student. Group members worked together to plan, produce, and present a multimedia project. Students were instructed to break their task down into subtasks to be performed by each group member. The results indicated that EMRs in the experimental groups were better accepted by their classmates than were control EMRs. There were no differences in sociometric rejections.

TEACHERS ON TEACHING

Cooperative learning methods have been very effective as means of mainstreaming students with academic handicaps. What kinds of experiences have you had in using cooperative learning with main-streamed students, and what specific strategies have you used to help integrate these students?

I presently use cooperative learning in various forms and adaptations for all subjects in my fifth grade classroom. In reading I am using self-made CIRC activities, combining Scott, Foresman "levels" and trade books. In science I use STAD in my class of twenty-six students, in addition to nine students mainstreamed from our EMR and LD classes. These are the only two subjects in which students earn team points for team and classroom rewards. However, I use the concepts of cooperative learning (team discussion, study, and practice) in *all* of my subjects.

Cooperative Learning is excellent for classes mainstreaming students. The pride and self-esteem that these students have in themselves and their accomplishments are so gratifying. And my "top" students are challenged in their commitment to their teammates' improvement. I also challenge them with research projects and creative projects.

I have found tremendous growth in my students this year. Their commitment to improvement, and the resulting rewards, is great, but I believe their growth is a direct result of the "other" concepts of cooperative learning. My students have learned that helping another classmate is not "cheating" by any means, but is rather a gift they all give of themselves. They have learned to evaluate their own and their teammates' strengths and weaknesses, and work together to bring out the best of all. Most importantly, they have learned that *everyone* has something of value to offer, and they have developed a very healthy dependence and support system among themselves. I have never been so impressed with a teaching method in my fourteen years of classroom experience. A student of mine expressed it very well in a recent evaluation of cooperative learning in our classroom: "For the first time in my life I am a *good* student. My mom can't believe it and I told her it's all 'cause of teams."

Debra Kauffman,
Fifth Grade Teacher
Taylor Elementary School,
Columbia, PA

Handicapped students typically have poor group skills. At the beginning of each year I devote an entire unit to communication skills (participation, turn taking, manners, body language, inflection, multi-meaning vocabulary, humor, assertive terms versus aggressive terms, pragmatics, and so on), using a TGT format.

It is not uncommon for the severely handicapped student to have a talent which isn't overly useful in isolation. For example, one of my Down's syndrome thirteen-year-olds has excellent fine motor skills and pretty printing. Her team works on the blackboard while she records the work that is turned in and graded. This child is in demand by other mildly handicapped students who hate to write. She was recruited to help with student council posters.

Another student has excellent auditory memory, discrimination, closure, and sequencing. Comprehension is a problem, but he can sound out any new vocabulary word.

His talent is appreciated by the visual learners with poor phonics skills.

I've found that the more severely handicapped students are, the more they need the security of a set routine. I keep groups together for the entire year and rotate TAI, STAD, and TGT for the review and evaluation. Some form of cooperative learning is done in fifteen-to-twenty-minute blocks each day. Monday, Tuesday, and Wednesday are for instruction and drill, Thursday is for review, and Friday is for evaluation. After Friday's test it is the students' choice to continue a cooperative learning procedure for extra-credit points. I've had to design the tests to be quick, because they are disappointed if we run out of time.

Mary Beth Ames,
Special Education Teacher
Laredo Middle School, Aurora, CO

Mainstreaming students has become much easier with cooperative learning. I emphasize that all team members must make a contribution and must show evidence of doing their part. Their part may be a drawing instead of writing, recording their portion on tape, helping to find resource materials, and so forth. Cooperative learning has helped to build self-esteem with the mainstreamed students. They are team members and thus are responsible to the team, not just the teacher. The team members soon learn the limitations of the mainstreamed students and help to adjust their contribution. The other members take it upon themselves to write for those who have trouble with written language. They realize others are counting on them to help with the assignments.

Phyllis McManus,
Third Grade Teacher
Hoagland Elementary School,
Hoagland, IN

A special education student in the sixth grade was transferred to our classroom, a fifth/sixth grade. The classroom she was in has several special education students. The girl—I'll call her Sara—was having behavior difficulties in her first classroom and was about to be expelled because of her unacceptable behavior with her peers. We offered her the opportunity to try our room with no special education students and with cooperative learning techniques being applied in various subjects along with TAI math. Sara was welcomed by her new classmates. We added her to one of the TAI math learning teams, and the students taught her the program's routine. Sara worked very steadily and methodically trying to catch up academically and to fit in socially. She began to take more pride in her dress and grooming habits. I have been working with Sara on her basic facts in preparation for the weekly facts quizzes. Her attitude toward her schoolwork and her self-concept have blossomed within the length of time she has been in our classroom.

Peer tutoring by other classmates has been most helpful in the other subjects in teaching Sara the routine and aiding her in understanding her assignments. The other students are learning by tutoring Sara. I am gathering feedback about the other classmates' comprehension pertaining to the concepts studied by their ability to tutor Sara. So far, she has not objected to having a tutor or partner. She tries to carry her full load and does not take advantage of the others' assistance.

All in all, mainstreaming utilizing cooperative learning techniques has worked well with Sara.

Nancy Chrest,
Fifth/Sixth Grade Teacher
George C. Weimer Elementary
School, St. Albans, WV

In implementing CIRC, we incorporate our special education teacher. As the need arises, the special-ed teacher works within the reading class and with the team or teams that have special-ed youngsters as members. This teacher provides another support base for not only the mainstreamed youngsters, but the other team members as well. Another outgrowth from this is that the mainstreamed youngsters do not stand out as being different; they are simply part of the team.

Maureen Sauter, Fourth, Fifth,
and Sixth Grade Teacher
Sacandaga Elementary School,
Scotia, NY

Studies in Self-Contained Classrooms. One issue related to cooperative learning and mainstreaming is the use of cooperative learning methods in special schools for emotionally disturbed adolescents. Two studies have evaluated TGT in such settings.

Slavin (1977b) compared TGT with a control group in two classes in a middle school for emotionally disturbed students of normal intelligence. Students were randomly assigned to classes, and both classes were taught by the same pair of teachers. Social studies achievement, in-class observations, and sociometric questions served as the dependent measures with respective pretests as covariates.

The results indicated no achievement differences, but the TGT students were on-task significantly more than control students. They also named significantly more of their classmates as friends and desired workmates. Five months after the conclusion of the study, when students had been reassigned to new classes, follow-up behavior observations indicated that former TGT students interacted with their peers significantly more than did former control students. Because appropriate peer interaction is a major goal of the special program, this was seen as a particularly important finding.

Janke (1978) replicated the Slavin (1977b) study in three schools for high school–aged emotionally disturbed students. Students were randomly assigned to three classrooms in each of three schools. Two of the classrooms in each school experienced TGT, while the third served as a control group. Students were in their treatments for eighteen weeks. The subject matter was mathematics.

The results of the Janke (1978) study, like those of the Slavin (1977b) study, indicated no achievement differences but more time on-task for the TGT classes. Also, behavioral observations indicated less disruptive behavior in the TGT classes than in control, and higher daily attendance.

Thus, the Slavin (1977b) and Janke (1978) studies are consistent in indicating that TGT can improve the behavior of emotionally disturbed adolescents in self-contained classes.

Conclusions

The research on cooperative learning and relations between academically handicapped and normal-progress students generally shows that cooperative learning can overcome barriers to friendship and interaction between these students. Further, these improvements can be obtained while achievement is being enhanced for all students in the class.

SELF-ESTEEM

Perhaps the most important psychological outcome of cooperative learning methods is their effect on student self-esteem. Students' beliefs that they are valuable and important individuals are of critical importance for their ability to withstand the disappointments of life, to be confident decision makers, and ultimately to be happy and productive individuals.

It hardly seems likely that a cooperative learning experience, typically in one class for a few weeks or months, would fundamentally change student self-esteem. On the other hand, two of the most important components of students' self-esteem are the feeling that they are well liked by their peers and the feeling that they are doing well academically. Cooperative learning methods affect both of these components: students typically are named as friends by more of their classmates, feel more successful in their academic work, and in fact achieve more than they do in traditional classrooms. For these reasons, cooperative learning would in fact increase students' self-esteem.

The evidence from the cooperative learning studies tends to bear this out, although there are many inconsistencies. In Jigsaw, students are made to feel important because they have information that is indispensable to the group. Blaney, Stephan, Rosenfield, Aronson, and Sikes (1977), Geffner (1978), and Lazarowitz, Baird, Bowlden, and Hertz-Lazarowitz (1982) found positive effects of Jigsaw on student self-esteem. On the other hand, no differences were found in two studies by Gonzales (1979, 1981).

Researchers of STAD and TGT have often used modifications of the Coopersmith Self-Esteem Inventory (Coopersmith, 1967) to study the effects of these methods on student self-esteem. The Coopersmith scales used in this research are general self-esteem, social self-esteem, and academic self-esteem. Madden and Slavin (1983a) found significantly greater general self-esteem in STAD than in control groups, but they found no differences on academic or social self-esteem. Oickle (1980) found positive effects of STAD on student self-esteem in a study using the Piers-Harris Children's Self-Concept Scale, but Allen and Van Sickle (1984) found no differences for STAD on this measure. DeVries, Lucasse, and Shackman (1980) found that TGT increased students' social self-esteem but not their academic self-esteem. In a study combining STAD, TGT, and Jigsaw II, Slavin and Karweit (1981) found greater general and academic self-esteem, but not social self-esteem, among the experimental group than among the control group. This study also found that students expressed less anxiety in the cooperative groups than in the control groups.

Because of its use of individualized instruction, where students can be successful working at their own levels, Slavin, Leavey, and Madden (1984) expected TAI to have especially strong effects on students' self-concepts in mathematics. And indeed they found large effects on a questionnaire measure of self-concept in mathematics in their first of two experiments (Experiment 1) but not in their second (Experiment 2). Another measure of self-esteem used in these studies of TAI was teacher ratings of student self-esteem behaviors. Teachers rated a sample of their students on such items as ''(Student) is extremely critical of himself/herself,'' ''(Student) lacks confidence,'' and ''(Student) quits when tasks become difficult,'' on a scale from 0 (not a problem) to 4 (extremely serious problem). The researchers found teacher ratings of students' self-concepts to be significantly higher in the TAI classes than in control in both of the TAI studies (Slavin, Leavey, and Madden, 1984).

Several of the Learning Together studies evaluated elements of self-esteem. Johnson, Johnson, and Scott (1978) found that students who had worked in groups were more likely than individualistically taught students to agree that ''I'm doing a good job of learning.'' Johnson and Johnson (1983) found that cooperation increased students' general and school self-esteem more than competition or individualization did, but they found no differences on peer self-esteem. Johnson, Johnson, Scott, and Ramolae (1985) found no differences in self-esteem between cooperative and individual methods.

Thus, the evidence concerning cooperative learning and self-esteem is not completely consistent. It should be noted, though, that in eleven of the fifteen studies in which the effects of cooperative learning on self-esteem were studied, positive effects on some aspect of self-esteem were found. The effects of cooperative learning on student self-esteem are probably specific to the settings in which they were obtained; it is difficult to imagine a dramatic change in such a central part of students' psychological makeup from an intervention of only a few weeks' duration. However, these results do suggest that if cooperative learning methods were used over longer periods as a principal instructional methodology, genuine, lasting changes in student self-esteem might result.

TEACHERS ON TEACHING

Research finds that cooperative learning methods can increase student self-esteem. Have you seen evidence of this in your own use of cooperative learning? Is there anything specific you do to enhance students' self-esteem when you are using cooperative learning methods?

We see evidence daily that cooperative learning techniques increase self-esteem. Students recognize that they are achieving in the classroom and enjoy recognition for their accomplishments. Themes of excellence and success are infused in the curriculum structure. A "Code to Success" program recognizes students for outstanding performance in certain areas such as leadership, cooperation, task completion, tutoring classmates, helping, organization, and even community service. Providing a positive classroom atmosphere that promotes pride, respect for each other, service, cooperation, encouragement, and a belief that "I can learn," and recognizing through various methods outstanding achievements nurtures the development of good self-esteem. The following are examples of some very effective types of recognition:

- filling a "success card"
- standing and receiving a "round of applause"
- having one's name placed on the "Cooperative Learning Honor Roll" for academic achievement
- receiving honors at a cooperative learning reception
- being a member of a Good-, Great-, or Superteam
- receiving a letter of recognition from the principal

Lynne Mainzer,
Special Education Teacher
Francis Scott Key High School,
Union Bridge, MD

BJ is a very quiet, timid, shy, nervous, and small fifth grade student. In the beginning of this school year BJ was very intimidated by working with his peers in a cooperative learning group. He would tell us that he was weak in math, or he didn't like math, or he couldn't do this part of the math very well, or he always did "mess up" in math, or people in his group worked faster than he did, and that he couldn't work for the talking in his group.

Slowly, BJ began asking for assistance from his teammates. Then, he asked for an explanation of the directions when he didn't understand. His teammates encouraged and praised his small successes as they occurred. BJ was finally experiencing success unit by unit. He became more comfortable working in a team. Soon BJ was gaining so much in confidence and math skills that he was passing some of his teammates. He began to really grow in math. Then, he missed ten problems with multiplication, three-digit numbers by a three-digit multiplier. Earlier this would have devastated him, but he just brought his paper to me and asked for an explanation of what he was doing wrong. He said, "Mrs. Chrest, I have the hang of it now. I'm going to get all of them correct this time!" And he did. I loved the display of confidence. BJ made an "A" in math on his report card this last nine-weeks grading period. He told us today that math is his favorite subject, and that this "A" was the first one he had ever earned in math on his report card.

I credit BJ's "A" in math and his newly developed self-esteem to the cooperative learning methods displayed in our room and the mastery learning technique used in TAI–math. We really stress team cooperation, team praise, recognition, and areas of enrichment in math throughout the room when the given objectives are met by the students. We have Superteam photographs on the

TAI–Math bulletin board each week. The students aid in designing the TAI–Math boards and have a lot of pride in "their TAI–Math program"!

Nancy Chrest,
Fifth/Sixth Grade Teacher
George C. Weimer Elementary
School, St. Albans, WV

PROACADEMIC PEER NORMS

One of the most important tenets of motivational theories of cooperative learning is that cooperative goals create peer norms that support high achievement. Essentially, the argument is that cooperative incentives motivate students to try to get each other to do academic work, and thereby gets students to feel that their classmates want them to do their best. These normative forces have been found in studies outside of the cooperative learning tradition to be powerful influences on student achievement (Coleman, 1961; Brookover, Beady, Flood, Schweitzer, and Wisenbaker, 1979). It seems likely that if the peer group can be enlisted to encourage achievement, then achievement should increase.

Early laboratory research demonstrated that norms can be changed by the use of cooperative incentive structures. Deutsch (1949) found that college students who discussed human relations problems under cooperative conditions felt more pressure to achieve from their groupmates, felt more of an obligation to their groupmates, and had a stronger desire to win their groupmates' respect than did students who worked under competitive instructions. These results indicate that in the cooperative groups, students wanted to achieve because their groupmates wanted them to do so. Thomas (1957) found that individuals in cooperative groups exerted social pressures on one another to achieve. These interpersonal sanctions–"responsibility forces," in Thomas's words—maintained behavior that helped the group to succeed.

The field experimental research also supports the findings of effects of cooperative learning on peer norms supporting individual achievement. Four STAD studies found such effects. Slavin (1978b) found positive effects of STAD on a questionnaire scale consisting of such items as "Students in this class want me to come to school every day," and "Other students want me to work hard in this class." Madden and Slavin (1983a) and Oickle (1980) also found positive effects of STAD on similar scales. Hulten and DeVries (1976) and Edwards and DeVries (1974) found similar results for TGT, but a few studies found no differences (DeVries and Mescon, 1975; DeVries, Mescon, and Shackman, 1975b; Slavin and Karweit, 1981). One study of the Johnsons' methods found significantly greater gains on measures of "peer academic support" in cooperative than in individualistic treatments (Johnson, Johnson, Scott, and Ramolae, 1985).

LOCUS OF CONTROL

The degree to which students believe that their academic success depends on their own efforts (internal locus of control) has been shown on many occasions to be the single personality variable most consistently related to high academic performance (see, for example, Brookover, Beady, Flood, Schweitzer, and Wisenbaker, 1979; Coleman et al., 1966). Attribution theory (Weiner, 1979) also predicts that individuals who perceive their successes or failures to be due to unchangeable features of themselves or their environments have less motivation and achieve less than students who feel that success or failure is due to their own efforts.

Cooperative learning might be hypothesized to influence locus of control for several reasons. The most obvious is that the cooperative learning methods tend to increase students' actual success, and individuals who experience success are much more likely than those who do not to believe that their efforts made the difference (Weiner and Kukla, 1970). In the Student Team Learning methods, the use of equal-opportunity scoring systems (see Slavin, 1980a) is specifically designed to reward students for additional effort, regardless of ability, and this should produce a (correct) perception that outcomes depend on academic efforts.

Several studies have found that internal locus of control is positively influenced by cooperative learning methods. Slavin (1978b) found that STAD increased students' feelings that their outcomes depended on their performance rather than on luck, and DeVries, Edwards, and Wells (1974) found similar effects for TGT. Gonzales (1979) found a positive effect of Jigsaw on internal locus of control. Johnson, Johnson, and Scott (1978) found that students who experienced the Learning Together model were less likely than control students to agree that "luck decides most things that happen to me," but they found no differences on the statement "If I work hard at something I will be good at it."

Several other cooperative learning studies examined other motivation-related attitudes or perceptions. Slavin (1978b) found that students in STAD reported more motivation than did control students. Johnson, Johnson, Johnson, and Anderson (1976) reported that students who had participated in Learning Together groups were more intrinsically motivated and less extrinsically motivated than were individualistically taught students. Hulten and DeVries (1976) and DeVries, Edwards, and Wells (1974) found that TGT students felt it was more important to do well in class than did control students, and Oickle (1980) found the same result for STAD. Slavin (1978b) found that STAD students felt they had a better chance to do well than did control students.

In sum, there is some evidence that cooperative learning methods make students feel that they have a chance to succeed, that their efforts will lead to success, and that success is a valued goal. These feelings are important in themselves and are the essential predictors of high achievement in many theories of achievement motivation, such as expectancy theory (DuCette, 1979; Kukla, 1972) and attribution theory (Weiner, 1979). It is likely that these changes in achievement-related perceptions partly explain the positive achievement outcomes of cooperative learning.

TIME ON-TASK AND CLASSROOM BEHAVIOR

One behavioral indication of student motivational involvement is the proportion of their class time they spend on-task. Behavioral observers have been used in several cooperative learning studies to collect information on this measure. The element of time on-task observed in all of these studies is *engaged time* (see Karweit and Slavin, 1981), the proportion of noninstructional time students are doing their assigned work within the time available for work.

Cooperative learning is hypothesized to increase time on-task by engaging students' attention (because of the social nature of the task) and by increasing their motivation to master academic materials. Most studies that have measured time on-task have found higher proportions of engaged time for cooperative learning students than for control students. This was found for STAD (Slavin, 1978b, 1980a), for TGT (Janke, 1978; Slavin, 1977b), and for Jigsaw II (Ziegler, 1981). The results for the Learning Together model have been less consistent. Johnson and Johnson (1981b) found more time on-task in Learning Together than in individualistic methods, but Johnson and Johnson (1981) and Johnson and Johnson (1982) found no differences on this variable.

The two TAI studies conducted by Slavin, Leavey, and Madden (1984) used teacher ratings of student classroom behavior. Teachers rated a sample of their class on a classroom behavior scale consisting of such items as "(student) does not attend to work" and "(student) constantly demands teacher's attention," on a scale from 0 (not a problem) to

---

TEACHERS ON TEACHING

How do you help students in your cooperative learning classes use their team practice time effectively?

With the entire class in a cooperative learning setting, any off-task problems can be localized and dealt with almost at once. I find that after the first strategy is used, the students get the idea that their team members can actually help them with their work. With some of the classes, group skills are much harder to teach. The students don't always get the cooperative idea at first. You might find two students doing all the work on a team with the others copying the answers. With some teacher prompting (I sometimes "join" the team for a practice session), these group skills are learned and the team functions as a unit. We have instructional aides (peer tutors) who can sometimes be used as team managers, making sure the team stays on-task.

At the peak of a group functioning effectively as a team unit, the students realize that the team practice is an essential and welcome aid to their learning. However, not all teams reach that peak at the same time in the same class, and consequently, some of them need some assistance from me.

Group dynamics are something to observe! But what terrific skills they teach these students!

Candy Nuzzolillo, Math Teacher
Gulf Middle School, Cape Coral, FL

---

4 (extremely serious problem) at pre- and posttest. The results indicated significantly higher ratings (controlling for pretests) for the TAI students in Experiment 1, but there were no differences in Experiment 2.

Finally, attendance is a major determinant of students' ultimate time on-task. Janke (1978) found that TGT increased student attendance (compared with control groups) in a school for emotionally disturbed adolescents.

LIKING OF CLASS

Various questionnaire measures of liking of class, liking of school, or liking of the subject matter being taught have been administered in research on cooperative learning. The hypothesis that students would enjoy working cooperatively more than individualistically is almost obviously correct: anyone walking into a class using any of the cooperative learning methods can see that the students enjoy working with each other. When the students are asked if they like working cooperatively and would like to do so again, they enthusiastically say that they would.

However, the research evidence on this variable is more inconsistent than that on any of the other noncognitive outcomes. Some studies have found significantly greater liking of class in cooperative than in control classes (DeVries, Edwards, and Wells, 1974a; Edwards and DeVries, 1972, 1974; Humphreys, Johnson, and Johnson, 1982; Johnson, Johnson, Johnson, and Anderson, 1976; Lazarowitz, Baird, Bowlden, and Hertz-Lazarowitz, 1982; Slavin and Karweit, 1981; Slavin, Leavey, and Madden, 1984 [Experiment 1]; Wheeler and Ryan, 1973). However, other studies have found no differences in liking of class between cooperative and control classes (for example, Slavin, 1978b; Madden and Slavin, 1983a; Oickle, 1980; DeVries, Mescon, and Shackman, 1975b; Hulten and DeVries, 1976; DeVries and Mescon, 1975; Slavin, Leavey, and Madden, 1984 [Experiment 2]; Gonzales, 1979; Janke, 1978; Johnson, Johnson, Scott, and Ramolae, 1985). Blaney, Stephan, Rosenfield, Aronson, and Sikes (1977) found that Anglos and blacks increased their liking of class more in Jigsaw than in control conditions, but Mexican-American students' liking of class increased more in the control group.

One of the problems in measuring liking of class is that most students, especially at the elementary level, tend to report on the pretest that they like class, and so the measurement on the posttest cannot discriminate students who like class more than they did before from those who like it the same as before. In the TGT studies that took place in third grades (DeVries and Mescon, 1975; DeVries, Mescon, and Shackman, 1975b) this is certainly part of the reason that no effects were found; more than 90 percent of the students in both experimental conditions agreed on the pre- and posttests that they liked class. Similar ceiling effects may account for many or most of the failures to find significant differences. Also, when students were directly asked whether they liked the method they experienced (cooperative or control), they did express greater liking for the cooperative method (Johnson, Johnson, Johnson, and Anderson, 1976; Humphreys, Johnson, and Johnson, 1982; Madden and Slavin, 1983a). This implies that part of the failure to find significant differences on the more global "liking of class" measures could be due to the fact that students were being asked not to compare experiences with different methods but to give their general feelings about school.

LIKING CLASSMATES AND FEELING LIKED BY CLASSMATES

Because cooperative learning methods are social interventions, they should produce social effects. The criteria for positive intergroup relations outlined by Allport (1954) are similar to the widely accepted antecedents of friendship formation or cohesion (see Lott and Lott, 1965). These include contact; perceived similarity; engaging in pleasant activities; and, once again, cooperation, where individuals who work toward the same goal come to see one another as providers of rewards (see Deutsch, 1949; Johnson and Johnson, 1972). Cooperative learning increases contact between students, gives them a shared basis of similarity (group membership), engages them in pleasant activities together, and has them work toward common goals. As such, it can clearly be hypothesized that they would increase positive affect among students.

Relationships between students have been measured in a variety of ways. In some studies, the number of names listed in response to a sociometric question such as "Who are your friends in this class?" is used as a measure of mutual attraction. Many studies use questionnaire scales with items such as "I like the other students in this class" and "The other students in this class like me."

Slavin (1978b) found positive effects of STAD on the number of friends named and on a "liking of others" questionnaire scale, but not on a "feeling of being liked" scale. Oickle (1980) also found positive effects of STAD on the number of students named as friends, but not on questionnaire scales measuring liking of others or feelings of being liked. DeVries and Edwards (1973) found that TGT increased student scores on a mutual-concern questionnaire scale, but not on a cohesiveness scale or on the number of friends named. Slavin (1977b) found that TGT increased the number of friends named in classes for emotionally disturbed adolescents.

In a combined study of STAD, TGT, and Jigsaw II, Slavin and Karweit (1981) found that the cooperative learning students named more friends than did control students, and they named fewer classmates as individuals with whom they would not like to work. However, there were no treatment differences on questionnaire scales measuring liking of classmates or feelings of being liked. In two TAI studies (Slavin, Leavey, and Madden, 1984), teachers rated a sample of their students on friendship-related problems such as "(Student) has few or no friends" and "(Student) is rejected by others," and on negative peer behaviors such as "(Student) fights with other students" and "(Student) picks on smaller or weaker students." Controlling for pretests, the researchers found that the TAI

TEACHERS ON TEACHING

In every class, there are a few teammates who have trouble getting along with each other at first. What successful strategies have you used to prevent or deal with interpersonal problems within teams?

We have had this experience, but not as frequently as we might have expected. Youngsters have skills of working with each other, and I believe CIRC simply enhances them.

What we have done is simply to remove the youngster from the team and insist he or she work alone until such time as he or she realizes that (1) it's easier to work with others, and (2) it's more fun.

It's been our experience that this youngster earns his or her way back on the team within a week.

Maureen Sauter, Fourth, Fifth,
and Sixth Grade Teacher
Sacandaga Elementary School,
Scotia, NY

---

students were rated significantly higher than the control students on the friendship scale in Experiments 1 and 2. On the negative peer behavior scale, the TAI students were rated significantly better in Experiment 1 and marginally better ($p < .10$) in Experiment 2.

The one Jigsaw study to investigate liking of classmates (Blaney, Stephan, Rosenfield, Aronson, and Sikes, 1977) found no differences on ratings of classmates, but it did find that Jigsaw students felt they were liked by their classmates more consistently than did control students. Many of the Learning Together studies have used responses to such statements as "Other students like me as I am" to assess students' feelings of being liked. Positive effects on such measures have been reported by Johnson, Johnson, Johnson, and Anderson (1976), Cooper, Johnson, Johnson, and Wilderson (1980), Johnson and Johnson (1981), and Johnson and Johnson (1982). A few studies (Slavin, 1978b; Madden and Slavin, 1983a; DeVries, Mescon, and Shackman, 1975b; DeVries and Mescon, 1975) found no effects on questionnaire scales measuring liking of classmates or feelings of being liked. However, all of these studies took place at the elementary level, where virtually all students report that they like their classmates very much, and this ceiling effect almost certainly accounts for these failures to find differences. The preponderance of the evidence, including the evidence from the race relations and mainstreaming studies, certainly supports the conclusion that cooperative learning promotes positive relationships between students.

COOPERATION, ALTRUISM, AND THE ABILITY TO TAKE ANOTHER'S PERSPECTIVE

One anticipated noncognitive outcome of a cooperative experience in schools is that students will become more cooperative or altruistic. Perhaps because this outcome is widely assumed, it has not been studied as often as many others.

One frequently used measure of a preference for altruism or cooperation as opposed to maximization of individual gain or competition is a choice board devised by Kagan and Madsen (1972) in which students allocate rewards to actual or imagined peers. The choices with which students are confronted are to give the "peer" more rewards (altruism), the same number of rewards (equality), or fewer rewards (competition) than the students receive themselves. Using measures based on this paradigm, Hertz-Lazarowitz, Sharan, and Steinberg (1980) showed that students who had experienced Group Investigation made more altruistic choices than did control students. They also found that when students who had worked in cooperative groups were reassigned to new groups for an experimental task, they cooperated better and their groups had higher productivity than groups made up from the control classes. A similar study (Sharan et al., 1984) failed to replicate the reward-allocation findings, but found that when new groups were made up from students in the experimental and control classes, there was more verbal and nonverbal cooperation and less competition on a construction task among students who had experienced Group Investigation than among control students. Students who had been in STAD classes also exhibited more verbal and nonverbal cooperation and less competition than control students, but less verbal and nonverbal cooperation than the Group Investigation students. Kagan, Zahn, Widaman, Schwarzwald, and Tyrell (1985) found that STAD and TGT increased cooperativeness toward others. Finally, Hertz-Lazarowitz, Sapir, and Sharan (1981) found that students who had experienced Group Investigation scored lower in competitiveness than did Jigsaw or control students. There were no differences between Jigsaw and control students on this measure.

Johnson, Johnson, Johnson, and Anderson (1976) found that when students engaged in Learning Together activities, they made more altruistic choices on a task similar

---

TEACHERS ON TEACHING

Not surprisingly, cooperative learning methods have been found to enhance students' abilities to work well with others. What specific strategies do you use to help students learn to work with others? How have you seen cooperative skills develop over time in your students? Have you seen carryover of cooperative behaviors into times other than those when you are using cooperative methods in the classroom?

I have very high expectations of students in cooperative learning. I am very pleased with the way most students rise to meet the expectations.

During the first month of cooperative learning I try to recognize every cooperative behavior I see and hear. Constant reinforcement of the behaviors leads to a habit of cooperative behaviors.

I circulate in the room constantly during team study time to ensure on-task behaviors. I have made a conscious effort to interact with students rather than intervene. This has been great for me to learn and has made my job easier as well as made the students responsible for their own behaviors.

I spend the first month to six weeks teaching cooperative behaviors and group processing. When I see the students have internalized the cooperative behaviors I remove the processing and move into the structured models of TGT and CIRC.

I am very aware of overflow cooperative behaviors such as the following:

1. I see children helping others to understand material even when they are not in the cooperative structure. The behaviors have become very natural and have carried over into individual learning tasks. It's wonderful to see.

2. At Christmas there is usually a problem with gift exchanges. Socially acceptable children do not want to exchange gifts with poorer children. This Christmas there was no observable dissatisfaction in gift exchange. I attribute that to well-defined cooperative behaviors which carried over into the social realm.

3. Recently I tried something that was really interesting. I provided pretzels and drinks as a reward for each group. However, there were not enough pretzels or drinks for every student in the group. I said nothing about the problem and just observed. The

groups immediately began to suggest ways to divide and share the food so that everyone would have some.

I did the same thing with a class that had not been involved in cooperative learning. Each child grabbed some food and was seemingly unaware of the other students in his group—indicating a marked lack of group interdependency.

The rewards are well worth the effort of teaching children cooperative behaviors!

Nancy Whitlock, Fifth Grade Teacher
Spencer County Elementary School,
Taylorsville, KY

Teamwork makes all the difference! When you explain to the children that they are working to earn the most points possible for their team and that they are responsible for how many points their partner earns, they work harder to help their partners. A great strategy is modeling exactly what you want and expect to see from the partners. As a teacher I choose one student and model every step for the class with that student when introducing CIRC or just reviewing procedures. With CIRC you will want to review and model steps periodically when beginning your first lessons. Over a period of time the noise level drops and the students become better judges of "Okay answers" and "great answers." Cooperative learning tends to carry over even when you aren't using it. The children tend to keep their partners even in other subjects. Many times in social studies and science they will want to discuss answers or have their partners check answers. They also like to review for a test in science and social studies by asking each other questions, sort of like a "story retell" review. They also become very upset if their partner is absent. I've heard students say, "How could you be absent?" However, the students adapt well to working with another set of partners for a day.

Holly Beers, Fifth Grade Teacher
Point Pleasant Elementary School,
Glen Burnie, MD

to the choice board than did students who had worked competitively or individualistically. Ryan and Wheeler (1977) found that students who had studied cooperatively made more cooperative and helpful decisions in a simulation game than did students who had studied competitively.

A study by Solomon, Watson, Schaps, Battistich, and Solomon (in press) introduced cooperative classroom activities along with other methods designed to develop prosocial norms in kindergarten classes, and then continued these interventions in subsequent years. As of this writing, the oldest children are in fourth grade. The form of cooperative learning used avoids both group rewards and individual accountability. The results after five years indicate mixed effects on many measures of prosocial behaviors and attitudes, but generally positive effects on such outcomes as the ability to resolve conflicts in groups, the tendency to cooperate with others, and interpersonal sensitivity.

Finally, an important component of the ability to cooperate with others is the ability to understand someone else's perspective. Bridgeman (1977) found that students who had worked cooperatively using Jigsaw were better able to take the perspective of another person than were control students, and Johnson, Johnson, Johnson, and Anderson (1976) found that students who had worked cooperatively were better able to identify feelings in taped conversations than were students who had worked individually.

Thus, it is clear that cooperative experiences do increase components of cooperative and altruistic behavior more than do competitive or individualistic experiences. These findings are very important, because they suggest that cooperative learning may enhance the kinds of prosocial behaviors that are increasingly needed in a society in which the ability to get along with others is more and more crucial.

CONCLUSION

The breadth of the outcomes affected by cooperative learning strategies is impressive. There exist special programs focused solely on improving student self-esteem, or internal locus of control, or race relations, or mainstreaming, or achievement; cooperative learning strategies have been shown to positively influence all of these outcomes and several others. What is more remarkable is that each of several quite different methods has been shown to have positive effects on a wide variety of outcomes. The differences in patterns of noncognitive outcomes between methods are not as interesting as their similarities. In general, for any desired outcome of schooling, administer a cooperative learning treatment, and about two-thirds of the time there will be a significant difference between the experimental and control groups in favor of the experimental groups (rarely, if ever, will differences favor a control group).

Although the effects of cooperative learning on the noncognitive outcomes reviewed in this chapter appear to be relatively strong and consistent, there is much work yet to be done in this area. The research conducted to date has dealt primarily with validation of the various cooperative learning models of the "brand X versus brand Y" variety, where brand X is some form of cooperative learning and brand Y is a competitive, individualistic, or untreated control treatment. There is a need both for careful analysis of what goes on in a cooperative classroom and for more attention to just how the various outcomes come about. A great deal is changed when a teacher adopts cooperative learning: the classroom incentive and task structures, feedback systems, and authority systems and the teacher's role all change substantially. Which of these changes accounts for the effects of cooperative learning on noncognitive outcomes? We have enough research to begin to identify which components of cooperative learning methods affect student achievement (see Chapter 2), but we have little to go on with respect to each of the noncognitive outcomes discussed in this chapter.

In summary, cooperative learning has been shown in a wide variety of studies to positively influence a host of important noncognitive variables. Although not every study has found positive effects on every noncognitive outcome, the overall effects of cooperative learning on student self-esteem, peer support for achievement, internal locus of control, time on-task, liking of class and of classmates, cooperativeness, and other variables are positive and robust.

FOUR

STAD and TGT

Two of the oldest and most extensively researched forms of cooperative learning are Student Teams–Achievement Divisions and Teams–Games–Tournaments. They are also among the most widely applicable forms of cooperative learning, having been used in grades two through twelve, in subjects from math to language arts to social studies to science. STAD and TGT are quite similar; the only difference between them is that STAD uses individual quizzes at the end of each lesson whereas TGT uses academic games.

STUDENT TEAMS–ACHIEVEMENT DIVISIONS

STAD is one of the simplest of all cooperative learning methods, and is a good model to begin with for teachers who are new to the cooperative approach.

Overview

STAD has five major components—class presentations, teams, quizzes, individual improvement scores, and team recognition.

Class Presentations. Material in STAD is initially introduced in a class presentation. This is most often direct instruction or a lecture-discussion conducted by the teacher, but could include audiovisual presentations. Class presentations in STAD differ from usual teaching only in that they must be clearly focused on the STAD unit. In this way, students realize that they must pay careful attention during the class presentation, because doing so will help them to do well on the quizzes, and their quiz scores determine their team scores.

Teams. Teams are composed of four or five students who represent a cross-section of the class in terms of academic performance, sex, and race or ethnicity. The major

This chapter is adapted from Slavin, 1986a.

TEACHERS ON TEACHING

What is the most important advice you would give to teachers who are about to use cooperative learning for the first time? What pitfalls should teachers watch out for, and how should teachers avoid them?

The most important advice I could give a teacher who is planning to use cooperative learning is *be prepared!* Study the handbook; thoroughly acquaint yourself with procedures, scoring, suggestions, and so on; thoroughly indoctrinate your students through practice sessions and demonstrations; get all the materials together far in advance of the actual implementation; be flexible; be prepared for frustration (yours and your students'); prepare your neighbors in the next classroom, invite their comments and suggestions; let the administrators know what you're doing; above all, *enjoy* the experience—TGT is the most exciting thing I, and many of my students, have ever experienced in a classroom.

Also, wait until you've gotten to know your students before you try to put them in groups. Again, be flexible; switch kids around until you've created good groups.

Wanda Sue Wansley, Math Teacher
Caloosa Middle School,
Cape Coral, FL

Start with just one strategy and pick just one class to start with. Teachers need to remember that hardly anyone will do everything right the first time, but by reading the manual carefully and planning thoroughly and taking each step slowly, the teacher should have a positive experience. Teachers should remember that cooperative learning is a tool to add to their repertoire. They should not abandon successful practices they have developed already in the classroom.

Steve Parsons, Math Teacher
West Frederick Middle School,
Frederick, MD

I recommend that a teacher think big but move slowly! I would remind her that when a teacher tries a new skill she will actually feel less competent for a period of time. I read that a new teaching skill takes twenty to thirty practices before a teacher reaches a comfort zone in its use.

Secondly, I recommend that teachers incorporate peer coaching to some degree. The transfer of learning is so much greater when shared and discussed with a colleague. I think it's a rare teacher who can work through the process without a peer support system.

Finally, I would recommend that teachers modify the programs to meet their specific needs. The basic elements must remain for the process of cooperative learning to be effective, but teachers often drop the idea completely because they cannot precisely follow the programs.

Nancy Whitlock, Fifth Grade Teacher
Spencer County Elementary School,
Taylorsville, KY

function of the team is to prepare its members to do well on the quizzes. After the teacher presents the material, the team meets to study worksheets or other material. Most often, the study takes the form of students discussing problems together, comparing answers, and correcting any misconceptions if teammates make mistakes.

The team is the most important feature of STAD. At every point, emphasis is placed on team members doing their best for the team, and on the team doing its best to help its members. The team provides the peer support for academic performance that is important

TEACHERS ON TEACHING

*How do you introduce the idea of cooperative learning to students'
parents? What kinds of responses do parents have to cooperative
learning? How have you dealt with parent concerns?*

In introducing cooperative learning to my parents, I held an open house and had a minilesson on a subject their children were learning. I staged a typical teacher-talk-and-student-listen report. I then asked parents to answer questions on the subject. I really praised the high "students" and said nothing about the others. I then had three minilessons introducing cooperative learning. We discussed the parents' scores, their ability to get along with their peers, self-esteem, and what they had learned. After each strategy, we changed groups and had another lesson. Before the end of the open house, all of my parents knew something about my class, my teaching strategies, and more importantly each other. Not only does this makes an ownership of my students with each other, but my parents have a real ownership with my class and each other. I have never had a problem with my teaching techniques or the fact I do not use workbook pages or worksheets.

Alta Blandford
Valley View Elementary School,
Rosewell, NM

for learning, and it provides the mutual concern and respect that are important for such outcomes as intergroup relations, self-esteem, and acceptance of mainstreamed students.

Quizzes. After one to two periods of teacher presentation and one to two periods of team practice, the students take individual quizzes. Students are not permitted to help one another during the quizzes. Thus, every student is individually responsible for knowing the material.

Individual Improvement Scores. The idea behind the individual improvement scores is to give each student a performance goal that the student can reach, but only if he or she works harder and performs better than in the past. Any student can contribute maximum points to his or her team in this scoring system, but no student can do so without showing improvement over past performance. Each student is given a "base" score, derived from the student's average performance on similar quizzes. Students then earn points for their teams based on how much their quiz scores exceed their base scores.

Team Recognition. Teams may earn certificates or other rewards if their average scores exceed a certain criterion. Students' team scores may also be used to determine up to 20 percent of their grades.

Preparation

Materials. STAD can be used with curriculum materials specifically designed for Student Team Learning and distributed by the Johns Hopkins Team Learning Project, or it can be used with teacher-made materials. Johns Hopkins materials are available for mathematics for grades two through ten, language arts for grades three through eight, junior high school life and physical science, and other topics.*

However, it is quite easy to make your own materials. Simply make a worksheet, a

*These materials are available from the Johns Hopkins Team Learning Project, 3505 N. Charles St., Baltimore, MD 21218. For more information on these materials, see the section on resources at the end of Chapter 7.

TEACHERS ON TEACHING

STAD uses a scoring system that emphasizes improvement rather than just percentage correct. How do students respond to the improvement scoring system? Do they understand it? Do they see it as fair? How do you explain it to students?

My students love getting what amounts to two scores for each quiz: the actual test grade goes in my grade book for later averaging, and their improvement points go on their team sheet. Students love receiving points for improvement: they're getting more mileage from each test paper. Through improvement points it's possible for the lower-scoring students to bring something back to their teams. Students have no problem understanding how the system works. They also understand that this system is fair.

When I introduce the improvement points concept, I explain that we all know some things more thoroughly than we know other things. I explain that today I may be knowledgable in a particular area but that on another day I may be confused about a particular concept. I explain that as a starting point, I will give everyone a base score computed by averaging his or her current grades. I explain that after three tests, each student will get a new base score determined by the last three test scores. Students appreciate the fact that they're not locked into a base score. They appreciate that their base score changes as their knowledge changes; students understand and appreciate this.

Jacquie Alberti,
Language Arts Teacher
Norman C. Toole Middle School,
N. Charleston, SC

worksheet answer sheet, and a quiz for each unit you plan to teach. Each unit should occupy three to five days of instruction. See Appendix 1 for examples of STAD worksheets and quizzes; these materials were developed by the Team Learning Project at The Johns Hopkins University. Guidelines for preparing your own materials appear at the end of this chapter.

Assigning Students to Teams. As we have seen, STAD teams represent a cross-section of the class. A four-person team in a class that is half male, half female, three-quarters white, and one-quarter minority might have two boys and two girls and three white students and one minority student. The team would also have a high performer, a low performer, and two average performers. Of course, *high performer* is a relative term: it means high for the class, not necessarily high compared with national norms.

You may take likes, dislikes, and "deadly combinations" of students into account in assigning students to teams, but do not let students choose their own teams, because they will tend to choose others like themselves. Instead follow these steps:

1. **Make copies of team summary sheets.** Make one copy of a team summary sheet (Appendix 2) for every four students in your class.
2. **Rank students.** On a sheet of paper, rank the students in your class from highest to lowest in past performance. Use whatever information you have to do this; test scores are best, grades are good, but your own judgment is fine. It may be difficult to be exact in your ranking, but do the best you can.
3. **Decide on the number of teams.** Each team should have four members if possible. To decide how many teams you will have, divide the number of students in the class by four. If the number is divisible by four, the quotient will be the number of four-member teams you should have. For example, if there are thirty-two students in the

class, you would have eight teams with four members each. If the division is uneven, the remainder will be one, two, or three. You will then have one, two, or three teams composed of five members. For example, if there are thirty students in your class, you would have seven teams; five teams would have four members and two would have five members.

4. **Assign students to teams.** In assigning students to teams, balance the teams so that (a) each team is composed of students whose performance levels range from low to average to high, and (b) the average performance level of all the teams in the class is about equal. Using your list of students ranked by performance, assign team letters to each student. For example, in an eight-team class you would use the letters A through H. Start at the top of your list with the letter A; continue lettering toward the middle. When you get to the last team letter, continue lettering in the opposite order. For example if you were using the letters A–H (as in Table 4–1), the eighth and ninth students would be assigned to team H, the tenth to team G, the next to team F, and so on. When you get back to letter A, stop and repeat the process from the bottom up, again starting and ending with the letter A.

Notice in Table 4–1 that two of the students (17 and 18) are not assigned at this point. They will be added to teams as fifth members, but first the teams should be checked for race or ethnicity and sex balance. If, for example, one-fourth of the class

Table 4–1 Assigning Students to Teams

	Rank	Team Name
High-Performing Students	1	A
	2	B
	3	C
	4	D
	5	E
	6	F
	7	G
	8	H
Average-Performing Students	9	H
	10	G
	11	F
	12	E
	13	D
	14	C
	15	B
	16	A
	17	
	18	
	19	A
	20	B
	21	C
	22	D
	23	E
	24	F
	25	G
	26	H
Students	27	H
	28	G
	29	F
	30	E
	31	D
	32	C
	33	B
	34	A

is black, approximately one student on each team should be black. If the teams you have made based on performance ranking are not evenly divided on both ethnicity and sex (they will hardly ever be balanced on the first try), you should change team assignments by trading students of the same approximate performance level, but of different ethnicity or sex, between teams until a balance is achieved.

5. **Fill out team summary sheets.** Fill in the names of the students on each team on your team summary sheets (Appendix 2), leaving the team-name space blank.

Determining Initial Base Scores. Base scores represent students' average scores on past quizzes. If you are starting STAD after you have given three or more quizzes, use students' average quiz scores as base scores. Otherwise, use students' final grades from the previous year (see Table 4–2).

Schedule of Activities

STAD consists of a regular cycle of instructional activities, as follows:

Teach. Present the lesson.

Team study. Students work on worksheets in their teams to master the material.

Test. Students take individual quizzes.

Team recognition. Team scores are computed based on team members' improvement scores, and individual certificates, a class newsletter, or a bulletin board recognize high-scoring teams.

Let's look at these activities in detail.

TEACH

Time: 1–2 class periods

Main idea: present the lesson

Materials needed: your lesson plan

Each lesson in STAD begins with a class presentation. The presentation should cover the opening, development, and guided-practice components of your total lesson; the

Table 4–2   Determining Initial Base Scores

Last Year's Grade	Initial Base Score
A	90
A−/B+	85
B	80
B−/C+	75
C	70
C−/D+	65
D	60
F	55

Average Three Test Scores	
Sara's Scores	90
	84
	87
	$\overline{261} \div 3 = 87$
Sara's Base Score =	87

TEACHERS ON TEACHING

STAD is one of the simplest and most broadly applicable of the Student Team Learning methods. What advice would you give a teacher who is considering this technique?

It's hard to select the most important piece of advice for teachers just starting out with cooperative learning. I am going to give several pieces of advice, my "Golden Rules of Implementing STAD":

1. Always completely explain the lesson before allowing students to get into their groups. Explain to the groups how to determine improvement points and determine new base scores. The time you spend with the initial instructions will greatly determine the success of your program. You cannot be successful with any program if you don't spend time explaining, demonstrating, or reexplaining in the beginning stages. This is true of all teaching, not just cooperative learning.

2. Always get students to figure their own improvement points and new base scores. I give every group a folder that contains the various forms. One person from each group is selected to average team scores, determine improvement points, and determine new base scores (when needed). Students enjoy doing this type of work. I spot-check their figures. It also helps to have a person from another team go over all figures before I look at them. Get students to lighten your paper load by doing any of the work they're capable of doing.

Jacquie Alberti,
Language Arts Teacher
Norman C. Toole Middle School,
N. Charleston, SC

---

team activities and quiz cover independent practice and assessment, respectively. In your lesson, stress the following (adapted from Good, Grouws, and Ebmeier, 1983):

Opening

- Tell students what they are about to learn and why it is important. Arouse student curiosity with a puzzling demonstration, real-life problem, or other means.
- Briefly review any prerequisite skills or information.

Development

- Stick close to the objectives that you will test.
- Focus on meaning, not memorization.
- Actively demonstrate concepts or skills, using visual aids, manipulatives, and many examples.
- Frequently assess student comprehension by asking many questions.
- Explain why an answer is correct or incorrect, unless this is obvious.
- Move rapidly to the next concept as soon as students have grasped the main idea.
- Maintain momentum by eliminating interruptions, asking many questions, and moving rapidly through the lesson.

TEACHERS ON TEACHING

Some teachers worry that they will not be able to cover as much material in cooperative learning as they ordinarily do. Has this been a problem for you? How do you organize your time to ensure adequate coverage of the content?

The question is not the quantity of the information covered but rather the amount of material that is retained by the student. Using cooperative learning strategies (particularly, in this case, TGT) has motivated students to retain more of the concepts and facts which are presented. I realize that most students do not "study" presented materials for homework. While most will produce a product for homework, study time is not a product. A forty-five-minute tournament does much to increase retention of material presented during class.

Gary Porter, Sixth Grade Teacher
Summitview Elementary School,
Waynesboro, PA

I really cover more material, because I don't get sidetracked as much as I used to, telling stories and repeating myself and trying to make things interesting. This method has helped me be more concrete–sequential instead of so abstract–random.

Bill Bollier, Science Teacher
Leo Junior/Senior High School,
Leo, IN

Guided Practice

- Have all students work problems or examples or prepare answers to your questions.
- Call on students at random. This makes all students prepare themselves to answer.
- Do not give long class assignments at this point. Have students work one or two problems or examples or prepare one or two answers, then give them feedback.

TEAM STUDY

Time: 1–2 class periods

Main idea: students study worksheets in their teams

Materials needed: two worksheets for every team

two answer sheets for every team

During team study, team members' tasks are to master the material you presented in your lesson and to help their teammates master the material. Students have worksheets and answer sheets they can use to practice the skill being taught and to assess themselves and their teammates. Only two copies of the worksheets and answer sheets are given to each team—this forces teammates to work together—but if some students prefer to work alone or want their own copies, you may make additional copies available.

On the first day of team work in STAD, you should explain to students what it means to work in teams. In particular, before beginning team work discuss the following team rules (which you may list on a bulletin board or chalkboard):

1. Students have a responsibility to make sure that their teammates have learned the material.

2. No one is finished studying until all *teammates* have mastered the subject.
3. Ask all teammates for help before asking the teacher.
4. Teammates may talk to each other *softly*.

You may encourage students to add additional rules if they like. Then proceed as follows:

- Have teammates move their desks together or move to team tables.
- Give teams about ten minutes to choose a team name. Any teams that cannot agree on a name in that time may choose one later.
- Hand out worksheets and answer sheets (two of each per team) with a minimum of fuss.
- Suggest that students work together in pairs or threes. If they are working problems (as in math), each student in a pair or three should work the problem individually and then check with his or her partner(s). If anyone missed a question, his or her teammates have a responsibility to explain it. If students are working on short-answer questions, they may quiz each other, with partners taking turns holding the answer sheet or attempting to answer the questions.
- Emphasize to students that they are not finished studying until they are sure their *teammates will make 100* on the quiz.
- Make sure that students understand that the worksheets are for *studying*—not merely for filling out and handing in. Thus, it is important for students to have the answer sheets to check themselves and their teammates as they study.
- Have students *explain* answers to one another instead of just checking each other against the answer sheet.
- Remind students that if they have questions, they must *ask all teammates* before asking you.
- While students are working in teams, *circulate through the class,* praising teams that are working well, sitting in with each team to hear how team members are doing, and so on.

TEST

Time: $\frac{1}{2}$–1 class period
Main idea: individual quiz
Material needed: one quiz per student

- Distribute the quiz and give students adequate time to complete it. *Do not let students work together on the quiz;* at this point students must show what they have learned as individuals. Have students move their desks apart if this is possible.
- Either allow students to *exchange papers* with members of other teams, or *collect the quizzes* to score after class. Be sure to have the quizzes scored and team scores figured in time for the next class.

TEAM RECOGNITION

Main idea: figuring individual improvement scores and team scores and awarding certificates or other team rewards

FIGURING INDIVIDUAL AND TEAM SCORES

As soon as possible after each quiz, figure individual improvement scores and team scores and award certificates or other rewards to high-scoring teams. If possible, announce team scores in the first period after the quiz. This makes the connection between doing well and receiving recognition clear to students, and in turn increases their motivation to do their best.

Improvement Points

Students earn points for their teams based on the degree to which their quiz scores (percentage correct) exceed their base scores:

Quiz Score	Improvement Points
more than 10 points below base score	0
10 points below to 1 point below base score	10
base score to 10 points above base score	20
more than 10 points above base score	30
perfect paper (regardless of base score)	30

Before you begin to figure improvement points, you will need one copy of a quiz score sheet (Appendix 3). Figuring improvement points is not at all difficult, and when you get used to it, it will take only a few minutes. Figure 4–1 shows how improvement points would be computed for one set of students.

The purpose of base scores and improvement points is to make it possible for all students to bring maximum points to their teams, whatever their level of past performance. Students understand that it is fair to compare each student with his or her own level of past performance, since all students enter class with different levels of skills and experience in mathematics.

Team Scores

To figure a team's score, record each team member's improvement points on the team summary sheet and divide team members' total improvement points by the number of team members who were present, rounding off any fractions (see Figure 4–2). Note that team scores depend on improvement scores rather than on raw quiz scores.

RECOGNIZING TEAM ACCOMPLISHMENTS

Three levels of awards are given. These are based on average team scores, as follows:

Criterion (Team Average)	Award
15	GOODTEAM
20	GREATTEAM
25	SUPERTEAM

Note that all teams can achieve the awards; teams are not competing with one another.

These criteria are set so that to be a Greatteam most team members must score above their base scores, and to be a Superteam most team members must score at least ten points above their base scores. You may change these criteria if necessary.

You should provide some sort of recognition or reward for achieving at the Greatteam or Superteam level. Attractive certificates to each team member may be used, a large, fancy certificate ($8\frac{1}{2}$ by 11 inches) for Superteams and a smaller one for Greatteams. Examples of certificates appear in Appendix 4. Goodteams should just receive congratulations in class. Many teachers make bulletin board displays listing the week's Superteams and Greatteams, or displaying Polaroid pictures of the successful teams. Others prepare one-page newsletters, give students special buttons to wear, or let Superteams and Greatteams line up first for recess or receive other special privileges. Use your imagination and

Student	Date: May 23 Quiz: Addition with Regrouping Base Score	Quiz Score	Improvement Points	Date: Quiz: Base Score	Quiz Score	Improvement Points	Date: Quiz: Base Score	Quiz Score	Improvement Points
Sara A.	90	100	30						
Tom B.	90	100	30						
Ursula C.	90	82	10						
Danielle D.	85	74	10						
Eddie E.	85	98	30						
Natasha F.	85	82	10						
Travis G.	80	67	0						
Tammy H.	80	91	30						
Edgar I.	75	79	20						
Andy J.	75	76	20						
Mary K.	70	91	30						
Stan L.	65	82	30						
Alvin M.	65	70	20						
Carol N.	60	62	20						
Harold S.	55	46	10						
Jack E.	55	40	0						

Figure 4–1   Quiz Score Sheet (STAD and Jigsaw II).

TEAM NAME Fantastic Four

TEAM MEMBERS	1	2	3	4	5	6	7	8	9	10	11	12	13	14
Sara A.	30													
Eddie E.	30													
Edgar I.	20													
Carol N.	20													
TOTAL TEAM SCORE	100													
TEAM AVERAGE	25													
TEAM AWARD	Super Team													

*Team Average = Total Team Score ÷ Number of Team Members

Figure 4–2   Team Summary Sheet.

TEACHERS ON TEACHING

Research on cooperative learning finds that group rewards are an important ingredient in cooperative learning. Have you used any innovative group rewards that other teachers might want to know about?

I have stumbled upon rewards that are extremely popular in my fifth grade class. One of these rewards *saves* me time! My Superteams in reading have an opportunity to create the rewards for other Super- and Greatteams. They use Print Shop, Award Ware, or Garfield Creates to design certificates, coupons, and tickets. Coupons can be redeemed for "free" assignments, and tickets can be used for "team time" on the computer—which is more often than not spent designing rewards! It remains a very special and very popular reward, even after months of use!

Debra Kauffman,
Fifth Grade Teacher
Taylor Elementary School,
Columbia, PA

I teach junior high (eighth) and senior high (ninth through twelfth), so I give *extra credit* toward students' nine-week grades. The idea that doing well as a team can help your grade but not hurt it seems to be some incentive for students to work well as a team. This is done only after a unit of study or over a period of time. Usually I change teams after this. As well as receiving credit points, students receive certificates or other rewards such as being recognized in front of the class and team names posted on a certificate on the bulletin board.

Bill Bollier, Science Teacher
Leo Junior/Senior High School,
Leo, IN

It is important that group (team) rewards are acknowledged in many meaningful and diversified ways. Each week members of the Superteam are given a certificate. These certificates are sent to the house principal's office, and the principal will sign or stamp the certificates. He will visit the classroom or invite the members of the team to visit his office, where he congratulates them.

The parents of the students are very pleased and appreciative. It is the first time many of the students have received a reward. Positive feedback is excellent.

Thelma Reiss, Math Teacher
North End Middle School,
Waterbury, CT

The children really vie to be Superteams. I have added a little extra incentive with a goodie box and homework passes. After the child has earned five Superteams, he or she gets to choose a prize from the goodie box. The prizes are various and sundry gems I have found at local yard sales. Children with six Greatteams get a homework pass, which allows them to skip one homework in one subject.

I have also had a sale with double Superteam awards or an extra ten points if everyone on the team has completed two units. These also act as incentives.

Joan Kotzin, Fifth Grade Teacher
Point Pleasant Elementary School,
Glen Burnie, MD

I give students "Berger Bucks" good for extra credit, free homework, time in the library (out of math), free milkshakes, or anything within reason (negotiable). These are given to TGT tournament winners and teams, as well as individuals, for something above and/or beyond the call of duty, or for *dramatic* improvement in achievement.

Edgar Berger, Math Teacher
Cypress Lake Middle School,
Ft. Myers, FL

creativity, and vary rewards from time to time; it is more important to be excited about your students' accomplishments than to give them large rewards.

Returning the First Set of Quizzes

When you return the first set of quizzes (with the base scores, quiz scores, and improvement points) to the students, you will need to explain the improvement point system. In your explanation, emphasize the following:

1. The main purposes of the improvement point system are to give everyone a minimum score to try to beat and to base that minimum score on past performance so that all students will have an equal chance to be successful if they do their best academically.
2. Students must realize that the scores of everyone on their team are important—that all members of the team can earn maximum improvement points if they do their best.
3. The improvement point system is fair because everyone is competing only with himself or herself—trying to improve his or her own performance—regardless of what the rest of the class does.

Recomputing Base Scores

Every marking period (or more frequently, if you like), recompute students' average quiz scores on all quizzes and assign students new base scores.

Changing Teams

After five or six weeks of STAD, reassign students to new teams. This gives students who were on low-scoring teams a new chance, allows students to work with other classmates, and keeps the program fresh.

Grading

Report card grades should be based on students' actual quiz scores, not on their improvement points or team scores. If you wish, you may make the students' team scores a part of (say, up to 20 percent of) their grades. If your school gives separate grades for effort, you might use team and/or improvement scores to determine the effort grades.

TEAMS–GAMES–TOURNAMENT

Overview

TGT is the same as STAD in every respect but one: instead of the quizzes and the individual improvement score system, TGT uses academic tournaments, in which students compete as representatives of their teams with members of other teams who are like them in past academic performance. A description of the components of TGT follows.

TEACHERS ON TEACHING

Because of its use of academic games as well as learning teams, TGT is often seen by students as one of the most exciting of the cooperative learning methods. How has TGT worked in your classes? What problems have come up, and how have you solved them?

In my opinion TGT is one of the best techniques I have ever used in my classroom. What TGT does is allow me as a teacher to use competition in a constructive/positive atmosphere. Students realize that competition is something they deal with all the time, but TGT gives them rules and strategies to compete as individuals after receiving help from their teammates. They develop a dependence or trust in their home team that allows them to feel confident when they compete in the tournament.

Students are always asking me when they are going to play TGT. This tells me that they enjoy the game atmosphere and like the chance to earn recognition for their team. The game itself sets a positive tone in the classroom because of the students' excitement over playing. Teachers do have to act as referees to settle disagreements over rules and answers, but if the teacher is circulating around the room and intervening quickly when problems arise, these disruptions will be minor. Again, the structure and rules of the game really set the tone and help keep a positive attitude. Also, the students realize that each tournament comes and goes. They will try their best each time whether they win or lose, because another tournament will be happening again soon.

Steve Parsons, Math Teacher
West Frederick Middle School,
Frederick, MD

I have definitely had no problems with maintaining students' interest or enthusiasm in TGT!

In fact, I hear "When are we going to have another tournament?" much more than I hear "Do we have to?" If for some reason we do not have a tournament at the regular time (the end of each chapter), we're talking major revolt! One time we had an extra, unscheduled tournament because some out-of-town guests wanted to observe, and the students were delighted! (The kids in the rest of my classes were very upset that they didn't get to have a tournament.)

One of the first questions I had this year from the eighth graders (who were in my seventh grade classes last year) was, "Do we get to do TGT this year?"

I always have the winning teams announced on the schoolwide PA system after a tournament. The students love hearing their names (and their team names—which they chose) in the announcements.

The results are also posted in my classroom, so they can see how everyone else is doing as well.

Wanda Sue Wansley,
Eighth Grade Teacher
Caloosa Middle School,
Cape Coral, FL

Class Presentations. (same as for STAD)

Teams. (same as for STAD)

Games. The games are composed of content-relevant questions designed to test the knowledge students gain from class presentations and team practice. Games are played at tables of three students, each of whom represents a different team. Most games are simply numbered questions on a ditto sheet. A student picks a number card and attempts to

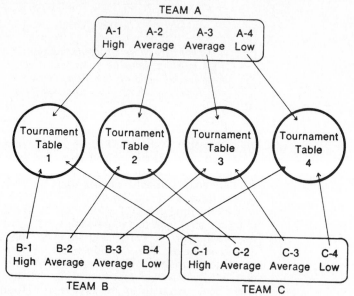

Figure 4–3 Assignment to Tournament Tables.

answer the question corresponding to the number. A challenge rule permits players to challenge one another's answers.

Tournaments. The tournament is the structure in which the games take place. It is usually held at the end of the week, after the teacher has made a class presentation and the teams have had time to practice with the worksheets. For the first tournament, the teacher assigns students to tournament tables—the top three students in past performance to table 1, the next three to table 2, and so on. This equal competition, like the individual improvement score system in STAD, makes it possible for students of all levels of past performance to contribute maximally to their team scores if they do their best. Figure 4–3 illustrates the relationship between heterogeneous teams and homogeneous tournament tables.

After the first week, students change tables depending on their own performance in the most recent tournament. The winner at each table is "bumped up" to the next higher table (for example, from table 6 to table 5); the second scorer stays at the same table; and the low scorer is "bumped down." In this way, if students have been misassigned at first, they will eventually be moved up or down until they reach their true level of performance.

Team Recognition. (same as for STAD)

Preparation

Materials. Curriculum materials for TGT are the same as for STAD, except that you will also need a set of cards numbered from 1 to 30 for every three students in your largest class. Teachers can obtain these materials from the Johns Hopkins Team Learning Project (see the resources section at the end of Chapter 7) or make their own by numbering colored index cards.

Assigning Students to Teams. (same as for STAD)

Assigning Students to Initial Tournament Tables. Make a copy of the tournament table assignment sheet (Appendix 5). On it, list students from top to bottom in past performance, using the same ranking you used to form teams (see Figure 4–4). Count the number of students in the class. If the number is divisible by three, all tournament

Student	Team	Tournament Number: 1	2	3	4	5	6	7	8	9	10	11	12	13
Sam	Orioles	1												
Sarah	Cougars	1												
Tyrone	Whiz Kids	1												
Maria	Geniuses	1												
Liz	Orioles	2												
John T.	Cougars	2												
Sylvia	Whiz Kids	2												
Tom	Geniuses	2												
John F.	Orioles	3												
Tanya	Whiz Kids	3												
Carla	Orioles	3												
Kim	Cougars	4												
Carlos	Geniuses	4												
Shirley	Whiz Kids	4												
Ralph	Cougars	5												
Ruth	Geniuses	5												
Zoe	Whiz Kids	5												

Figure 4–4   Tournament Table Assignment Sheet.

tables will have three members; just assign the first three students on the list to table 1, the next three to table 2, and so on. If there is a remainder to the division, one or two of the top tournament tables will have four members. For example, a class of twenty-nine students would have nine tournament tables, two of which would have four members. The first four students on the ranked list will be assigned to table 1, the next four to table 2, and three each to the other tables (see Figure 4–4).

How to Start TGT

Begin with the schedule of activities described in the following section. After teaching the lesson, announce team assignments and have students move their desks together to make team tables. Tell students that they will be working in teams for several weeks and competing in academic games to add points to their team scores, and that the highest-scoring teams will receive recognition in a class newsletter.

Schedule of Activities

TGT consists of a regular cycle of instructional activities, as follows:

Teach. Present the lesson.

Team study. Students work on worksheets in their teams to master the material.

Tournaments. Students play academic games in ability-homogeneous, three-member tournament tables.

Team recognition. Team scores are computed based on team members' tournament scores, and a class newsletter or bulletin board recognizes high-scoring teams.

These activities are described in detail on the following pages.

TEACH

Time: 1–2 class periods

Main idea: present the lesson

Materials needed: your lesson plan

See the section on teaching for STAD, pp. 59–61.

TEAM STUDY

Time: 1–2 class periods

Main idea: students study worksheets in their teams

Materials needed: two worksheets for every team

two answer sheets for every team

See the section on team study for STAD, pp. 60–61.

TOURNAMENTS

Time: one class period

Main idea: competition at three-member, ability-homogeneous tournament tables

Materials needed: tournament table assignment sheet, filled in

one copy of game sheet and game answers (same as the quiz and quiz answers for STAD) for each tournament table

one game score sheet (Appendix 6) for each tournament table

one deck of number cards, corresponding to the number of questions on the game sheet, for each tournament table.

At the beginning of the tournament period, announce students' tournament-table assignments and have them move desks together or go to tables serving as tournament tables. Scramble the numbers so that students won't know which are the "top" and "bottom" tables. Have selected students help distribute one game sheet, one answer sheet, one deck of number cards, and one game score sheet to each table. Then begin the game. Figure 4–5 describes the game rules and procedures.

To start the game, the students draw cards to determine the first reader—the student drawing the highest number. Play proceeds clockwise from the first reader.

The first reader shuffles the cards and picks the top one. He or she then reads aloud the question corresponding to the number on the card, including the possible answers if the question is multiple-choice. For example, a student who picks card 21 answers question 21. A reader who is not sure of the answer is allowed to guess without penalty. If the content of the game involves math problems, all students (not just the reader) should work the problems so that they will be ready to challenge. After the reader gives an answer, the student to his or her left (first challenger) has the option of challenging and giving a different answer. If he or she passes, or if the second challenger has an answer different from the first two, the second challenger may challenge. Challengers have to be

Reader
1. Picks a numbered card and finds the corresponding question on the game sheet.
2. Reads the question out loud.
3. Tries to answer.

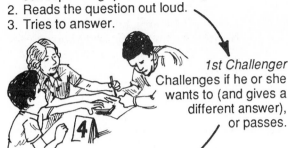

1st Challenger
Challenges if he or she wants to (and gives a different answer), or passes.

2nd Challenger
Challenges if 1st challenger passes, if he or she wants to. When all have challenged or passed, 2nd challenger checks the answer sheet. Whoever was *right* keeps the card. If the *reader* was wrong, there is no penalty, but if either challenger was wrong, he or she must put a previously won card, if any, back in the deck.

Figure 4–5   Game Rules (TGT).

careful, however, because they lose a card (if they have one) if they are wrong. When everyone has answered, challenged, or passed, the second challenger (or the player to the reader's right) checks the answer sheet and reads the right answer aloud. The player who gave the right answer keeps the card. If either challenger gave a wrong answer, he or she must return a previously won card (if any) to the deck. If no one gave a right answer, the card returns to the deck.

For the next round, everything moves one position to the left: the first challenger becomes the reader, the second challenger becomes the first challenger, and the reader becomes the second challenger. Play continues, as determined by the teacher, until the period ends or the deck is exhausted. When the game is over, players record the number of cards they won on the game score sheet in the column for game 1. If there is time, students reshuffle the deck and play a second game until the end of the period, recording the number of cards won under "Game 2" on the score sheet (See Figure 4–6).

All students should play the game at the same time. While they are playing, move from group to group to answer questions and be sure that everyone understands the game procedures. Ten minutes before the end of the period, call "Time" and have students stop and count their cards. They should then fill in their names, teams, and scores on the game score sheet, as in Figure 4–6.

Have students add up the scores they earned in each game (if they played more than one) and fill in their day's total. For younger children (fourth grade or below), simply collect the score sheets. If students are older, have them calculate their tournament points.

PLAYER	TEAM	Game 1	Game 2	Game 3	DAY'S TOTAL	TOURNAMENT POINTS
Eric	Giants	5	7		12	20
Lisa A.	Geniuses	14	10		24	60
Darryl	B. Bombs	11	12		23	40

TABLE #_____   GAME SCORE SHEET (TGT)   ROUND #_____

Figure 4–6   Sample Game.

Table 4–3 Calculating Tournament Points

For a Four-Player Game

Player	No Ties	Tie for Top	Tie for Middle	Tie for Low	3-Way Tie for Top	3-Way Tie for Low	4-Way Tie	Tie for Low and High
Top Scorer	60 points	50	60	60	50	60	40	50
High Middle Scorer	40 points	50	40	40	50	30	40	50
Low Middle Scorer	30 points	30	40	30	50	30	40	30
Low Scorer	20 points	20	20	30	20	30	40	30

For a Three-Player Game

Player	No Ties	Tie for Top Score	Tie for Low Score	3-Way Tie
Top Scorer	60 points	50	60	40
Middle Scorer	40 points	50	30	40
Low Scorer	20 points	20	30	40

For a Two-Player Game

Player	No Ties	Tied
Top Scorer	60 points	40
Low Scorer	20 points	40

Table 4–3 summarizes tournament points for all possible outcomes. In general, at a three-person table with no ties have students give the top scorer sixty points, the second scorer forty points, and the third scorer twenty points. If there are more or less than three players or if there are any ties, use Table 4–3 to tell students what to do. When everyone has calculated his or her tournament points, have a student collect the game score sheets.

TEAM RECOGNITION

Main idea: figuring team scores and preparing a class newsletter or bulletin board

FIGURING TEAM SCORES

As soon as possible after the tournament, figure team scores and prepare team certificates or write a class newsletter to announce the standings. To do this, first check the tournament points on the game score sheets. Then, simply transfer each student's tournament points to the summary sheet for his or her team, add all the team members' scores, and divide by the number of team members present. Figure 4–7 shows the recording and totaling of scores for one team.

TEAM SUMMARY SHEET

TEAM NAME *GENIUSES*

TEAM MEMBERS	1	2	3	4	5	6	7	8	9	10	11	12	13	14
Mark	60	20	20	40										
Kevin	40	40	20	60										
Lisa A.	50	20	40	60										
John F.	60	60	20	40										
Dewanda	40	40	60	20										
TOTAL TEAM SCORE	250	180	160	220										
TEAM AVERAGE	50	36	32	44										
TEAM AWARD	Super Team			Good Team										

*Team Average = Total Team Score ÷ Number of Team Members

Figure 4–7 Sample Team Summary Sheet.

RECOGNIZING TEAM ACCOMPLISHMENTS

As in STAD, three levels of awards are given, based on average team scores:

Criterion (Team Average)	*Award*
40	Goodteam
45	Greatteam
50	Superteam

You may give certificates (such as those in Appendix 4) to teams that meet Greatteam or Superteam criteria. Goodteams should just be congratulated in class. Instead of or in addition to team certificates, you may wish to display each week's successful teams on a bulletin board, posting their pictures or team names in a place of honor. Many teachers use class newsletters in TGT (see Figure 4–8 for an example). However you recognize

The Weekly Planet

4th Week March 28

FLASH! Fantastic Four Sweeps Language Arts Tournament!

The Fantastic Four was the winning team this week with a total of 55 points. John T., Kris, and Alvin put in outstanding performances for the Four, each contributing sixty points to their team. Their victory brings the Four to second place in the National League standings, only six points behind the leading Giants! Mary said, "We won because our team works well together."

Hot on the heels of the Fantastic Four were the Brain Busters with 52 points. Anita and Tanya helped the team out with victories at their tables, while Peter tied for first at his. The Brain Busters are still in third place in National League competition, but are moving up fast! Darryl was overheard telling Peter, "We really learned to cooperate with each other."

Third this week were the American League Geniuses with 44 points. They were helped out by Kevin and Lisa A., both table winners. Mark told his teammates he had more of a chance to help others this week.

Other table winners were Lisa P. of the Daredevils and Mike of the Grammar Haters.

THIS WEEK'S SCORES

1st--Fantastic Four		2nd--Brain Busters		3rd--Geniuses	
John T.	60	Anita	60	Mark	40
Mary	40	Peter	50	Kevin	60
Kris	60	Darryl	40	Lisa A.	60
Alvin	60	Tanya	60	John F.	40
	220		210	Dewanda	20
					220

Daredevils		Giants		Chipmunks		Grammar Haters	
Lisa P.	60	Robert	40	Caroline	50	Sarah	20
Henry	20	Eric	20	Jerry	20	Willy	20
Cindi	40	Sharon	20	Charlene	30	Mike	60
Fred	40	Sylvia	40	James	20	Theresa	30
	160		120		120	John H.	20
							150

SEASON'S STANDING FOURTH WEEK

National League		American League	
TEAM	SEASON SCORE	TEAM	SEASON SCORE
Giants	195	Grammar Haters	185
Fantastic Four	180	Geniuses	162
Brain Busters	165	Daredevils	142
Chipmunks	147		

Figure 4–8   Sample TGT Newsletter.

team accomplishments, it is important to communicate that team success (not just individual success) is what is important, as this is what motivates students to help their teammates learn.

Bumping

Bumping, or reassigning students to new tournament tables, must be done after each tournament to prepare for the next tournament. It is easiest to do the bumping when you are figuring team scores.

To bump students, use the steps that follow. Figure 4–9 diagrams the procedure, and Figure 4–10 illustrates a completed tournament table assignment sheet, showing how bumping works for a hypothetical class after two tournaments (one tournament per week).

1. Use the game score sheets to identify the high and low scorers at each tournament table. On the tournament table assignment sheet, circle the table assignments of all students who were high scorers at their tables. If there was a tie for high score at any table, flip a coin to decide which number to circle; do not circle more than one number per table. In Figure 4–10, Tyrone, Maria, Tom, Carla, and Ralph were table winners in the first tournament, so their table numbers are circled in the first column; Tyrone, Liz, John T., Tanya, and Ruth were winners in the second tournament, so their numbers are circled in the second column.

2. Underline the table numbers of students who were low scorers. Again, if there was a tie for low score at any table, flip a coin to decide which to underline; do not underline more than one number per table. In Figure 4–10, Sarah, John T., John F., Kim, and Shirley were low scorers at their respective tables in the first tournament.

3. Leave all other table assignments as they were, including numbers for absent students.

4. In the column for the next tournament, transfer the numbers as follows: If the number is *circled,* reduce it by one (4 becomes 3). This means that the winner at table 4 will compete the following week at table 3—a table where the competition will be more difficult. The only exception is that ①remains 1, because table 1 is the highest table. If the number is *underlined,* increase it by one (4 becomes 5), except at the lowest table, where the low scorer stays at the same table (for example, 10 remains 10). This means that the low scorer at each table will compete the next week at a table where the

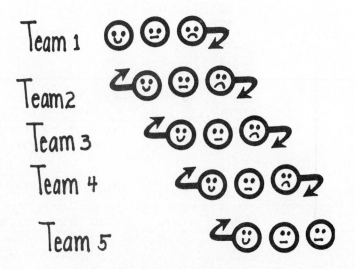

Figure 4–9   Bumping.

(Five Tournament Tables)
TOURNAMENT TABLE ASSIGNMENT SHEET (TGT)
Tournament Number:

Student	Team	1	2	3	4	5	6	7	8	9	10	11	12	13
SAM	Orioles	1	1	2										
SARAH	Cougars	1	2	2										
TYRONE	Whiz Kids	①	①	1										
MARIA	Geniuses	②	1	1										
LIZ	Orioles	2	②	1										
JOHN J.	Cougars	2	③	2										
SYLVIA	Whiz Kids	3	3	4										
TOM	Geniuses	③	2	3										
JOHN F.	Orioles	3	4	5										
TANYA	Whiz Kids	4	④	3										
CARLA	Orioles	④	3	3										
KIM	Cougars	4	5	5										
CARLOS	Geniuses	4	4	4										
SHIRLEY	Whiz Kids	5	5	5										
RALPH	Cougars	⑤	4	4										
RUTH	Geniuses	5	⑤	4										

Note:
③ indicates *high* scorer at Table 3
3 indicates *middle* scorer at Table 3
<u>3</u> indicates *low* scorer at Table 3

Results of ↑   ↑ Tournament Table
Most Recent | | Assignment for
Tournament | | Next Tournament

Figure 4–10   Sample Tournament Table Assignment Sheet with Bumping.

competition will be less difficult. If the number is neither underlined nor circled, do not change it for the next tournament; transfer the same number.

In Figure 4–10, note that Tom won at table 3 in the first tournament and was bumped up to table 2. At table 2 he was the low scorer, so for the third week's tournament he will compete at table 3 again. Sylvia was the middle scorer at table 3 in the first tournament, so she stayed at table 3; then she lost in the second tournament and was moved to table 4.

Count the number of students assigned to each table for the next week's tournament. Most tables should have three students; as many as two may have four. If table assignments do not work out this way because of student absences or other problems, make some changes so that they do.

Note that in Figure 4–10, Tyrone won twice at table 1 but did not change tables, because there was no higher place to go than table 1. Shirley and Kim lost at table 5 but were not bumped down, because table 5 was the lowest table.

Changing Teams

After five or six weeks of TGT, assign students to new teams.

Combining TGT with Other Activities

Teachers may wish to use TGT for one part of their instruction and other methods for other parts. For example, a science teacher might use TGT three days a week to teach basic science concepts, but use related laboratory exercises on the other two days. TGT can also be used in combination with STAD, either by having quizzes one week and tournaments the next, or by having a quiz the day after each tournament and counting both the quiz score and the tournament score toward the team score. This procedure gives the teacher a better idea of student progress than the tournament alone.

Grading

TGT does not automatically produce scores that can be used to compute individual grades. If this is a serious problem, consider using STAD instead of TGT. To determine individual grades, many teachers using TGT give a midterm and a final test each semester; some give a quiz after each tournament. Students' grades should be based on quiz scores or other individual assessments, not on tournament points or team scores. However, students' tournament points and/or team scores can be made a small part of their grades. Or, if the school gives separate grades for effort, these scores can be used to determine the effort grades.

TEACHERS ON TEACHING

Sometimes teachers express a concern that students will get tired of cooperative learning after the initial novelty wears off. Have you experienced this? What specific strategies do you use to maintain students' interest in team work and team success?

In two years, we have not experienced any youngsters getting "tired of cooperative learning after the initial novelty wears off."

I believe this has happened because as I work with the classroom teacher at grade levels four, five, and six, we try to vary not the concept but the awards system. Each teacher has his or her particular likes and strengths:

1. Grade four: When a team responds well to oral discussion, it is awarded a marble. An accumulation of marbles gives the team lunch with the teacher, plus ice cream.

2. Grade five: When the six-week term is completed, this class holds an award assembly. After the awards are issued, they have a BYO party—"Bring Your Own" goodies. These parties have contributed to a weight gain of five pounds for the teachers.

3. Grade six: These teams are rewarded with homework-exemption certificates to be used anytime over the year. Last year one smart sixth grader accumulated his certificates and used them during the month of June.

Maureen Sauter, Fourth, Fifth, and Sixth Grade Teacher Sacandaga Elementary School, Scotia, NY

I have not found that my students tire of cooperative learning. Here are some of the things I have done to keep my students keenly interested.

1. Change the rewards often.
2. Let students suggest things they would like to work toward:
   a. extra play time
   b. additional computer time
   c. first choice of playground equipment
   d. line leaders
   e. additional library time
   f. treats for high-point teams
   g. names in school newspaper
   h. picture taken to send home and/or put in newspaper
   i. lunch with teacher, principal, nurse
   j. suggest their favorite dessert to cafeteria personnel (once a month)
3. Reward at the end of each lesson with points for positive behavior. (My students like big numbers, so I usually start with fifty and build on this.)

When we have visitors I try to encourage them to send a note to the students telling how they enjoyed seeing the class working together, what they liked, and so on. I share the letters with the students. Positive feedback is very important for the students.

Phyllis McManus,
Third Grade Teacher
Hoagland Elementary School,
Hoagland, IN

Having students tire of cooperative learning has never been a problem for me. I use a great variety of strategies, and I imagine that in itself accounts for the fact that students don't get tired of them. The Co-op Co-op book report we do just once a year, though it extends over a period of several weeks. Each quarter I use different group-building strategies when we form new groups. And when I plan a unit of work I try to include many different types of learning situations: for example, in a poetry unit recently I had students learn figures of speech by using color-coded cards, and then, in dealing with individual poems, they used Partners, Numbered Heads, and Jigsaw. Also included was some direct instruction.

Now that we're working on a short story unit, I'm using Blooming Worksheets, Roundtable, and Numbered Heads.

Ruth Werfel, English Teacher
Wilcox High School, Santa Clara, CA

MAKING WORKSHEETS AND QUIZZES FOR STAD OR TGT

Making curriculum materials for STAD or TGT is very much like making worksheets and quizzes for any instructional unit. In fact, you may use any worksheets and quizzes you already have, or you may take items from other sources instead of creating entirely new worksheets and quizzes. To make materials for STAD or TGT, follow these steps:

1. **Make a worksheet and a worksheet answer sheet for each unit.** A worksheet is usually a series of items that provide students with practice and self-assessment that will directly help them prepare for the quiz (STAD) or game (TGT) to follow. The number of worksheet items to make depends on the material you are teaching. For short-answer items, such as irregular verb tenses, multiplication facts, or multiple-choice questions, you would probably make a longer worksheet than you would for a unit in which each item takes a long time to do, as in a long-division unit. The Johns

Hopkins Team Learning Project curriculum materials always use thirty-item worksheets (see Appendix 1), but there is no particular reason to make that exact number of items. Also, note that a set of items is not the only possible kind of worksheet. For example, in a geography unit the students could be asked to fill in country names on a blank map, and a math-facts or spelling unit might use flash cards. The main idea is to be sure that the worksheet or other material provides *direct* practice for the quiz or game. For example, a crossword puzzle might give students some help with a spelling test, but it does not give them the kind of drill and practice that will enable them to master the spelling words. As such, it could be used as a supplementary activity, but should not be used to replace a worksheet or flash cards that do directly prepare students for a spelling test.

As soon as you have made a worksheet, make a worksheet answer sheet. Students will use this answer sheet to check themselves as they study.

2. **Make a game/quiz and a game/quiz answer sheet for each unit.** The same sheet is used as a game in TGT and a quiz in STAD. The game/quiz items should closely parallel the worksheet items, as in the following examples:

Worksheet	*Game/Quiz*
1. $\frac{1}{2} + \frac{1}{2} =$	1. $\frac{1}{3} + \frac{1}{3} =$

2. The car crept _____ up the hill.
   a. slow
   b. slowly
	2. Even though he was nervous, he got a _____ score on the test.
	   a. good
	   b. well

3. A combination of hydrogen and fluorine would be written:
   a. H_2F
   b. HF
   c. HF_2
   d. H_2F_2
	3. A combination of calcium and chlorine would be written:
	   a. Ca_2Cl
	   b. $CaCl$
	   c. $CaCl_2$
	   d. Ca_2Cl_2

4. The capital of Canada is _____.	4. The capital of Canada is _____.

Note that in questions 1–3, the parallel items tested the same skill or concept (addition of simple fractions with like denominators, correct use of adjectives and adverbs, writing of chemical formulas with elements of different valences) but used different items. This avoids the possibility that students will memorize the *items* instead of learning the *concepts*. However, in item 4, the task is to memorize capitals of countries, and so it is appropriate to give the same item twice; it would of course be unfair to have a capital on the game/quiz that did not appear on the worksheet.

For TGT, the number of items on the game/quiz should be thirty, since this is the number of cards used in the TGT games. For STAD any number of items may be used.

You will need to make a game/quiz answer sheet for TGT so that students can check themselves during the game. For STAD, you will need a correction key. If you are allowing students to correct each other's papers, you could put the answers on an overhead projector sheet or a large piece of paper to show the class, although most teachers simply read the answers to the students for correction.

Examples of STAD and TGT units (worksheets, worksheet answers, games and quizzes, and game and quiz answers) are found in Appendix 1.

FIVE

TAI and CIRC

Most of the cooperative learning methods currently in widespread use, including STAD, TGT, Jigsaw, and the Johnsons' methods, are what might be called generic techniques. That is, they are applicable to a wide range of grade levels, subjects, and school and classroom characteristics. The broad applicability of these models is a strength, and certainly accounts in large part for their popularity. However, methods that are appropriate for *all* subjects and grade levels are unlikely to be optimal for any *particular* subject and grade level. For example, cooperative learning methods designed specifically for elementary mathematics or reading, middle school science, or high school composition would certainly be different from one another. One size can't possibly fit all.

Generic forms of cooperative learning also ignore issues of curriculum, creating a situation in which cooperative learning methods may be used to do a better job of teaching material that is not worth teaching. But cooperative learning can serve specifically as a vehicle for introducing improved practices or content, such as an emphasis on metacognitive activities in reading, writing for revision in composition, or conceptually rich instruction in mathematics. It can also be designed specifically to accommodate a wide range of student skills in one classroom—a particularly important objective where cooperative learning is introduced as an alternative to ability grouping or is used to facilitate mainstreaming of academically handicapped students.

This chapter describes two programs, TAI and CIRC, that combine the use of cooperative learning with other practices and that directly address issues of teaching methods and content as well as classroom organization.

TEAM ASSISTED INDIVIDUALIZATION*

Rationale

Whether to adapt instruction to individual differences in student ability or achievement, and if so, how, has been one of the most long-standing controversies in American education. Opinion has alternately favored such practices as tracking, within-class ability grouping, programmed instruction, computer-assisted instruction, and mastery learning as a means of attempting to insure that the needs and readiness of every student are taken into account in instruction. The need for some sort of individualization has been perceived as particularly great in mathematics, where learning of each skill depends in large part on mastery of prerequisite skills.

The rationale behind individualization of mathematics instruction is that students enter class with widely divergent knowledge, skills, and motivation. When the teacher presents a single lesson to a diverse group, it is likely that some students will not have the prerequisite skills to learn the lesson, and will fail to profit from it. Others will already know the material, or will learn it so quickly that additional time spent going over the lesson will be wasted for them.

It is clear that teaching a single lesson at a single pace to a heterogeneous class incurs certain inefficiencies in the use of instructional time. In theory, maximum instructional efficiency should be achieved when material presented to students is exactly appropriate to their level of readiness and proceeds at as rapid a pace as students can assimilate information. The substantial effects of one-to-one tutoring on student achievement (see, for example, Glass, Cahen, Smith, and Filby, 1982) probably arise in part from the ability of the adult tutor to establish a level and pace of instruction that is closely tailored to the needs of the student.

However, almost all students learn in class groups, not in individual tutoring sessions. Individualizing instruction in class groups entails costs in instructional efficiency that may equal or exceed the inefficiencies introduced by the use of a single level and pace of instruction. For example, programmed instruction provides complete individualization of instruction, allowing students to proceed at their own rates on materials appropriate to their level of prior knowledge. Yet programmed instruction inevitably reduces the amount of time teachers can spend in direct instructional activities and increases the amount of time students spend doing seatwork. In studies of group-paced instruction, time spent on seatwork has typically been negatively associated with learning, whereas time spent on direct instruction has had positive effects on learning (see Brophy and Good, 1986). Time spent checking materials and managing the program is largely time lost from instruction. Motivation is often lacking in programmed instruction: students may place little value on progress for its own sake, and may become bored with endless interaction with written materials alone (see Kepler and Randall, 1977; Schoen, 1976).

Reviews of research on individualized instruction in mathematics (for example, Miller, 1976; Schoen, 1976) uniformly conclude that individualized instruction is no more effective than traditional methods in increasing student achievement. Given the costs and difficulties of implementing individualized instruction, one might argue that this approach should be abandoned as unworkable and ineffective.

Yet the problems of student heterogeneity that individualized instruction was designed to address will not go away. If anything, classes are becoming more, not less heterogeneous as a consequence of such movements as mainstreaming and desegregation. Tracking itself is increasingly being questioned as an effective means of dealing with student heterogeneity. Studies of tracking find that it offers few achievement benefits (Slavin, 1987c).

---

*This is the name under which TAI was originally developed and researched; TAI is currently distributed as Team Accelerated Instruction.

TEACHERS ON TEACHING

TAI–Math combines cooperative learning with individualized instruction. How do the elements of TAI work together to accelerate student achievement in math? What problems do you see in TAI, and how have you dealt with them?

TAI–Math allows students to advance at an individual or small-group pace of instruction. The pace of instruction can vary, allowing a teacher opportunities to use manipulatives or to repeat a lesson several times or just give a brief overview of material during the direct teacher presentation. The teacher has flexibility to vary from group to group or individual to individual.

TAI lets students process a lot of the paperwork that ties a teacher down. Students check each other's work as they progress through the units. This is important because it provides the immediate feedback students need and it identifies problems that often can be handled in the group or answered by the teacher if further help is needed.

Finally, at our school TAI has provided opportunities for handicapped students to work with the mainstream. It lets students establish goals and achieve goals.

The one problem I see is grading. We have dealt with grading on an individual basis, establishing goals with our students and grading them subjectively on what they have accomplished.

Steve Parsons, Math Teacher
West Frederick Middle School,
Frederick, MD

Individual accountability as well as group rewards are important in increasing student achievement. Cooperative learning uses this strategy very well. In TAI, this is very noticeable, especially in children who previously disliked math. Many times students are very frustrated because they don't understand and as a result fail tests and quizzes. By using TAI in math the child is able to work at his or her own level and achieve success.

The children want to do well to achieve the team points and are able to do well because they are working on their own level. As a result, the group receives a reward and the child feels self-satisfaction for doing well and receives positive reinforcement from the teacher as well as the team. Parents also give the child positive reinforcement for doing so well in school, especially in a subject the child did not enjoy.

Holly Beers, Fifth Grade Teacher
Point Pleasant Elementary School,
Glen Burnie, MD

The students realize increased achievement because they work at their own level. They don't move on to the next level until they're ready, which provides a stronger foundation for the building of skills. They also know that they will move ahead to something new when they're ready. They can excel as quickly as they master, which keeps them from becoming bored if they're on the "bottom."

One problem with TAI is ensuring that students have really mastered the concepts. I have found it important to meet with the teaching groups frequently—every day if possible. This also "slows down" the students; in their efforts to produce points for the team, they sometimes get carried away, and the quality of their work suffers.

Claudia Phillips,
Fourth Grade Teacher
Summitview Elementary School,
Waynesboro, PA

The first few weeks of TAI are very critical in setting the tone for the program. I spend the first week going over all of the procedures with the students, explaining the "How to Do TAI" flow chart, the progress form, and the score sheets. I make sure that they understand the proper procedures for going to the monitor's station, taking tests, and getting the teacher's attention. Time is also spent looking at the skill-practice sheets. Students need to know where the guide pages, the unit numbers, the skill-practice pages, and the formative tests are.

The class needs to learn how to set up their papers. Using a sample on the overhead projector, I show them where to place their name, the date, and the unit number. I make sure it is clear to the students that they need to number their problems and label the skill practices and formative tests. I go over how to check each others's work and where their initials should go.

There are several ways to help reinforce the procedures for TAI. One way is to pose hypothetical situations and have students tell what they should do when these certain situations arise. During TAI it can be help- ful to positively reinforce a student or team that is following the procedures properly.

For at least the first two weeks the class reviews the steps for TAI at the beginning of each session. At the end of each session we discuss how the day went. I let the students tell about the good things that happened, where we might need improvement, and any problems that might have occurred. This helps them to feel good about themselves and know what they need to work on the next time. Letting them tell about any problems that have occurred lets them know that I care and that as a class we can try to solve those problems.

To set a positive tone and help team relations, I like to spend some time doing team-building activities in the first week and each time the teams are changed. I allow the students time to make up a team name and a team poster. They do some activities that help them get to know each other better. Each team also comes up with a creative team handshake which they use at the start and finish of each session of TAI. These and other activities can boost team spirit and lessen the occurrence of team conflicts.

Theresa Brown,
Fourth Grade Teacher
Point Pleasant Elementary School,
Glen Burnie, MD

Students working in TAI understand that the primary way to increase a team's score is to complete tests. Consequently, students encourage one another to work at a rapid rate to complete class assignments and tests. Due to the requirement of 80 percent mastery on formative tests and unit tests the quality of the work is not sacrificed. Individualized math programs used in the past at our high school, especially in the special education resource programs, did not have the element of group motivation. Students were less motivated and worked at a much slower pace.

PROBLEMS	SOLUTIONS
Maryland Project Basic Competency Testing format different from TAI materials.	Inclusion of worksheets and tests of MD Functional Math curriculum into TAI format.
Due to individualized nature of TAI program, teamwork process can be limited.	Assign students specific roles with group- and self-evaluation component: • supervisor • coach • recorder • go-getter (roles rotate weekly)

| Limitations of curriculum units; units needed in:
   geometry
   problem solving
   algebra
   measurement
   time
   money | Supplement program with curriculum resources. |
| Curriculum resources needed:
   computer software
   manipulatives | Supplement program with curriculum resources. |

Lynne Mainzer,
Special Education Teacher
Francis Scott Key High School,
Union Bridge, MD

TAI math began as an attempt to design a form of individualized instruction that would solve the problems that had made earlier individualized programs ineffective. By having students work in cooperative learning teams and take responsibility for routine management and checking, for helping one another with problems, and for encouraging one another to achieve, teachers can free themselves to provide direct instruction to small, homogeneous groups of students drawn from the heterogeneous teams. The instructional focus is on the *concepts* behind the algorithms students are learning in their individualized work. This arrangement provides for the direct instruction lacking in most individualized methods.

In addition to solving the problems of management and motivation in individualized programmed instruction, TAI was created to take advantage of the considerable socialization potential of cooperative learning. Previous studies of group-paced cooperative learning methods have consistently found positive effects of these methods on such outcomes as race relations and attitudes toward mainstreamed academically handicapped students (see Chapter 3). There was good reason to expect that similar outcomes could be achieved in a method combining cooperative learning and individualized instruction.

TAI was designed to satisfy the following criteria for solving the theoretical and practical problems of individualized instruction:

- The teacher would be minimally involved in routine management and checking.
- The teacher would spend at least half of his or her time teaching small groups.
- Program operation would be so simple that students in grades three and up could manage it.
- Students would be motivated to proceed rapidly and accurately through the materials, and could not succeed by cheating or finding shortcuts.
- Many mastery checks would be provided so that students would rarely waste time on material they had already mastered or run into serious difficulties requiring teacher help. At each mastery checkpoint, alternative instructional activities and parallel tests would be provided.
- Students would be able to check one another's work, even when the checking student was behind the student being checked in the instructional sequence, and the checking procedure would be simple and not disrupt the checker.
- The program would be simple to learn for teachers and students, inexpensive, and flexible, and would not require aides or team teachers.
- By having students work in cooperative, equal-status groups, the program would establish conditions for positive attitudes toward mainstreamed academically handicapped students and between students of different racial or ethnic backgrounds.

The TAI program that was developed to meet these criteria was piloted in a single class, extensively revised, studied in two full-scale but brief (eight and ten weeks, respectively) field experiments (Slavin, Leavey, and Madden, 1984), revised again, and then successfully evaluated in three large-scale field experiments (Slavin, Madden, and Leavey, 1984; Slavin and Karweit, 1985). The program as it now exists is described in the following sections.

Program Elements

Unlike STAD and TGT, TAI depends on a specific set of instructional materials and has its own implementation guide. For this reason, it is not possible to use TAI simply by reading this chapter. For more information on TAI materials and training, see "Resources for Cooperative Learning" in Chapter 7.

Teams. Students in TAI are assigned to four-to-five-member heterogeneous teams, just as in STAD or TGT.

Placement Test. Students are pretested at the beginning of the program on mathematics operations. They are placed at the appropriate point in the individualized program based on their performance on this test.

Curriculum Materials. For most of their mathematics instruction, students work on individualized curriculum materials covering addition, subtraction, multiplication, division, numeration, fractions, decimals, ratio, percent, statistics, and algebra. Word problems and problem-solving strategies are emphasized throughout the materials. Each unit has the following parts:

- A guide page reviewing the concepts introduced by the teacher in the teaching groups (to be discussed shortly) and giving a step-by-step method of solving the problems.
- Several skill-practice pages, each consisting of sixteen problems. Each skill practice introduces a subskill that leads to final mastery of the entire skill.
- Formative tests—two parallel sets of ten items.
- A fifteen-item unit test.
- Answer pages for the skill-practice pages and formative and unit tests.

Team Study. Following the placement test, the teacher teaches the first lesson (see "Teaching Groups" below). Then the students are given a starting place in an individualized mathematics unit. The units are printed in student books. Students work on their units in their teams, following these steps:

1. The students form pairs or triads within their teams for checking.
2. Students read their guide pages and ask teammates or the teacher for help if necessary. Then they begin with the first skill practice in their unit.
3. Each student works the first four problems in his or her own skill practice and then has a teammate check the answers against an answer page, printed upside down in the student books. If all four are correct, the student may go on to the next skill practice. If any are wrong, the student must try the next four problems, and so on, until he or she gets one block of four problems correct. Students who run into difficulties at this stage are encouraged to ask for help within their teams before asking the teacher for help.
4. When a student gets a block of four problems correct on the last skill practice, he or she takes formative test A, a ten-item quiz that resembles the last skill practice. On the formative test, the student works alone until he or she is finished. A teammate scores the test. If the student gets eight or more problems correct, the teammate signs

TEACHERS ON TEACHING

Many teachers who use cooperative learning have a particular success story—a child who was turned around, a new perspective on teaching, markedly improved grades or test scores. If you have such a success story, please briefly tell it.

There are "individual" success stories and there are "group" success stories. Cooperative learning meets the social needs of so many students, let alone meeting their academic needs. In our TAI math class, we see so many students come in to the remedial math class with a low "math" opinion of themselves, plus sometimes a low "self" opinion. We notice the head starts to pick up about the third week of TAI—there's success finally for the student. The math is individualized and helps the student narrow in on his or her own particular skill problem, but at the same time, provides the student with the opportunity to contribute successfully to a special unit—the team. When first-quarter marks come out, some of the students are ecstatic with the "A" or "B" they've earned—for some the first ever.

Individual successes come from the social growth these students make in their cooperative teams. One in particular was an educably retarded tenth grader, who became the inspiration of the team with his successes—they even named their team after him!

We have students who are looked on as leaders in our cooperative classes, who never would have achieved that status in a traditional classroom—these qualities would not have been nurtured.

After six years of cooperative learning, I could give you numerous individual success stories, even at the top level with high-ability students finally learning that they can share some of their intellectual ability with others—it doesn't have to be kept to themselves. Peer tutoring works wonders with those high-ability students' realization of their gift and how they can now share it.

Patricia Robinson Baltzley,
Math Teacher
Francis Scott Key High School,
Union Bridge, MD

the test to indicate that the student is certified by the team to take the unit test. If the student does not get eight correct, the teacher is called in to respond to any problems the student is having. The teacher might ask the student to work again on certain skill-practice items and then to take formative test B, a second ten-item test comparable in content and difficulty to formative test A. Otherwise, the student may go straight to the unit test. No student may take the unit test until he or she has been passed by a teammate on a formative test.

5. Students take their signed formative tests to a student monitor from a different team to get the appropriate unit test. The student then completes the unit test, and the monitor scores it. Each day two different students serve as monitors.

Team Scores and Team Recognition. At the end of each week, the teacher computes a team score. This score is based on the average number of units covered by each team member and the accuracy of the unit tests. Criteria are established for team performance. A high criterion is set for a team to be a Superteam, a moderate criterion for a team to be a Greatteam, and a minimum criterion for a team to be a Goodteam. The teams meeting the Superteam or Greatteam criteria receive attractive certificates.

Teaching Groups. Everyday the teacher works for ten or fifteen minutes with each of two or three small groups of students drawn from the heterogeneous teams who are at the same point in the curriculum. Teachers use specific concept lessons provided with the program. The purpose of these sessions is to introduce major concepts to the students. Teachers make extensive use of manipulatives, diagrams, and demonstrations. The lessons are designed to help students understand the connection between the mathematics they are doing and familiar, real-life problems. In general, the students have concepts introduced to them in the teaching groups before they work on them in their individualized units. While the teacher works with a teaching group, the other students continue to work in their teams on their individualized units. This direct instruction to teaching groups is made possible in an individualized program by the fact that students take responsibility for almost all checking, materials handling, and routing.

Facts Tests. Twice each week, the students take three-minute tests on facts (usually multiplication or division facts). The students are given facts sheets to study at home to prepare for these tests.

Whole-Class Units. After every three weeks, the teacher stops the individualized program and spends a week teaching the entire class such skills as geometry, measurement, sets, and problem-solving strategies.

COOPERATIVE INTEGRATED READING AND COMPOSITION

Rationale

Although cooperative learning methods have been researched and used in a wide variety of subjects, two of the most important subjects in the elementary school curriculum—reading and writing—have been conspicuously lacking in this research. This section describes the rationale, development, and evaluation of Cooperative Integrated Reading and Composition (CIRC), a comprehensive program for teaching reading, writing, and language arts in the upper elementary grades. As in the case of TAI, the development of CIRC focused simultaneously on curriculum and on instructional methods in an attempt to use cooperative learning as a vehicle for introducing state-of-the-art curricular practices derived primarily from basic research on the practical teaching of reading and writing. The cooperative learning approach followed the findings of the earlier research, emphasizing group goals and individual accountability. Also, the research on TAI had demonstrated that the combined use of homogeneous teaching groups and heterogeneous work groups could be both practical and effective.

Additionally, the development of CIRC proceeded from an analysis of the problems of traditional reading, writing, and language arts instruction. The principal issues addressed in the development process are discussed in the following sections (see Stevens, Madden, Slavin, and Farnish, 1987).

Follow-up. An almost universal feature of elementary reading instruction is the use of reading groups composed of students of similar performance levels (see Hiebert, 1983). The major rationale for the use of homogeneous ability groups in reading is that students need to have materials appropriate to their levels of skill. However, use of reading groups creates a problem: When the teacher is working with one reading group, the other students in the class must be occupied with activities they can complete with minimal teacher direction. Research on these "follow-up" activities, or unsupervised seatwork, indicates that they are often of poor quality, are rarely taken seriously by teachers or students, and are poorly integrated with other reading activities (see, for example, Beck, McKeown, McCaslin, and Burkes, 1979) and that student time on-task during follow-up periods is typically low (see, for instance, Anderson, Brubaker, Alleman-Brooks, and Duffy, 1985). Yet it has been found that in a class with three reading groups, two-thirds or more of the reading period is spent on follow-up activities.

One major focus of the CIRC activities prescribed for basal stories is on making more effective use of follow-up time: Students work within cooperative teams on these activities, which are coordinated with reading-group instruction, in order to meet objectives in such areas as reading comprehension, vocabulary, decoding, and spelling. Students are motivated to work with one another on these activities by the use of a cooperative reward structure in which they may earn certificates or other recognition based on the learning of all team members.

Oral Reading. Reading out loud is a standard part of most reading programs. Research on oral reading indicates that it has positive effects on students' decoding and comprehension skills (Dahl, 1979; Samuels, 1979), probably because it increases their ability to decode more automatically and therefore focus more on comprehension (La-Berge and Samuels, 1974; Perfetti, 1985). However, in traditionally structured classrooms students get to do very little oral reading. For example, Thurlow, Groden, Ysseldyke, and Algozzine (1984) found that on average, second graders read out loud only ninety seconds per day. Further, most oral reading takes place in reading groups, where one student reads while others wait; the time of the reading group members other than the reader is largely wasted. One objective of the CIRC program is to greatly increase students' opportunities to read aloud and receive feedback on their reading by having students read to teammates and by training them in how to respond to one another's reading.

Reading Comprehension Skills. Several descriptive studies of elementary reading instruction have noted an overemphasis on literal comprehension instead of interpretive and inferential comprehension (see, for example, Guszak, 1967; Hansen, 1981) and a lack of explicit instruction in reading comprehension skills (Durkin, 1978–1979, 1981). Studies of good and poor readers have consistently found that poor readers lack comprehension strategies and metacognitive control of their reading, and that these strategic deficits play a large part in their comprehension problems (see, for instance, Baker and Brown, 1984; Brown and Palincsar, 1982; Myers and Paris, 1978; Pace, 1981; Ryan, 1982).

Several experimental studies have demonstrated that explicit instruction in reading comprehension strategies and metacognitive monitoring processes can increase students' comprehension skills, or at least those skills specifically taught in the interventions (Brown and Palincsar, 1982; Day, 1980; Hansen, 1981; Palincsar and Brown, 1984; Raphael, 1980). For example, Palincsar and Brown (1984) found that comprehension could be improved by teaching students summarizing, questioning, clarifying, and predicting skills.

A major objective of CIRC is to use cooperative teams to help students learn broadly applicable reading comprehension skills. Several components of CIRC are directed toward this end. During follow-up, students work in pairs to identify five critical features of each narrative story: characters, setting, problems, attempted solutions, final solution. Instruction in story structure has been found to increase reading comprehension of low-achieving students (see, for example, Fitzgerald and Spiegal, 1983; Short and Ryan, 1982). Students in CIRC also make and explain predictions about how problems will be resolved and summarize main elements of stories to one another, both of which are activities found to increase reading comprehension (see, for instance, Palincsar and Brown, 1984; Weinstein, 1982). One day each week, students in CIRC receive direct instruction in such comprehension-fostering strategies and metacognitive strategies. This instruction incorporates specially developed materials different from those used in basal-related instruction.

Writing and Language Arts. Research on instruction in elementary writing and language arts has indicated that the time allocated to these subjects focuses primarily on isolated language mechanics skills, with little time allocated to actual writing (see, for example, Bridge and Hiebert, 1985; Graves, 1978). However, two parallel but related trends have created the potential for a substantial change in elementary writing and language arts instruction. First, basic research is developing a clearer understanding of the cognitive processes involved in writing (see, for instance, Bereiter and Scardamalia, 1982; Flower and Hayes, 1980; McCutchen and Perfetti, 1983; Scardamalia and Bereiter, 1986). Second, there has been a rapid expansion in the use of writing process models, in which students are taught to use a cycle of planning, drafting, revising, editing, and publishing compositions (Gray and Myers, 1978; Calkins, 1983; Graves, 1983).

A major objective of the developers of the CIRC writing and language arts program was to design, implement, and evaluate a writing-process approach to writing and language arts that would make extensive use of peers. Peer response groups are a typical component of most writing-process models, but peer involvement is rarely the central activity. In the CIRC program, however, students plan, revise, and edit their compositions in close collaboration with teammates. Language mechanics instruction is completely integrated with and subordinated to writing, and writing is integrated with reading comprehension instruction both by the incorporation of writing-process activities in the reading program and by the use of newly learned reading comprehension skills in writing instruction.

Program Elements

CIRC consists of three principal elements: basal-related activities, direct instruction in reading comprehension, and integrated language arts and writing. In all of these activities, students work in heterogeneous learning teams. All activities follow a regular cycle that involves teacher presentation, team practice, independent practice, peer preassessment, additional practice, and testing. As with TAI, CIRC has its own manual and materials (see "Resources for Cooperative Learning" in Chapter 7), and therefore cannot be implemented from the information in this chapter alone. The major components of CIRC are as follows.

Reading Groups. Students are assigned to two or three reading groups according to their reading level, as determined by their teachers.

Teams. Students are assigned to pairs (or triads) within their reading groups, and then the pairs are assigned to teams composed of partnerships from two reading groups. For example, a team might be composed of two students from the top reading group and two from the low group. Team members receive points based on their individual performances on all quizzes, compositions, and book reports, and these points form a team score. Teams that meet an average criterion of 95 percent on all activities in a given week are designated Superteams and receive attractive certificates; those meeting an average criterion of 90 percent are designated Greatteams and receive smaller certificates.

Basal-Related Activities. Students use their regular basal readers. Basal stories are introduced and discussed in teacher-led reading groups that meet for approximately twenty minutes each day. In these groups, teachers set a purpose for reading, introduce new vocabulary, review old vocabulary, discuss the story after students have read it, and so on. Presentation methods for each segment of the lesson are structured. For example, vocabulary presentation requires a demonstration of understanding of word meaning by each individual, a review of methods of word attack, and repetitive oral reading of vocabulary to achieve fluency. Story discussions are structured to emphasize such skills as making and supporting predictions and identifying the problem in a narrative.

After the stories are introduced, students are given a story packet, which lays out a

---

TEACHERS ON TEACHING

Some people are concerned that students in TAI–Math or CIRC reading will know that others are at different math or reading levels and that this will lead to putdowns and negative labeling. Does this occur in your classes? How do you prevent it?

In the past I have realized that my fourth grade students are aware of their abilities and realize whether they are in the bottom, top, or middle group. In order to alleviate any putdowns or labeling, I do the following:

1. When I introduce the groups, they are not labeled by ability. For example, each reading group is referred to by the name of their reading text; each math group is assigned a color.
2. Just before I introduce the class to their reading groups we have a discussion about how each student in the room is important. We discuss how we all have different interests and talents. I elicit from the students that we all have things that we are good in and things we are not so good in. Then we talk about how we all have different abilities in reading. I tell them that they are divided into groups by what they are good and not so good at in reading. Finally, I tell them that it does not matter which reading group they are in as long as they each do their best work. I let them know that they all will be expected to do their share of the work no matter which group they are in. When I take time to do this, students seem to feel more positive about themselves and negative comments are alleviated. This also helps the students know what is expected of them.

Theresa Brown,
Fourth Grade Teacher
Point Pleasant Elementary School,
Glen Burnie, MD

---

series of activities for them to do in their teams when they are not working with the teacher in a reading group. The sequence of activities is as follows:

Partner Reading. Students read the story silently and then take turns reading the story aloud with their partner, alternating each paragraph. The listener corrects any errors the reader may make. The teacher assesses student performance by circulating and listening in as students read to each other.

Story Grammar and Story-Related Writing. Students are given questions ("Treasure Hunts") related to each story that emphasize the story grammar—the structure that underlies all narratives. Halfway through the story, they are instructed to stop reading and to identify the characters, the setting, and the problem in the story, and to predict how the problem will be resolved. At the end of the story students respond to the story as a whole and write a few paragraphs on a topic related to it (for example, they might be asked to write a different ending to the story).

Words Out Loud. Students are given a list of new or difficult words used in the story; they must be able to read these words correctly in any order without hesitating or stumbling. Students practice these word lists with their partner or other teammates until they can read them smoothly.

Word Meaning. Students are given a list of story words that are new in their speaking vocabularies and are asked to look them up in the dictionary, paraphrase the definition, and write a sentence for each that shows the meaning of the word (for example, "An *octopus* grabbed the swimmer with its eight long legs," rather than "I have an *octopus*").

Story Retell. After reading the story and discussing it in their reading groups, students summarize the main points of the story to their partner.

Spelling. Students pretest one another on a list of spelling words each week, and then over the course of the week help one another master the list. Students use a "disappearing list" strategy, in which they make new lists of missed words after each assessment until the list disappears. Then they go back to the full list, repeating the process until no words are missed.

TEACHERS ON TEACHING

CIRC is one of the most effective of the cooperative learning methods in reading, writing, and language arts. How has this program worked in your class? What problems have come up in implementing CIRC, and how have you solved them?

I have no problems implementing CIRC. This is the best reading program I've ever seen. I never realized what a waste of time it was for kids to only look up or memorize definitions of words until I started having kids write meaningful sentences and say the words out loud.

I was shocked that even some of the good students couldn't say the words correctly, never mind use them appropriately in a meaningful sentence. What a disaster those first sentences were!

We stuck with it, and I'm happy to report that the meaningful sentences are very good now and getting better.

This has been wonderful practice for the students and really the only "meaningful," thorough, useful, and lasting way to learn new vocabulary.

Ann Heathman,
Sixth Grade Teacher
Village Woods Middle School,
Fort Wayne, IN

The most important advice I would give a teacher using CIRC is don't give up! At first CIRC will seem very loud and you won't feel like you're getting very much out of the kids. Don't worry! It takes several weeks to "break" the kids into the routine and for them to learn what you expect from them. It also takes you time to learn the routine and to organize your time. After all, you are learning right along with the children. As you become adjusted, the children become better adjusted. One pitfall some teachers fall into is that they feel they cannot do some of the activities they used to do in reading. (Example: I can't do a special writing activity I used to use with this story.) This is not true. The CIRC program is flexible enough that teachers can use their own activities with the program. If you want to throw in extra activities with CIRC it's okay. Do not feel you are limited by CIRC. CIRC can actually leave you more time to do extra activities successfully.

Holly Beers, Fifth Grade Teacher
Point Pleasant Elementary School,
Glen Burnie, MD

CIRC has worked well in all our classes. The initial problem was to adapt our reading series to the CIRC methods. I have spent two years writing these lessons and also writing lessons using children's literature materials, so the classroom teacher has some options when deciding how he or she will accomplish the teaching of reading.

I think one of the most important factors in implementing CIRC is the time necessary for planning. Every class in grades four, five, and six in our building is using CIRC. We accomplished that because of the support given to me by our building principal to take the time to develop the curriculum. In addition, I have worked with every one of the teachers to help them be more comfortable and knowledgeable about these techniques. I found that once classroom teachers realized that modification of any process without changing the objective is acceptable, they all took the

concepts of CIRC and implemented them. At the same time, many veteran teachers began enjoying teaching reading, and that can only mean that:

1. students enjoy it;
2. students achieve greater success because they are a part of the process; and
3. everyone leaves the program a better reader.

Maureen Sauter, Fourth, Fifth, and Sixth Grade Teacher Sacandaga Elementary School, Scotia, NY

It is so easy to fit the components of our reading series into the CIRC format. My favorite thing about CIRC is that it does not depend upon a particular text; once I have learned it I can use it with any program. (That's

really not my favorite thing about CIRC—it's really that the children love it so much and comprehension goes way up!) It is such a time saver to make a CIRC lesson instead of preparing lessons the way I used to.

Nancy Whitlock, Fifth Grade Teacher Spencer County Elementary School, Taylorsville, KY

Partner Checking. After students complete each of these activities, their partners initial a student-assignment form indicating that they have completed and/or achieved criterion on that task. Students are given daily expectations as to the number of activities to be completed, but they can go at their own rate and complete the activities earlier if they wish, creating additional time for independent reading (to be discussed shortly).

Tests. At the end of three class periods, students are given a comprehension test on the story, asked to write meaningful sentences for each vocabulary word, and asked to read the word list aloud to the teacher. Students are not permitted to help one another on these tests. The test scores and evaluations of the story-related writing are major components of students' weekly team scores.

Direct Instruction in Reading Comprehension. One day each week, students receive direct instruction in specific reading comprehension skills, such as identifying main ideas, understanding causal relations, and making inferences. A step-by-step curriculum was designed for this purpose. After each lesson, students work on reading comprehension worksheets and/or games as a team, first gaining consensus on one set of worksheet items and then assessing one another and discussing any remaining problems on a second set of items.

Integrated Language Arts and Writing. During language arts periods, teachers use a curriculum on language arts and writing developed especially for CIRC. In it, students work as teams on language arts skills that lead directly to writing activities. The emphasis of this curriculum is on writing, and language mechanics skills are introduced as specific aids to writing rather than as separate topics. For example, students study modifiers during a lesson on writing descriptive paragraphs, and quotation marks when writing dialogue for a narrative story. The writing program uses both ''writers' workshops'' in which students write on topics of their choice, and specific, teacher-directed lessons on such skills as writing compare/contrast paragraphs, newspaper articles, mystery stories, and letters. On all writing assignments students draft compositions after consulting team-mates and the teacher about their ideas and organizational plans, work with teammates to revise the content of their compositions, and then edit one another's work using peer editing forms emphasizing grammatical and mechanical correctness. The peer editing forms begin very simply but become increasingly complex as students cover successive skills. Finally, students "publish" their final compositions in team and/or class books.

Independent Reading and Book Reports. Students are asked to read a trade book of their choice for at least twenty minutes every evening. Parents initial forms indicating that students have read for the required time, and students contribute points to their teams if they submit a completed form each week. Students also complete at least one book report every two weeks, for which they also receive team points. Independent reading and book reports replace all other homework in reading and language arts. If students complete their story packets or other activities early, they may read their independent reading books in class.

SIX

Task Specialization Methods

Several forms of cooperative learning are designed so that students take on specific roles in accomplishing an overall group task. For example, in a group report on the beginnings of aviation, one group member might focus on the development of balloons and gliders, a second on powered flight, a third on early military aviation, and a fourth on early civil aviation. Task specialization solves the problem of individual accountability by having each student be uniquely accountable for his or her own contribution to the group. An important rationale for task specialization is that when each student is responsible for a separate part of the overall group task, each can be proud of his or her contribution to the group; the group's task is inherently interdependent, rather than being artificially made interdependent by the use of a group scoring system. Further, giving students different tasks may help avoid invidious comparisons among groupmates. One task specialization method, Finding Out/Descubrimiento, explicitly emphasizes that there is no one continuum of ability; rather, each child has something unique to contribute to the group's task (see Cohen, 1986).

One problem of task specialization methods is the danger that students will learn only about the subtopic or subtask for which they were personally responsible. To solve this problem, most task specialization methods include a procedure whereby students share information they have gathered with groupmates and, in many cases, with the class as a whole. In Jigsaw II, students are quizzed on all topics and the quiz scores are averaged to form team scores. So if the team is to succeed, team members must not only accomplish their subtasks but also do a good job of sharing information with their teammates. In Group Investigation and Co-op Co-op, teams prepare information and then report it to the class.

This chapter presents detailed guides to three task specialization methods—Group Investigation, Co-op Co-op, and Jigsaw II—and briefly describes other task specialization methods, including several versions of Jigsaw.

GROUP INVESTIGATION

The most extensively researched and successful of the task specialization methods is Group Investigation, a form of cooperative learning that dates back to John Dewey (1970), but has been refined and researched in more recent years by Shlomo and Yael Sharan and Rachel Hertz-Lazarowitz in Israel.*

Rationale

Group Investigation has its origins in philosophical, ethical, and psychological writings dating to the early years of this century. First among the prominent forebears of this educational orientation is John Dewey. Dewey viewed cooperation in the classroom as a prerequisite for dealing with the complex problems of life in a democracy. The classroom is a cooperative enterprise where teacher and pupils build the learning process on mutual planning based on their respective experiences, capacities, and needs. Learners are active participants in all aspects of school life, making decisions that determine the goals toward which they work. The group affords the social vehicle for this process. Group planning is one method for ensuring maximum pupil involvement.

A cooperative-investigation method of classroom learning derives from the premise that in both the social and intellectual domains the school learning process incorporates the values it advocates. Group Investigation cannot be implemented in an educational environment that does not support interpersonal dialogue or that disregards the affective-social dimension of classroom learning. Cooperative interaction and communication among classmates are best achieved within the small group, where exchange among peers and cooperative inquiry can be sustained. The social-affective aspect of the group, its intellectual exchange, and the meaning of the subject matter itself provide the primary sources of meaning for students' efforts to learn.

Acquiring Group Skills. Successful implementation of Group Investigation requires prior training in communication and social skills. This phase is often called *laying the groundwork* or *team building*. The teacher and students experience a variety of academic and nonacademic activities that establish norms of appropriate cooperative behavior in the classroom. Team-building activities are discussed in Chapter 7 (See also Cohen, 1986; Graves and Graves, 1985; Johnson and Johnson, 1986; Kagan, 1985; Sharan and Sharan, 1976).

As the name implies, Group Investigation is appropriate for integrated study projects that deal with the acquisition, analysis, and synthesis of information in order to solve a multi-faceted problem. The academic task should allow for diverse contributions from group members, and not be designed simply to obtain answers to factual questions (who, what, when, and so on). For example, Group Investigation would be ideal for teaching about the history and culture of a country or about the biology of the rain forest, but would not be appropriate for teaching map skills or the periodic table of the elements. Generally, the teacher designates a broad topic, which the students then break down into subtopics. These subtopics are an outgrowth of student backgrounds and interests, as well as of the exchange of ideas among the students.

As part of the investigation the students seek information from a variety of sources inside and outside the classroom. Such sources (books, institutions, people) offer a range of ideas, opinions, data, solutions, or positions regarding the problem being studied. The students then evaluate and synthesize the information contributed by each group member in order to produce a group product.

*The description of Group Investigation presented in this chapter is adapted with permission from Y. Sharan and S. Sharan, *Group Investigation: A Strategy for Expanding Cooperative Learning.* 12 Oppenheimer St., Tel-Aviv, Israel. Book in preparation.

Cooperative Planning. Central to Group Investigation is students' *cooperative planning* of their inquiry. Group members take part in planning the various dimensions and requirements of their project. Together they determine what they want to investigate in order to "solve" their problem; which resources they require; who will do what; and how they will present their completed project to the class. Usually there is division of labor in the group that enhances positive interdependence among members.

Cooperative planning skills should be introduced gradually into the classroom and practiced in a variety of situations before the class undertakes a full-scale investigation project. Teachers can conduct discussions with the whole class or with small groups, eliciting ideas for carrying out any aspect of classroom activity. Students can help plan short-term activities that last only one period, or long-term activities. Anything from naming a goldfish to organizing a class trip or student council group is appropriate for cooperative planning.

The Teacher's Role. In a class conducting a Group Investigation project the teacher serves as a resource person and facilitator. He or she circulates among the groups, sees that they are managing their work, and helps out with any difficulties they encounter in group interaction and the performance of the specific tasks related to the learning project.

The teacher's role is learned by practice over time, as is the students' role. First and foremost, the teacher must model the social and communication skills expected from students. There are many opportunities in the course of the school day for the teacher to assume a variety of leadership roles, as in discussions with the entire class or with small groups. In these discussions the teacher models a variety of skills: listening, paraphrasing, reacting nonjudgmentally, encouraging participation, and so forth. These discussions can be aimed at determining short-term learning goals and the means to reach them.

No doubt some aspects of curricula may not be amenable to Group Investigation. Furthermore, the subtopics selected by the students for research need not be the only material that students study about a subject. The investigation of subtopics of the students' choice may be supplemented by the teacher's instruction of other topics he or she feels are important. The teacher can then expand the unit by direct whole-class instruction, individualized instruction in learning centers, or any combination of methods. These lessons may be presented before, after, or during the time the class is conducting Group Investigation (Cohen, 1986; Sharan and Sharan, 1976). For example, in a class studying World War I the teacher might present lessons to the class on the geography and history of Europe just before the war and then begin a Group Investigation unit in which students focus on topics of interest to them.

Implementation

In Group Investigation, pupils progress through six stages. These stages and their components are outlined below and then described in detail. Of course teachers will have to adapt these guidelines to their pupils' backgrounds, ages, and abilities, as well as the constraints of time, but the guidelines are sufficiently general to apply in a wide range of classroom conditions.

Stage 1: Identifying the Topic and Organizing Pupils into Groups

- Students scan sources, propose topics, and categorize suggestions.
- Students join the group studying the topic of their choice.
- Group composition is based on interest and is heterogeneous.
- Teacher assists in information gathering and facilitates organization.

Stage 2: Planning the Learning Task

- Students plan together:

    What do we study?

    How do we study? Who does what? (division of labor)

    For what purpose or goals do we investigate this topic?

Stage 3: Carrying Out the Investigation

- Students gather information, analyze the data, and reach conclusions.
- Each group member contributes to the group effort.
- Students exchange, discuss, clarify, and synthesize ideas.

Stage 4: Preparing a Final Report

- Group members determine the essential message of their project.
- Group members plan *what* they will report and *how* they will make their presentation.
- Group representatives form a steering committee to coordinate plans for the presentation.

Stage 5: Presenting the Final Report

- The presentation is made to the entire class in a variety of forms.
- Part of the presentation should actively involve the audience.
- The audience evaluates the clarity and appeal of presentation according to criteria determined in advance by the whole class.

Stage 6: Evaluation

- Students share feedback about the topic, about the work they did, and about their affective experiences.
- Teachers and pupils collaborate in evaluating student learning.
- Assessment of learning should evaluate higher-level thinking.

Stage 1: Identifying the Topic and Organizing into Research Groups. This stage is devoted to organizational matters. The teacher presents a broad problem or issue (for example, understanding South America's geography, economics, and culture) and the students identify and select the various subtopics for study, based on their interests and backgrounds. This stage begins with classwide cooperative planning, which can proceed in several ways:

1. The teacher presents a problem to the entire class and asks, "What do you want to know about this problem?" Each student raises questions about the aspect of the problem he or she would like to investigate.
2. Students meet in buzz groups where each person expresses his or her ideas about what to investigate. A recorder in each buzz group writes down all ideas and then reports them to the whole class. A short class discussion results in a shared list of suggestions for subtopics to be investigated.
3. Planning begins with each student writing down his or her suggestions, and continues in progressively larger groups, from pairs to quartets or even groups of eight. At each step the group members compare their lists, eliminate repetitions, and compile a single list. This final list represents the interests of all members.

The next step is to make all the suggestions available to the whole class. The teacher or students can do this by writing all the suggestions on the board or on newsprint hung on the walls, or by copying them and distributing a copy to each student. After each student has a list of everyone's suggestions, the class classifies them into several categories. This step can be conducted by one of the three methods just outlined. The resulting list, organized into categories that are presented as the subtopics for separate group investigation, incorporates the ideas and interests of all class members. For example, if the class were studying South America, different groups might choose different countries, or one group might choose the physical geography of South America, another the natural resources, and so on.

Participation in this stage enables students to express their own interests and to exchange ideas and opinions with their classmates. It is important for the teacher to allow the students to determine the parameters of the investigation by not imposing his or her own suggestions and by not rejecting pupils' ideas. Full, unhurried implementation of this initial planning stage demonstrates that the group learning process is based on individual members' experiences and needs. It is likely that in two classrooms investigating the same general topic, the subtopics would be different, reflecting the unique interests of the members of each class.

In the final step of this stage the subtopics are presented to the whole class, usually on the board. Groups are formed based on students' interests; each student joins the group studying the subtopic of his or her choice. The teacher may wish to limit the number of students in a group. If one particular subtopic is very popular, two groups may be formed to investigate it. Because of group members' different interests and needs, each of the two groups will produce a unique product, despite the common subtopic.

Stage 2: Planning the Investigation in Groups. After joining their respective research groups, students turn their attention to the subtopic of their choice. At this stage group members determine the aspect of the subtopic each one of them (singly or in pairs) will investigate. In effect, each group must formulate a researchable problem, decide how to proceed, and determine which resources it will need to carry out its investigation.

Many groups find it useful to fill out a worksheet containing questions relevant to this planning stage. The worksheet may look like this:

OUR RESEARCH TOPIC:
GROUP MEMBERS: (names)
WHAT DO WE WANT TO INVESTIGATE?
WHAT ARE OUR RESOURCES?
HOW WILL WE DIVIDE THE WORK?

The teacher can post a copy of each group's worksheet in order to present graphic evidence that the class is a "group of groups." Each student contributes to the small group's investigation, and each group contributes to the whole class's study of the larger unit.

Stage 3: Carrying Out the Investigation. In this stage each group carries out the plans it formulated earlier. Typically this is the longest stage. Although students may be given a time limit, it is not always possible to foresee the exact number of sessions they will need to complete their investigation. The teacher should make every effort to enable a group project to proceed uninterrupted until the investigation is accomplished, or at least until the bulk of the work is done.

During this stage students, singly or in pairs, gather, analyze, and evaluate information, reach conclusions, and apply their share of new knowledge to the resolution of the group's research problem. Each student investigates that aspect of the group project that interests him or her most, and in so doing contributes one of the parts necessary to create a group "whole."

When individuals or pairs complete their portion of the task, the group reconvenes and members share their knowledge. Members may also help each other and discuss their work while it is in progress. Groups may choose to have one member record their conclusions, or each member may present a written summary of his or her findings. Groups carrying out their first investigation, especially in the lower grades, may simply have each member present a short summary in response to the question that was to be investigated. With experience, this presentation of summaries becomes a problem-solving discussion.

Stage 4: Preparing a Final Report. This stage is a transition from the data-gathering and clarifying stage to the stage where the group reports the results of its activities to the class. Primarily it is an organizational stage, but like stage 1 it also entails such intellectual activities as abstracting the main idea of the group's project, integrating all of its parts into a whole, and planning a presentation that will be both instructive and appealing.

How does the class plan its final presentation? At the conclusion of the investigation stage the teacher asks each group to appoint a representative to a *steering committee*. This committee will hear each group's plan for its report. It will collect all requests for materials, coordinate time schedules, and make sure that the ideas for presentation are realistic and interesting. The teacher continues in the role of adviser, helping the committee where needed and ensuring that each group's plan enables all members to be involved. Some groups determine the nature of their final report when they start their work. In others the plan for the final report emerges in stage 4, or it develops while the group is engaged in investigation. Even if groups do begin to generate ideas about their final report during the investigation phase, they still will require time for a systematic discussion of their plan. During this transitional planning session the pupils begin to assume a new role—the role of the teacher. Of course, students have been telling their groupmates all along about what they are doing and learning, but now they begin to plan how to teach their classmates in a more organized fashion the essence of what they have learned.

When the teacher meets with the steering committee, he or she may wish to highlight the following guidelines to help the groups plan their reports:

- Emphasize the *main ideas* and conclusions of the investigation.
- Inform the class about the sources the group consulted and how it obtained information.
- Allow for questions and answers.
- Involve classmates as much as possible in the presentation by giving them roles to perform; don't have them sit and listen for long periods.
- Make sure everyone in the group plays an important role in the presentation.
- Make sure all necessary equipment or materials have been requested.

Stage 5: Presenting the Final Report. The groups are now prepared to present their final report to the class. At this stage, they convene and reconstitute the class as a whole.

The students making the presentation must fill a role to which they are largely unaccustomed. They must cope not only with the demands of the task—ideas and procedures—but also with the organizational problems of coordinating the work and planning and carrying out the presentation. The following guidelines might prove helpful:

- Speak clearly and succinctly when addressing the class, but lecture as little as possible.
- Use the blackboard to illustrate concepts.
- Use audiovisual equipment, such as an overhead projector.
- Conduct formal debates in front of the class if appropriate.
- Think of preparing learning stations where classmates can perform tasks prepared by the group.
- Consider dramatizing some portion of the work, or simulating certain events.
- Consider quiz programs as one way to get an audience interested.
- Consider displays of pictures, drawings, or photographs to liven up the presentation.

A sixth-grade group studying the legacy of ancient Greece decided to conduct a trial exactly as it was held in ancient Greece. The class became a meeting of citizens, and judges were selected from the "populace" by lot. The pupils reproduced as many details in the trial as they could reconstruct from their texts. Another group in the same class prepared a quiz show about the Olympic gods. The group had made figurines of the best-known Greek gods and used them in the show. A third group displayed a large model of the Parthenon that it had built. Other groups' presentations were a series of Olympic games; a dictionary of Greek words used in modern English and a learning center where pupils wrote sentences using these words; and a skit depicting the battle of Achilles and Hector and demonstrating principles of Greek drama.

These final reports afforded an experience in which intellectual pursuits were accompanied by a moving emotional experience. All members of the class could participate in many of the presentations, by performing tasks or answering questions; the presentations were not just a matter of performing rehearsed roles and reciting lines.

Stage 6: Evaluating Achievement. Group Investigation challenges teachers to employ innovative approaches in assessing what pupils have learned. In traditional classroom instruction all students are expected to learn the same material and acquire a uniform set of concepts. The manner in which they are to demonstrate their understanding of the subject is also largely uniform. That such expectations are clearly inappropriate in Group Investigation reinforces the fear of some teachers that not every pupil has actively participated or done his or her best and that in the absence of uniform evaluation these students will not be identified.

In Group Investigation teachers should evaluate students' higher-level thinking about the subject they studied—how they investigated certain aspects of the subject, how they applied their knowledge to the solution of new problems, how they used inferences from what they learned in discussing questions requiring analysis and judgment, and how they reached conclusions from sets of data. This kind of evaluation is best achieved through a cumulative view of the individual's work during the entire investigation project.

Group Investigation exposes pupils to constant evaluation both by peers and by the teacher more than does traditional whole-class instruction. The pupil's ideas, grasp of a subject, and work investment are all very visible in this approach. In the traditional classroom, many students are never heard from until the final test. In the Group Investigation classroom, teachers should be able to form reliable student evaluations on the basis of frequent conversations and observations of the student's academic activity.

If testing is desired, the tests should take into consideration different levels or types of learning. Tests that focus exclusively on information gathering and recall are not likely to reflect the learning that actually took place. Pupils' affective experiences during their study also should be evaluated, including their level of motivation and involvement.

TEACHERS ON TEACHING

When students are working together on group projects, there is always a danger that not all students will participate in the activity. How do you ensure individual accountability when your students are doing group projects?

The past two years I have used cooperative learning almost exclusively in ninth grade honors classes, and these classes, as a rule, do not present the problems of nonparticipation that many classes do. Still, there are those who sit back and relax, and what I usually do is to have each member in the group work with one aspect of a work, problem, and so forth. For example, if each group is assigned a short story or a poem, each member will be given one aspect, such as tone, imagery, or theme, and will report to the group as a whole on his or her part . . . in the case of a written assignment (a short one), group members each prepare an individual assignment and then take the best from all four papers and prepare a group paper to hand in.

I have had good success with the Co-op Co-op book report, for which each member of the group "specializes" in one aspect of the book, and then all four members are required to participate in a presentation to the class.

Ruth Werfel, English Teacher
Wilcox High School, Santa Clara, CA

My students have really been excited about cooperative learning. Each student in our thematic unit does individual research on a project. Students then bring to the group their individual information and compile it into one report. The team will report its findings to the rest of the class with a list of ten important facts. The facts are then used as test questions as in Jigsaw, or tournament cards as in TGT.

The team recognition comes by doing the reports in a finished folder to be placed in the library for minilessons with other classes.

Alta Blandford, Valley View
Elementary School, Roswell, NM

Feedback from the pupils themselves should convey how they feel about the topic and about the work they did.

The teacher of the sixth-grade class on ancient Greece gave a quiz on democracy that included the following questions: "If you could turn back the wheels of time and prepare a plan for the history of ancient Greece, what mistakes would you try to avoid that the Greeks did not avoid? Which elements in their history would you want to strengthen and improve? If you could plan a better democracy for our country today, what would it be like, and why would you want it to be the way you suggest?"

Teachers and pupils can collaborate in evaluating student learning. One possible suggestion is peer evaluation. The students and teacher cooperate in formulating an exam, with each research group submitting questions about the most important ideas it presented to the class. Such a test, comprising questions from all groups, would cover the entire topic the class investigated. Each group is given the pupils' written answers to the questions and must correct those answers. In this way the group becomes a committee of experts who must evaluate their classmates' achievement.

The teacher may wish to reconvene the steering committee to assist in the evaluation. For example, each research group might submit five questions, from which the teacher and the steering committee would select two. With seven research groups in the class, the final exam would consist of fourteen questions. In the meantime, all pupils are given a copy of all the questions composed by the various groups and told that the exam will consist of fourteen of the thirty-five questions. The date for the exam is set for a week or two weeks later to give everyone time to prepare. During this preparation pupils must carefully review the material presented in the group reports, because the groups have prepared the exam questions on the basis of these reports. The pupils are free to discuss their answers with members of each research group after the exams have been returned to them. This examination can become an important learning experience for all involved.

Another approach to evaluation could have the students reconstruct the process of investigation and map out the steps they followed in their work. They should also analyze the way different groups contributed to each other's progress. Each student might be asked to prepare a reconstruction of his or her own activities and write how this work complemented the work of other group members and contributed to the progress of the research group as a whole. This kind of evaluation is probably beyond the abilities of children in the early elementary grades and is more appropriate for those in sixth grade or higher. Reconstructive evaluation should help students develop a broad and critical perspective of their own study procedures and achievements, improving their ability to plan investigation projects in the future.

CO-OP CO-OP

Co-op Co-op is quite similar to Group Investigation. It places teams in cooperation with one another (hence the name) to study a class topic.*

Co-op Co-op allows students to work together in small groups, first to advance their understanding of themselves and the world, and then to provide them with the opportunity to share that new understanding with their peers. The method is simple and flexible. Once a teacher grasps the philosophy behind Co-op Co-op, he or she may choose any of a number of ways to apply the approach in a given classroom. Nevertheless, following nine specific steps increases the probability of success of the method.

Step 1: Student-Centered Class Discussion. At the beginning of a class unit in which Co-op Co-op is used, encourage students to discover and express their own interests in the subject to be covered. An initial set of readings, lectures, or experiences can serve this purpose. Then conduct a student-centered class discussion. The aim of this discussion should be to increase students' involvement in the learning unit by uncovering and stimulating their curiosity, not to lead them to specific topics for study. The discussion should lead to an understanding among the teacher and all the students about what the students want to learn and experience in relation to the topic to be covered.

The time needed for this first step depends in part on the extent to which the students have differentiated interests in the topic. The importance of the initial student-centered discussion cannot be underestimated; it is unlikely that Co-op Co-op will be successful for any students who are not actively interested in a topic related to the unit and who are not motivated to learn more about the topic.

Step 2: Selection of Student Learning Teams and Team Building. If students are not already working in teams, assign them to four-to-five-member heterogeneous teams as in STAD. Use the team-building exercises described in Chapter 7 or have them work for a few weeks on STAD or Jigsaw II units before starting a Co-op Co-op unit. Students need to have developed trust and good group working skills before beginning Co-op Co-op.

Step 3: Team Topic Selection. Allow students to select topics for their team. If the team topic selection does not directly follow the student-centered class discussion, remind students (via blackboard, overhead, or handout) which topics the class as a whole

*The following description of Co-op Co-op is adapted from S. Kagan (1989), *Cooperative Learning Resources for Teachers*. San Juan Capistrano, CA: Resources for Teachers.

has indicated are of greatest interest. Point out that the team can cooperate most fully in realizing the class goals if they choose a topic related to the interests of the class. Encourage students to discuss the various topics among themselves so they can settle on the topic of most interest to their team.

As the teams discuss their interests and begin to settle on topics, circulate among them and act as a facilitator. If two teams begin to settle on the same topic, you can point this out and encourage the teams to reach a compromise, either by dividing that topic or by having one of the teams choose some other topic of interest. If no team settles on a topic that the class deems important, you can point this out too and encourage the students to respond to the need.

When this third step of Co-op Co-op is successfully completed, each team has a topic and feels identified with it. The teacher may facilitate class unity by pointing out how each of the topics makes an important contribution to the class goal of mastering the learning unit.

Step 4: Minitopic Selection. Just as the class as a whole divides the learning unit into sections to create a division of labor among the teams in the class, each team divides its topic to create a division of labor among members. Each student selects a minitopic that covers one aspect of the team topic.

Minitopics may overlap, and team members are encouraged to share references and resources, but each minitopic must provide a unique contribution to the team effort. Teacher involvement in student minitopic selection may vary, depending on the level of the students. The teacher may require that minitopics meet his or her approval to ensure that they are appropriate to the level of the interested student or that sufficient resources are available on them.

Because of differences in abilities and interests, it is acceptable and natural for some students to contribute more than others to the team effort, but all members need to make an important contribution. Teachers can accomplish this by (1) allowing the students to evaluate the contributions of their fellow teammates; (2) assigning an individual paper or project to the students on their minitopics; and (3) monitoring the individual contributions. If the minitopics are selected properly, each student will make a unique contribution to the group effort, and will thereby have peer support for mastering their minitopics.

Step 5: Minitopic Preparation. After the students have divided the team topic into minitopics, they work individually. They each know that they are responsible for their minitopic and that the group is depending on them to cover an important aspect of the team effort.

The preparation of minitopics takes different forms, depending on the nature of the class unit being covered. The preparation may involve library research, data gathering through interviews or experimentation, creation of an individual project, or an expressive activity such as writing or painting. These activities take on a heightened interest because students know they will be sharing their product with their teammates and that their work will contribute to the team presentation.

Step 6: Minitopic Presentations. After the students complete the individual work they present their minitopic to their teammates. This step is similar to the team report of Jigsaw. The minitopic presentations within teams should be formal. That is, each team member is allotted a specific time, and stands while presenting his or her minitopic.

Minitopic presentations and discussion within teams are carried out in a way that affords all teammates the knowledge or experience acquired by each. Following the presentations, teammates discuss the team topic like a panel of experts. The students know that the minitopics, like the pieces of a jigsaw puzzle, must be put together in a coherent whole for a successful team presentation to the class. Interaction with peers over a topic of common concern provides an opportunity for some of the most important learning to occur.

During the minitopic presentations, a division of labor within the teams may be encouraged so that one teammate takes notes, another plays critic, another plays supporter, and another checks for points of convergence and divergence in the information presented.

Time may be allotted for feedback; students may report back to the team after they research, redo, or rethink their minitopics in light of the feedback they receive from the team. Team members are encouraged to let teammates know which questions regarding the minitopic remain unanswered; team members are responsible to their group.

Step 7: Preparation of Team Presentations. Students are encouraged to integrate all minitopic material in the team presentation. There must be an active synthesis of the minitopics so that during the team discussion the team presentation will become more than the sum of the minitopic presentations.

Discussion of the form of the team presentation should follow the synthesis of the minitopic material. Panel presentations in which each team member reports on his or her minitopic are discouraged, as they may represent a failure to reach high-level cooperative synthesis. The form of the presentation should be determined by the content of the material. For example, if a group cannot come to consensus, the ideal form for their presentation would be to present a debate for the class. Nonlecture formats such as displays, demonstrations, learning centers, skits, and team-led class discussion are encouraged. The use of blackboard, overhead, audiovisual medias, and handouts are also encouraged.

Step 8: Team Presentations. During its presentation, the team takes control of the classroom. Team members are responsible for how the time, space, and resources of the class are used during their presentation; they are encouraged to make full use of the classroom facilities.

Because teams have difficulty managing time, the teacher must generally appoint a class timekeeper who is not a member of the presenting team. The timekeeper holds up warning cards when there are just five, one, and no minutes remaining.

TEACHERS ON TEACHING

What do you do to prevent students who do really well from giving up when the other members of their team do not produce enough quality work?

I have discovered that sometimes one student does really well but his or her teammates prevent the team from being a Superteam. Other times a team may earn a Superteam award because one or two people did exceptionally well that week while the others really did not do their share of the work. When either of these situations occurs, the students who do really well deserve some extra credit.

When I announce the team awards I also give awards for Superpeople. I make students aware of the criteria for being a Superperson. This makes it possible for people to get two awards, but I think the awards are well deserved. I have found that this helps keep the Superpeople motivated and may also motivate others to try to be Superpeople.

Theresa Brown,
Fourth Grade Teacher
Point Pleasant Elementary School,
Glen Burnie, MD

The team may wish to include in its presentation a question–answer period and/or time for comments and feedback. In addition, following the presentation the teacher may find it useful to lead a feedback session and/or to interview the team so that other teams can learn something of what was involved in the development of the presentation. Particularly successful teams are held up as models. During postpresentation interviews, the teacher uncovers strategies that might be useful to other teams in future Co-op Co-op units.

Step 9: Evaluation. Evaluation takes place on three levels: (1) team presentations are evaluated by the class; (2) individual contributions to the team effort are evaluated by teammates; and (3) a write-up or presentation of the minitopic by each student is evaluated by the teacher.

Following each presentation, the teacher may guide a class discussion of the strongest and weakest elements in the content and format of the presentation. Formal evaluation forms are also sometimes used for teammate and team contributions.

Some Co-op Co-op teachers and classes prefer to make learning and sharing their own reward; others prefer formal evaluation. In either case, the class should have considerable say in determining the form of the evaluation.

JIGSAW II

Jigsaw Teaching was developed by Elliot Aronson and his colleagues (1978). His original method, briefly described later in this section, required extensive development of special materials. A more practical and easily adapted form of Jigsaw, Jigsaw II (Slavin, 1986a), is described here in more detail.*

Overview

Jigsaw II can be used whenever the material to be studied is in written narrative form. It is most appropriate in such subjects as social studies, literature, some parts of science, and related areas in which concepts rather than skills are the learning goals. The instructional "raw material" for Jigsaw II should usually be a chapter, story, biography, or similar narrative or descriptive material.

In Jigsaw II, students work in heterogeneous teams, as in STAD and TGT. The students are assigned chapters or other units to read, and are given "expert sheets" that contain different topics for each team member to focus on when reading. When everyone has finished reading, students from different teams with the same topic meet in an "expert group" to discuss their topic for about thirty minutes. The experts then return to their teams and take turns teaching their teammates about their topic. Finally, students take quizzes that cover all the topics, and the quiz scores become team scores, as in STAD. Also as in STAD, the scores that students contribute to their teams are based on the individual improvement score system, and students on high-scoring teams may receive certificates or be recognized in a newsletter or on the bulletin board. Thus, students are motivated to study the material well and to work hard in their expert groups so that they can help their team do well. The key to Jigsaw is interdependence: every student depends on his or her teammates to provide the information he or she needs to do well on the quizzes.

Preparation

Materials. At present, Johns Hopkins Team Learning Project materials are available for Jigsaw only in junior high school U.S. history. But preparation of Jigsaw materials is not difficult. An example of a complete Jigsaw II unit appears in Appendix 7.

*This section is adapted from Slavin, 1986a.

To make materials for Jigsaw II, follow these steps:

1. Select several chapters, stories, or other units, each covering material for two or three days. If students are to read in class, the selections should not require more than a half hour to complete; if the reading is to be assigned for homework, the selections can be longer.

2. Make an expert sheet for each unit. This tells students what to concentrate on while they read, and which expert group they will work with. It identifies four topics that are central to the unit. For example, an expert sheet for the Level Four Harcourt Brace Jovanovich social studies book might refer to a section on the Blackfoot Indian tribes that is used to illustrate a number of concepts about groups, group norms, and leadership. The expert sheet for that section might be as follows:

The Blackfoot

To read: pages 3–9 and 11–12

Topics:

1. How were Blackfoot men expected to act?
2. What is a group and what does it do? What are the most important groups for the Blackfoot?
3. What did Blackfoot bands and clubs do?
4. What were the Blackfoot customs and traditions?

As much as possible, the topics should cover themes that appear throughout the chapter, instead of issues that appear only once. For example, if the class were reading *Tom Sawyer,* a good topic might be ''How did Tom feel about his community?'' which appears throughout the book, as opposed to ''What happened to Tom and Huck Finn when they ran away?'' which a student could learn by reading only a section of the book. The expert topics may be put on ditto masters and one copy run off for each student, or they may be put on the chalkboard or poster paper.

3. Make a quiz for each unit. The quiz should consist of at least eight questions, two for each topic, or some multiple of four (twelve, sixteen, twenty, and so on), so that there is an equal number of questions for each topic. Teachers may wish to add two or more general questions. The questions should require considerable understanding, because students will have had ample time to discuss their topics in depth, and easy questions would fail to challenge those who have done a good job in preparation. However, the questions should not be obscure. In the Blackfoot example, the first two questions might be as follows:

1A. Which of the following was not an expected way of behaving for a Blackfoot man?
    a. He was expected to be brave.
    b. He was expected to brag about how many of the enemy tribe he had touched.
    c. He was expected to clean buffalo meat.
    d. He was expected to share buffalo meat.

1B. What are norms of behavior?
    a. All the ways of acting that people in a group have.
    b. The ways people in a group expect themselves and other members of the group to act.
    c. Records of great deeds.
    d. Sharing food with the very old.

All students must answer all questions. The quiz should take no more than ten minutes. Teachers may wish to use an activity other than a quiz or in addition to a quiz as an opportunity for team members to show their learning—for example, an oral report, a written report, or a crafts project.

4. Use discussion outlines (optional). A discussion outline for each topic can help guide the discussions in the expert groups. Such an outline lists the points that students should consider in discussing their topics. For example, a discussion outline for a topic relating to the settlement of the English colonies in America might be as follows:

Topic: What role did religious ideals play in the settlement of America?

- Puritan beliefs and religious practices
- Puritan treatment of dissenters
- Founding of Connecticut and Rhode Island
- Quakers and the establishment of Pennsylvania
- Catholics and religious toleration in Maryland

Assignment of Students to Teams. Assign students to four- or five-member heterogeneous teams, exactly as in STAD.

Assignment of Students to Expert Groups. You may wish to assign students to expert groups simply by distributing roles at random within each team. Or you may wish to decide which students will go to which expert group, ensuring that there are high, average, and low achievers in each group. If your class has more than twenty-four students, you should have two expert groups on each topic, so that there will not be more than six students in each expert group; an expert group larger than six can be unwieldy. Place team members' names on team summary sheets (Appendix 2), leaving the name blank.

Determination of Initial Base Scores. Assign students initial base scores exactly as for STAD. Use a quiz score sheet to record the scores.

Schedule of Activities

Jigsaw II consists of a regular cycle of instructional activities:

Reading. Students receive expert topics and read assigned material to locate information.

Expert-group discussion. Students with the same expert topics meet to discuss them in expert groups.

Team report. Experts return to their teams to teach their topics to their teammates.

Test. Students take individual quizzes covering all topics.

Team recognition. Team scores are computed as in STAD.

These activities are described in detail in the following pages.

READING

Time: half a class period to one class period (or assign for homework)

Main idea: Students receive expert topics and read assigned material to locate information on their topics.

Materials needed: an expert sheet for each student, consisting of four expert topics

a text or other reading assignment on which the expert topics for each student are based

The first activity in Jigsaw II is distribution of texts and expert topics, assignment of a topic to each student, and then reading. Pass out expert sheets and then go to each team and point out which students are to take which topic. If any team has five members, have two students take topic 1 together.

When students have their topics, let them read their materials, or assign the reading as homework. Students who finish reading before others can go back and make notes.

EXPERT-GROUP DISCUSSIONS

Time: half a class period

Main idea: Students with the same expert topics discuss them in groups.

Materials needed: expert sheet and texts for each student

(optional) discussion outlines for each topic: one for each student with that topic

Have all students with expert topic 1 get together at one table, all students with expert topic 2 at another table, and so on. If any expert group has more than six students (that is, if the class has more than twenty-four students), split the expert group into two smaller groups.

If students are to use a discussion outline, distribute it to them in each expert group.

Appoint a *discussion leader* for each group. The discussion leader need not be a particularly able student, and all students should have an opportunity to fill this role at some time. The leader's job is to moderate the discussion, calling on group members who raise their hands and trying to see that everyone participates.

Give the expert groups about twenty minutes to discuss their topics. Students should have already tried to locate information on their topics in their texts, and they share this information with the group. Group members should take notes on all points discussed.

While the expert groups are working, the teacher should spend time with each group in turn. He or she may wish to answer questions and resolve misunderstandings, but should not try to take over leadership of the groups—that is the discussion leaders' responsibility. The teacher may need to remind discussion leaders that part of their job is to see that everyone participates.

TEAM REPORT

Time: half a class period

Main idea: Experts return to their teams to teach their topics to their teammates.

Students should return from their expert-group discussions and prepare to teach their topics to their teammates. They should take about five minutes to review everything they have learned about their topics from their reading and their discussions in the expert groups.If two teammates shared topic 1, they should make a joint presentation.

Emphasize to students that they have a responsibility to their teammates to be good teachers as well as good listeners. You may wish to have experts question their teammates after they have reported to them to see that they have learned the material and are ready for the quiz.

TEST

Time: half a class period

Main idea: Students take a quiz.

Materials needed: one copy of the quiz for each student

Distribute the quizzes and allow enough time for almost everyone to finish. Have students exchange quizzes with members of other teams for scoring, or collect the quizzes and score them yourself. If students do the scoring, have the checkers put their name at the bottom of the quizzes they checked. After class, spot-check several quizzes to be sure that the students did a good job of checking.

Team Recognition. Scoring for Jigsaw II is the same as scoring for STAD, including base scores, improvement points, and team-scoring procedures. Also as in STAD, certificates, newsletters, bulletin boards, and/or other rewards are given in recognition of high-scoring teams.

Original Jigsaw

Aronson's original Jigsaw resembles Jigsaw II in most respects, but it also has some important differences. In the original Jigsaw, students read sections different from those read by their teammates. This has the benefit of making the experts possessors of unique information, and thus makes the teams value each member's contribution more highly. For example, in a unit on Chile, one student might have information on Chile's economy, another on its geography, a third on its history, and so forth. To know all about Chile, students must rely on their teammates. Original Jigsaw also takes less time than Jigsaw II; its readings are shorter, only a part of the total unit to be studied.

The most difficult part of original Jigsaw is that each section must be written so that it is comprehensible by itself. Existing materials cannot be used, in contrast with Jigsaw II: books can rarely be divided neatly into sections that make sense without the other sections. For example, in a biography of Alexander Hamilton, the section describing his duel with Aaron Burr would assume that the reader knew who both men were—knowledge the students would be unlikely to have unless they had read the rest of the biography. Preparing an original Jigsaw unit involves rewriting materials to fit the Jigsaw format. The advantage of Jigsaw II is that all students read all the material, which may make unified concepts easier to understand.

Teachers who wish to capitalize on the special features of original Jigsaw can do so by using Jigsaw II with these modifications:

1. Write units that present unique information about a subject but make sense by themselves. You can do this by cutting apart texts and adding information as needed, or by writing completely new material.
2. Assign students to five- or six-member teams and make five topics for each unit.
3. Appoint team leaders, and emphasize team-building exercises before and during use of the technique. See the section on team building in Chapter 7.
4. Use quizzes less frequently and do not use team scores, improvement scores, or newsletters. Simply give students individual grades.

For more information on original Jigsaw, see Aronson, Blaney, Stephan, Sikes, and Snapp (1978).

Other Ways of Using Jigsaw

Jigsaw is one of the most flexible of the cooperative learning methods. Several modifications can be made that keep the basic model but change the details of implementation:

1. Instead of having students refer to narrative materials for information on their topics, have them search a set of classroom or library materials for the information.
2. After the experts' reports, have students write essays or give oral reports instead of taking quizzes.

3. Instead of having all teams study the same material, give each team a unique topic to learn together and each team member a subtopic. The team could then prepare and make an oral presentation to the class. For methods of this type, see the preceding discussion of Group Investigation and Co-op Co-op.

4. For other Jigsaw modifications, see Kagan (1989).

TEACHERS ON TEACHING

What special issues need to be considered in using cooperative learning with middle/junior high school and high school students? What special adaptations are needed for students of this age?

Senior high school students should be educated in the basic principles of cooperative learning at the very beginning of the program. It is important that they understand that the principles relate to the world of work and the sports arena. Avoiding associations with the elementary school is wise since these students want to be treated as young adults. Receptivity to cooperative learning is usually increased when the students are told it is used and researched at the college level. Fostering positive feelings toward the cooperative class structure from the onset will significantly enhance the effectiveness of using cooperative learning structures.

Besides giving a brief background of cooperative learning to high school students it is essential that the class standards, procedures, and disciplinary system be explained in the introductory stage. Using the cooperative learning techniques to learn these "ground rules" accomplishes a two-fold purpose. Students rapidly understand both the nature of the cooperative class and some of the strategies involved.

Essential to the success of a cooperative learning program at the high school level is not only that the administering teachers believe these motivating strategies will enhance achievement, but that they also view building self-esteem and fostering mutual concern as important elements of the learning process. If teachers provide a well-defined set of cooperative learning principles, clear expectations, and an appropriate reward structure, then students, even high school students, will respond in a positive manner and find the classroom motivating and fun!

Lynne Mainzer,
Special Education Teacher
Francis Scott Key High School,
Union Bridge, MD

There are no adaptations that are necessary for high school students. They are more point/grade-oriented and will take a greater degree of sophistication in your explanations, but the techniques will work throughout the grades. The techniques that I would use for elementary math work with high school students.

Joe Mahood, Science Teacher
Wilcox High School, Santa Clara, CA

The greatest consideration when trying cooperative learning with middle school students is their initial desire to visit with their friends during group time. I have reduced this problem in two ways. First of all, the first time the students are grouped together, I decide the groups. I pay particular attention to putting students in groups away from their closest friends. I do also allow them the opportunity to move if they get placed into a group with another person they know they cannot work with. Secondly, I make sure that the first group work is high-interest, such as a lab experiment, and has enough work to keep the students very involved and on-task. After a few trials, when the students have demonstrated their ability to work in groups and understand my expectations, I usually allow them to pick their own groups. So far, I have seen little difficulty with this approach.

The reward system used is another concern. I usually let the class determine their reward from a list of ideas. Candy, free time, and extra-credit points are possibilities. If the students buy into the reward, and feel as if they have some control over their situation, they are generally very cooperative.

Jim Cronin, Science Teacher
Laredo Middle School, Aurora, CO

FINDING OUT/DESCUBRIMIENTO

Another cooperative learning method based on inquiry and investigation is Finding Out/Descubrimiento, a discovery-oriented elementary school science program developed by Edward DeAvila and Elizabeth Cohen. This method, used particularly in bilingual classes, involves students in small-group, hands-on science activities directed toward discovery of important scientific principles. Students may work together on experiments to derive principles of magnetism, sound, light, and so on. Materials for Finding Out/Descubrimiento are available in English and Spanish, so that monolingual and bilingual students can work together cooperatively. In addition to learning science, students in Finding Out/Descubrimiento apply mathematics skills in real-life situations and engage in focused discussions that help develop English skills for limited-English-speaking children.

For information on Finding Out/Descubrimiento, see DeAvila and Duncan (1980) and Cohen (1986).

SEVEN

Other Cooperative Learning Methods and Resources

LEARNING TOGETHER

Among the most widely used cooperative learning methods are those developed and researched by David and Roger Johnson and their colleagues at the University of Minnesota. Their methods emphasize four elements (Johnson, Johnson, Holubec, and Roy, 1984):

1. **Face-to-face interaction:** Students work in four-to-five-member groups.
2. **Positive interdependence:** Students work together to achieve a group goal.
3. **Individual accountability:** Students must show that they have individually mastered the material.
4. **Interpersonal and small-group skills:** Students must be taught effective means of working together and of discussing how well their groups are working to achieve their goals.

The Johnsons' methods are similar to STAD in that they use heterogeneous learning groups and emphasize positive interdependence and individual accountability. However, they also highlight team building and group self-assessment, and recommend team grades rather than certificates or other recognition.

Research on these methods has found that when they involve rewards to groups based on the individual learning of all group members, they increase student achievement more than individualistic methods and they have positive effects on such outcomes as race relations and acceptance of mainstreamed classmates (see Johnson and Johnson, 1985). For practical guides to these methods, see Johnson, Johnson, Holubec, and Roy (1984) and Johnson and Johnson (1984).

The Johnsons and their colleagues have also developed and researched methods for engaging students in "cooperative controversy." Students in four-member groups are given study materials on a controversial issue, such as whether the hunting of wolves should be permitted in northern Minnesota. Two group members take one side of the issue and two take the other. Then they switch roles and argue the opposite side. Finally, the entire group comes to a consensus. Students follow seven rules as they work (Smith, Johnson, and Johnson, 1981, p. 654):

1. I am critical of ideas, not people.
2. I remember that we are all in this together.
3. I encourage everyone to participate.
4. I listen to everyone's ideas, even if I do not agree with them.
5. I restate what someone said if it is not clear.
6. I try to understand both sides of the issue.
7. I first bring out all the ideas, then I put them together.

Research on the constructive controversy methods has generally found them to be more effective than traditional debate or individual study methods in increasing retention of information, changing attitudes, and other outcomes. See Johnson and Johnson (1979, 1986) for more on constructive controversy.

GROUPS OF FOUR

Groups of Four is a cooperative mathematics program developed by Marilyn Burns. It emphasizes problem solving, applications, and discovery. Students work together to solve complex math problems and to discover mathematical principles and operations. For more on Groups of Four, see Burns, 1981.

GROUP DISCUSSION AND GROUP PROJECTS

Among the oldest and most widely used forms of cooperative learning are group discussion and group projects. For example, most science teachers use cooperative lab groups, and many social studies and English teachers use discussion or project groups.

Whenever you are using a cooperative learning method, you have already assigned students to small teams; it is easy to use the same teams for discussions or projects as well. Many teachers use a mix of strategies. For example, a science teacher might use TGT or STAD to teach science information and vocabulary, Jigsaw II for expository material about science, and lab groups for lab work, all with the same teams. A social studies teacher might use TGT or STAD for geography and graph reading, Jigsaw for history, and discussion groups for contemporary social problems.

Discussion Groups

The main task in setting up a discussion group is to make sure that each group member participates. If the group is to write a report, it is also very important for each member to have a well-defined part of that task, so that all the work (and learning) does not fall on the shoulders of one member.

It is important to select a leader of the discussion group. This person should be chosen for leadership ability and organizational skills, *not* on the basis of academic performance alone. The leader should insure that everyone participates and that the group stays on-task.

One good way to get every team member to participate is to have each one write an opinion or an idea before the group starts discussing. For example, if the group is discussing capital punishment, you might have each student first write three advantages of capital punishment, three disadvantages, and his or her own opinion. The group members could then read their lists of advantages and disadvantages to the group, and the discussion could focus on each student's lists in turn. The key to this procedure is that if you force all students to state an opinion, they will have a commitment to the group discussion and are much more likely to participate in it.

Another way to insure participation is to make students experts on some part of the topic, as in Group Investigation, Co-op Co-op, and Jigsaw, by having them do research on their area of expertise. In the capital punishment discussion, one student could be an expert on the history of capital punishment, another on alternatives to capital punishment, another on its effects, and so on.

In addition to broad participation, another main task in setting up a group discussion is *focus*. Nothing is worse than a discussion with no aim. The job of the group should be clearly expressed. For example, the group could be charged to come to a consensus on an issue—for example, "Resolved: The United States Should Outlaw Strikes in Vital Industries," or "Resolved: The United States Should Not Have Entered World War I"—with reasons for the position taken. In these cases, it would be important to have a class discussion based on positions presented by each group.

If the group is to write a report, make sure that each student participates. One way to do this is to break the report into parts that different students write, as in Group Investigation or Co-op Co-op (see Chapter 6).

Group Projects

The basic principle behind a good group project is the same as the basic principle for a good discussion: get everyone to participate, and do not allow one or two students in the group to take all the responsibility. A group leader is as important for projects as for discussions, but again the teacher should emphasize that the leader's job is to get every group member to participate, and not to be personally responsible for the outcome.

The best ways to get every group member to participate in a group project are the same as for a group report: either give each member a specific part of the task, if the task can be divided, or give each member a part of the report to write or to present to the class. If group members do not each feel an individual responsibility for the group product, they are unlikely to participate fully.

If the group project can be divided into parts, you might ask that the groups do this, but then allow them to do so as they wish. For example, you could simply assign a group the task of writing a report on the development of aviation, and let the students decide how to break it down for research and for presentation to the class. For more on group projects of this kind, see the discussions of Group Investigation and Co-op Co-op in Chapter 6.

INFORMAL METHODS

This book has focused thus far on complete cooperative learning methods that can be used over extended periods. However, many teachers weave cooperative activities into their otherwise traditional lessons or use them when presenting lessons in STAD, TGT, or other cooperative techniques. A description of some of the most useful of these informal cooperative activities follows.*

Spontaneous Group Discussion

If students are sitting in groups, it is easy to ask them at various times during a lecture or presentation to discuss what something means, why something works, or how a problem

*This section is adapted from Kagan (1989).

might best be solved. This simple cooperative learning structure complements a traditional lesson, and the group work can vary from a few minutes to a full class session.

Numbered Heads Together

Russ Frank, a teacher at Chaparral Middle School in Diamond Bar, California, was teaching a grammar lesson. He put a sentence on the overhead projector and asked, ''Where should the comma go? Put your heads together and consult with your group.'' The students did just that. There was a buzz of animated talking. After a short time Russ flipped off the lights. Total silence. Then he called out a number. The hand of one student in each group shot up. Russ called on one of these group representatives. A correct answer led to points for that team.

Each student in a group had a number and the students knew that only one student would be called on to represent the group. The buzz of animated discussion was the attempt of the students to share the information so that everyone knew the answer. That way they would receive a point no matter which number was called.

Numbered Heads Together is basically a variant of group discussion; the twist is having only one student represent the group but not informing the group in advance whom its representative will be. That twist insures total involvement of all the students. Russ Frank's method is an excellent way to add individual accountability to a group discussion.

Team Product

Have student teams make a learning center, write an essay, draw a mural, work a worksheet, make a presentation to the class, design a better government, list possible solutions to a social problem, or analyze a poem. To maintain individual accountability, assign team members specific roles or individual areas of responsibility.

Cooperative Review

It is the day before the exam. Student groups make up review questions. They take turns asking the other groups the questions. The group asking the question gets a point for the question. The group initially called on gets a point for a correct answer. Then a second group can receive a point if it can add any important information to the answer.

In a variation on cooperative review, the teacher brings in the questions. Another variation combines Numbered Heads Together with cooperative review. That is, when the teacher or students ask the review question, students first discuss their answers with their teammates. After this brief ''heads together'' time, a number is called—1, 2, 3, or 4. Students with the corresponding numbers have the opportunity to come up with the right answer. A second number is called after a correct answer is provided, and another student can earn a point for his or her team by adding information to the original correct answer. If the teacher feels there is still important information to be brought out, a third number may be called, and so on.

Think–Pair–Share

This simple but very useful method was developed by Frank Lyman of the University of Maryland. When the teacher presents a lesson to the class, students sit in pairs within their teams. The teacher poses questions to the class. Students are instructed to *think* of an answer on their own, then to *pair* with their partners to reach consensus on an answer. Finally, the teacher asks students to *share* their agreed-upon answers with the rest of the class. For more on Think–Pair–Share, see Lyman (1981).

TEACHERS ON TEACHING

Many teachers use cooperative learning methods all year, while others use them on and off. Which characterizes your use of the methods? If you use them for some topics and not others, how do you decide which topics to use cooperative methods for and which not?

My two remedial math classes (ninth and tenth mixed) use TAI on a daily basis. My team partners (both special educators) and I have also incorporated simple cooperative strategies into our class with fact practice, and we have done much to emphasize the team-building aspect of cooperative learning. We have assigned roles to the students on a weekly basis: Supervisor, Coach, Recorder, and Go-Getter. We find that the team-building activities set the tone for an effective use of TAI.

In my other classes, I go in and out of cooperative strategies on a regular basis. In my advanced classes I find that some topics lend themselves to the methods more readily than others. Particularly, those topics that require some brainstorming and problem solving are facilitated much more easily with the cooperative teams. Sometimes we culminate with a tournament using TGT, or a quiz using STAD improvement points, or a research project using Jigsaw. Or maybe just a team activity where all team members are accountable for some aspect of the activity.

I find a nice flow in these classrooms, in and out of all kinds of cooperative strategies. Once the teams are built, the activities are easy to use at any given moment, from a warmup to a structured peer practice strategy.

Candi Nuzzolillo, Math Teacher
Gulf Middle School, Cape Coral, FL

I use cooperative learning on and off all year in my language arts classes. In language arts it's relatively easy to know when to use cooperative learning materials. Whenever I work on grammar, I use my STAD materials. Whenever I'm working on writing, I use a writing-process approach.

I use cooperative learning materials for all my objective drills. I do not use STAD materials when the answers can vary. The switching from objective to subjective activities has worked very well for me. My students don't get bored with any one activity because our activities change so often.

Jacquie Alberti,
Language Arts Teacher
Norman C. Toole Middle School,
N. Charleston, SC

The more difficult the content, the more appropriate it is to use cooperative learning. Student Team Learning is a special tool in my classroom. I use it for the most important learning tasks (the ones that have traditionally given the students trouble).

When I put them into cooperative groups they know this is serious business and extremely important material to be learned. Overuse of cooperative learning for routine lessons diminishes the impact, I believe.

Nancy Whitlock, Fifth Grade Teacher
Spencer County Elementary School,
Taylorsville, KY

COOPERATIVE CLASSROOM MANAGEMENT

Most cooperative learning classrooms are well behaved, because students are motivated to learn and are actively engaged in learning activities. However, many teachers may wish to take additional steps to ensure that students will use class time effectively and direct their energies toward productive activities. This section describes classroom management methods adapted from Kagan (1989).

Theory: Group-Based Positive Reward

The most effective approach to classroom management for cooperative learning is to create a group-based positive reward system. The teacher gives his or her attention to the group behavior he or she most wants in the classroom. Quickly the other groups begin to model themselves after the group that is receiving the teacher's positive attention.

Studies demonstrate that in a whole-class setting, if teachers pay attention to undesired behaviors such as leaving one's seat or talking, the frequency of those behaviors increases. It does not matter if the attention is positive or negative. That is, even if the teacher severely scolds students who get out of their seats without permission, other students will model themselves after the students who are receiving the attention.

So it is in a cooperative classroom. If a teacher gives his or her attention to a team that is too noisy or not on-task, other teams will follow the lead of the team that has managed to win the attention of the teacher, even if the attention is negative. Conversely, if the teacher ignores the teams who are least on-task and gives special recognition to those who are, soon most or all teams will be on-task. This is especially so if the special recognition is specific, public, and recorded. The teacher does well to articulate to the whole class exactly why the model team is receiving special recognition and to record the instance on a class recognition chart.

Another important element in a successful cooperative learning management system is clear expectations. The teacher needs to define clearly and in advance those behaviors that are necessary for successful classroom functioning and those behaviors that are appreciated. Necessary behaviors include quickly coming to full, quiet attention whenever the teacher asks. Appreciated behaviors include extra peer helping, cooperation with teammates, and attention to the needs, opinions, and desires of others.

Management Techniques

1. The Zero-Noise Signal. After groups are formed the teacher will explain that there is a natural tendency for a classroom of teams to become too noisy. As one team talks, a nearby team needs to talk a bit louder to be heard, which forces the first team to talk even louder. Noise levels can escalate. The teacher needs to be able to bring the noise level quickly back to zero. He or she indicates that the class can solve this problem if it can learn to respond quickly to a zero-noise signal.

The zero-noise signal is a signal to students to stop talking, to give their full attention to the teacher, and to keep their hands and bodies still. Teachers choose different signals for their students. Some may simply ask for attention by saying "May I have your attention, please." Others may flip the lights on and off or ring a bell. One effective method is for the teacher to raise one hand. That signal is convenient because the teacher does not have to talk over the group noise level, and because he or she does not have to walk over to the bell or light switch. An additional advantage of the raised-hand signal is that the teacher can indicate that when students see the teacher's raised hand they too should raise their hands. Thus, when the teacher needs the attention of the class, she or he raises a hand. The students nearby quickly raise their hands, which leads to yet other students doing so. The raised hand of the teacher is like the pebble dropped in the pond: quiet attention spread from the teacher across the class like a ripple.

Some variations of the zero-noise signal:

1. Use a timer, and time how long it takes to come to zero noise. The seconds are summed each week and are taken away from team or class fun time (to be discussed shortly).

2. Have different signals, one to simply bring the noise level down (for example, arm up, palm horizontal), another to bring the noise level down and get students' attention for an announcement you wish to make (arm up, palm vertical).

3. Use a random timer to bring noise levels down. Tell students that the first team to come to zero noise when the timer goes off will receive five recognition points, the second team three, and the third team one. Points earned may be applied toward class rewards or special recognition.

Remember: The effectiveness of the zero-noise signal will depend on the effectiveness of the positive group reward. The reward must be clear and public, and should follow desired behavior as soon as possible. If you use a hand signal, give special recognition to the first team or teams to have all members quiet with full attention after you raise your arm. The effectiveness of the zero-noise signal, like that of all elements in a cooperative classroom, depends a great deal on the way special recognition is given.

2. Group Praise. It is hard to overemphasize the power of praising groups. One day Spencer Kagan visited the classroom of a teacher who was trying Jigsaw for the first time. She had all of the elements right. The class would come to full attention when she raised her hand, and she was giving special recognition to the first teams to do so.

But something was terribly wrong. The noise level was high. Over in one group the expert was using her new authority to bawl out the other students for being stupid. In another group, as soon as the teacher was looking away the expert stuffed some paper in his nose, which led to loud giggles and laughter. And the zero-noise signal was really not much help: the kids responded by quickly coming to attention, but right afterwards they would return to loud talking and off-task behaviors.

What was wrong? What could be done? Kagan walked over to the teacher and said, "I am going to sit down again, but I want you to walk over to the best group in the class, give the zero-noise signal, and draw everyone's attention to the group, praising them for their good work and saying exactly what you like about their behavior. Don't give points; just say clearly what you like."

She did. The power of the praise was astonishing. For about ten minutes after the group praise, all the teams were markedly more on-task. When they began to slip, the teacher used group praise again. This time they stayed on-task longer. By the end of the period, the class had turned around. Jigsaw was working the way it should. The teacher was thrilled; she had a powerful tool for shaping the class. Group praise establishes the norms for the classroom; students learn which behaviors are valued and receive special recognition for exhibiting them. It is as if all they really need is a very clear message about how to behave well in the new setting. Holding up as a model the groups that are behaving best is the clearest way to give that message and to show students what is valued.

3. Special-Recognition Bulletin. A very effective way to give special recognition in the classroom is to use a chart or poster to record special-recognition points. Whereas a positive comment is valued at the moment, if it is recorded it has additional power to motivate students toward desired behaviors. The recorded recognition points may be turned in for a team reward, applied toward a class reward, or simply stand on their own as a form of special recognition. In any case, teammates will work hard and encourage each other toward desired behaviors if they know their efforts will be recognized. A teacher may simply walk over to the recognition chart and mark in points, explaining to the class the reason a certain team is receiving special recognition.

4. Special-Recognition Ceremony. Teachers may hold a special-recognition ceremony each week in which outstanding teams and individuals are recognized by the teacher and students. The ceremony can be quite brief but still very important. In the ceremony, students and teams who have earned the most recognition points write in or post their

TEACHERS ON TEACHING

Cooperative learning inevitably involves more noise than traditional teaching. Has this been a problem for you? How have you dealt with the noise issue?

Cooperative learning does involve a *little* more noise than traditional teaching. However, this has not been a real problem for me. The way I have dealt with this problem began the first day that I decided to use cooperative learning. By this, I mean that much preplanning took place before I started cooperative learning groups. My first step was to decide on a room arrangement that would allow me to see all students at all times and a traffic pattern that would not interfere with movement. Next, rules and procedures were decided. These were discussed with the students at the beginning of the year and practiced every day to insure understanding. At first much feedback is needed, but as the school year progresses, the transitions are smoother and shorter, until it becomes routine. Last, I start the period by explaining the procedures and directions on exactly what the groups are to accomplish that day. If the noise level seems to be escalating as the class progresses, I give a clapping signal which the students return. I then have everyone's attention. We talk about the noise level, what we can do about it, and everyone goes back to work. In my opinion, the key to a successful cooperative learning atmosphere is good management and organization skills. If you are a good manager and organizer, the noise level will take care of itself.

Georgiann Ash
Fifth–Sixth Grade Teacher
George C. Weimer Elementary
School, St. Albans, WV

The zero-noise-level signal that I use is very helpful in coping with the noise level in cooperative learning. The signal is that I raise my hand. Every student who sees the signal stops talking, raises his or her hand, and *gently* taps others in her or his group to make them aware of the signal. I can have my classroom completely quiet and ready to listen in about three seconds. When I first explain and use the signal I give points or tickets to the first one or two groups who respond.

Rose Marie Wise,
Fifth Grade Teacher
Laurelwood School, Santa Clara, CA

The noise level in my classroom is usually *less* of a problem when using cooperative learning, especially when conducting a TGT tournament.

I am lucky enough to have my own classroom this year, which means I am able to leave tables in team arrangement.

In the past, I have used a clapping system to control noise and behavior—two claps means "freeze." Sometimes this is needed for interruptions on the PA system, too much noise, or just time to quit. Currently I am experimenting with green, yellow, and red flags for "all's well," "caution," and "stop everything."

Wanda Sue Wansley, Math Teacher
Caloosa Middle School,
Cape Coral, FL

What better noise than the noise of minds learning! It's nice to "hear" minds at work!

Denise Campbell,
English Teacher
Laredo Middle School, Aurora, CO

names on the weekly special-recognition chart, and receive applause from the rest of the class. For the individual-recognition categories, the recognized individuals come forward with their teams and write in or post both their team name and their own name.

5. Class or Team Fun Time. Special-recognition points may be traded for class or team rewards. It is often helpful to have the students choose fun-time activities, such as first out for recess or time at a fun-activity table. The teacher may announce that whenever any team earns a certain number of points, it may cash them in for extra recess or fun activities. Or, if a cooperative between-time format is adopted, the recognition points are summed and the whole class receives the reward when the total reaches the predetermined criterion.

It is important to provide a visible measure of how the class is progressing toward the class reward. For example, the teacher may drop marbles (loudly) into a clean jar to represent the accumulation of special-recognition points. When the jar is full, the class gets its fun time. A bright thermometer that rises toward a predetermined goal is another attractive addition to the cooperative class.

TEACHERS ON TEACHING

Student misbehavior is a problem in many classes, and while cooperative learning usually improves student time on-task, it is not a magic cure for misbehavior. What do you do to prevent or deal with student misbehavior in classes using cooperative learning?

Looking back, I feel the key to our success in getting students to work so cooperatively with others was that we began slowly. Each day we were very careful to establish what we wanted them to do and the manner in which we expected them to perform. For example, we quickly learned that just moving the desks into cooperative learning teams was going to be a major task for those students who wanted to drag their desks the length of the room to their team spot. We took "time out" to explain and demonstrate how to move yourself to your group's location and utilize the desk nearest to you. We praised students when the mechanics of the program, the STAD technique or the TAI–Math, flowed well. On days that confusion persisted, we just stopped, pointed out the problem we saw, and brainstormed with the students how to solve the problem. The next day, we began again with the modification or improvement incorporated. Each day we were careful to see that the students understood what they were going to do and how to carry it out.

A technique we followed when a group socialized too much or one person was not pulling his or her share of group responsibility was to stop again, discuss the problem, and brainstorm how to improve their group, with ideas coming from the team members themselves. This gave the team ownership to the suggested solution, which was then accepted more readily than if it were administered by the teachers.

If one student continued to disrupt the team and failed to cooperate, he or she was pulled away from the group a few feet to work independently for an indefinite, hopefully short, length of time. Then, when the student felt he or she could work as a team member as expected, he or she would be moved back into the group.

As cooperative skills have developed over time, different students have displayed cooperative behaviors during times other than those when we are using cooperative methods in the classroom. For example, Debi is always eager to help someone in her group. She says it makes her feel good when she shows someone how to do a math problem, and then he or she scores well on the unit test. She says it makes her feel partly responsible. In our split fifth/sixth classroom we were introducing string art for a follow-up geometry enrichment activity. Seven of the fifth graders were in a health unit in another classroom when this lesson was introduced. When they returned, Debi demonstrated to the group of fifth graders how to draw the angles and number the rays for the specific design they wanted to create with the string art.

Another example of cooperation being carried over is with those students who are still struggling to pass their facts quizzes in TAI math. Three or four students will go to the Math Lab during any extra time throughout the day to drill with each other on the computer and facts machines for practice before the quizzes are administered. They work very well together as a small group or just with a partner. I see the cooperative learning skills being utilized while they are drilling each other on facts.

We have had a minimum of misbehavior during cooperative learning compared with other classrooms in our school and compared with other schools. We credit this to the slow pace with which we began and the time set aside each day in which we were careful to see that the students understood what they were going to do and how to carry it out. We strongly feel this procedure has enhanced the students' abilities and desires to work well with others.

Nancy Chrest, Fifth/
Sixth Grade Teacher
George C. Weimer Elementary
School, St. Albans, WV

When first placing the student on his or her team, not only do I create a good heterogeneous mix but I look very carefully at the personalities on that team, trying to find students who are easy to work with, are good at encouraging, and will not be cutting or spiteful. Also once teams have been formed I will try to use some team-building exercises to allow students time to work together, get to know one another, and so on, prior to starting one of the STL structures. If this still does not get a student active, I work with the student separately, but this has hardly ever happened. Usually students want to become a part of the group because they see the excitement, cooperation, and fun others are experiencing working in their groups.

Steve Parsons, Math Teacher
West Frederick Middle School,
Frederick, MD

I use a chart on the wall to keep track of group points. The students have a goal of 250 points in order to earn a class party. Each team must achieve the 250 points in order for the class to have the party. Teams who achieve the required number of points first are very encouraging to the other teams. I give points for good behavior on rainy days, passing multiplication facts tests, returning papers on time, having homework completed, good citizenship, and/or getting ready to work quickly, as well as for practicing good social skills on particular assignments. The children respond very positively. The class I have this year has become the "best-behaved" class in school. I attribute this to cooperative learning. The PE teacher has commented on the feeling of teamwork and cooperation in the group.

Rose Marie Wise,
Fifth Grade Teacher
Laurelwood School, Santa Clara, CA

TEAM BUILDING

Many teachers and proponents of cooperative learning advocate extensive training of students in how to work in groups, and there are many techniques for developing team spirit and cohesiveness. This section presents a few simple team-building methods that you may wish to use before beginning to use cooperative learning methods. Many teachers want to get student teams right into learning rather than taking time out for cohesiveness building; they find that simply starting students off in their team activities is as good a team-building method as anything. However, others feel that students need to be prepared to work cooperatively before beginning cooperative learning activities.

The team-building activities that follow are just a few of the many included in Kagan (1989). For additional methods, see Dishon and O'Leary (1984); Johnson, Johnson, Holubec, and Roy (1984); or Schmuck and Schmuck (1983).

1. Name Learning

Each group is given a set amount of time to learn the names of their teammates. They then take a test and the average percentage of correct names per group is announced.

Variations: Include more information, such as favorite hobby or most unusual experience. Following 100-percent mastery by all groups, have teams pair and repeat the exercise. This time, though, the goal is for each team to learn the names of all the members of the other team.

2. Interview

Interview introduces teammates to each other in some depth and classmates to each other superficially. It gives students some basis for relating to others with common interests or experiences, it gives them the opportunity to feel welcome in the group, and it helps overcome initial resistances that some students have to participating in groups. Interview consists of the following steps:

1. The teacher has students gather in teams.
2. Teammates count off—1, 2, 3, 4, or more, one number for each teammate.
3. The teacher informs the students that it is 1's job to interview 2, 3's job to interview 4, and so on, for five minutes. The aim of the interview is to gather information that will be used to introduce each person to his or her teammates. Interview topics may be suggested, such as hobbies, unusual experiences, favorite movies, and life goals. Interviewing tips may be provided, such as how to follow the lead of the other person rather than suggesting topics of interest to yourself.
4. Introductions are carried out within groups. Each interviewer has one minute to present to the group the person he or she has interviewed.
5. Steps 3 and 4 are repeated with students switching roles: 2 interviews and presents 1, 4 interviews and presents 3, and so on.
6. The team attempts to discover through discussion the ''positive essence'' of each teammate so that he or she can be described in an adjective or very brief phrase, such as ''gutsy,'' ''adventuresome,'' ''caring,'' or ''nature girl.'' Students are instructed to look for themes in the interview responses that will help them capture the positive essence of the person.
7. Team members introduce their teammates to the class by taking turns stating the adjective or phrase that best captures the positive essence of the team member and providing a sentence or two of explanation.

3. Team Name, Banner, Logo, and/or Mural

When teams are first formed they are asked to name themselves. This process can be used as a teambuilding exercise. Three simple rules for the group process are stated: Each team member must have a say; no decision can be reached unless everyone consents; no member consents to the group decision if he or she has a serious objection. These rules set the tone for future group processes, which must include participation, consensus, and respect for individual rights.

In addition to choosing a name, you may wish to have teams create a team mural, banner, or logo. If you do, the same rules apply. Each member must contribute, and the group cannot proceed without consensus. The teacher may facilitate the process by giving each member a different-colored marking pen and calling for an integrated product with all colors represented. The task can be structured so that other teams will judge how well all colors are integrated into a meaningful and artful whole.

4. Group Brainstorming. Any task that has many possible solutions may be set up for group brainstorming. The instructions are simply that the group members put their heads together and come up with as many correct or interesting solutions as they can. One fun activity that lends itself to group brainstorming is Hanky Panky. The problem is to come up with as many two-word rhymes as possible. For example:

A flexible tree is *limber timber.*
An immobile large vehicle is a *stuck truck.*
A bee is a *nectar collector.*
Butter is a *bread spread.*

After groups have had time to brainstorm, they may get points for their number of correct solutions; they may rate the creativeness of each group's best solution; or they may simply share their most creative products.

IMPROVISING YOUR OWN COOPERATIVE LEARNING MODIFICATIONS

Once you have had some experience with cooperative learning, you may wish to adapt team techniques to your own situation or needs. If you do, try to follow these basic principles:

1. Make sure you offer some kind of recognition or reward to successful teams. The stronger the desire of team members to have their team succeed, the more likely they will cooperate with and help one another to do well.

2. Make each student responsible for his or her own performance. Avoid team tasks in which there is a single "team product" that can be completed by one or two team members. We all remember being in "lab groups" that were supposed to prepare a single report; somehow, one student always wound up doing most of the work (and thus most of the learning). That is why the team scores in all of the Student Team Learning techniques are composed of the sum of individual performances on individual quizzes or games. *All* students must do well if the team is to do well, and the team knows which students need help and which have done the most to help the team.

3. Set up a scoring system that allows students of all performance levels to contribute meaningfully to the team scores or products. This is the purpose of the individual improvement score system in STAD and Jigsaw II, and the tournament system in TGT. There are two reasons for this. First, it is important to set up a system of rewards in which a student is likely to be rewarded for improving his or her level of performance over his or her usual level; all students are thereby motivated to do their best. In a system that rewards *improvement* in performance rather than ability, every student can succeed or fail based on his or her own efforts. Second, a system that rewards improvement in performance is particularly important in a Student Team Learning technique, as it makes every team member's potential contribution large. This motivates team members to tutor the low-performing students, who might

otherwise be ignored because they would be perceived as unlikely to contribute much to the team score.

SOLVING PROBLEMS WITH COOPERATIVE LEARNING

As you begin to use cooperative learning, you may experience a few problems. Some of these problems and the solutions that teachers have found effective for them are discussed in this section.*

1. Failure to get along. This problem often comes up in the first week or two of cooperative learning. Remember, teams usually consist of the most unlikely combinations possible. Students differ from one another in sex, ethnicity, and academic performance.

The primary solution for this problem is time. Some students will be unhappy about their team assignments initially, but when they get their first team scores and realize that they really are a team and need to cooperate to be successful, they will find a way to get along. This is why it is important not to allow students to change teams except in extreme circumstances; students should be focusing their attention on making their teams work, not on getting out of them.

However, some students will need constant reminding that their task is to cooperate with their teammates. You must set a firm tone that cooperation with teammates is what is appropriate behavior during team practice. No one should be forced to work with a team; individuals who refuse (this happens rarely) should be allowed to work alone until they are ready to join the team. However, you should make it clear to students that putdowns, making fun of teammates, or refusing to help teammates is not a very effective way for teams to succeed and is not acceptable to you.

One effective way to get students to cooperate better is to provide extra rewards to winning teams. Sometimes students will not care how the team or their teammates are doing until they know that the winning team will get refreshments, time off, release from a test, and so on.

It is also a good idea to have students who work in pairs within their teams to switch partners every once in a while, to reemphasize that it is a team effort that is needed, not just individual preparation.

If some teams just do not work out, you may change teams after three or four weeks instead of waiting for six. When you reassign the teams, take care to avoid the problems you encountered in your first team assignments.

2. Misbehavior. One way to encourage students to behave appropriately is to give each team up to three additional team points per day based on the team's behavior, cooperativeness, and effort. If you do this, make sure that you also move from team to team and tell the teams what they are doing right—for example, "I see the Cougars are working well together. . . . The Fantastic Four are all in their seats and doing their work. . . . The Chiefs are working quietly." The points teams earn for their behavior should definitely *not* be a surprise, but should reflect what you were saying during the period. (For more on this, see the section on cooperative classroom management.)

3. Noise. Noise is more of a problem in some schools than in others, depending on acoustics, open versus traditional construction, and school attitudes toward noise. A cooperative learning classroom should sound like a beehive, not a sports event. A busy sound is fine, but you should not be able to pick out individual voices. Cooperative learning does not mix well with a teacher who shushes students every five minutes, but if things are so noisy that students cannot hear each other, something should be done.

*This section derives from Slavin (1986a).

TEACHERS ON TEACHING

Absences are a problem in any classroom. Does cooperative learning increase attendance in your classes? How do you deal with absences in your cooperative learning classes?

Absences can be a problem, particularly during a team practice activity. However, I find that if I make the team responsible for "catching" their member up when he or she returns (on the high school level), it helps the student more than in a traditional classroom, where so little time is available for one-on-one tutoring. Chronic absenteeism presents a serious problem to some cooperative learning strategies, but I have found through the years that I try not to penalize the team if the problem is a serious one. Cooperative learning entices more of the low-level absentee problems "back to the fold" in our Basic Math classes. These students find the success factor a strong encouragement. We have instituted a SUCCESS CARD for the individual students which, among other codes, has a code for absenteeism. The SUCCESS CARD was designed to reward individuals for excellence in a particular area (on-task, enthusiasm, achievement, homework, tutoring, and so forth). A code is signed by the teacher on a card with sixteen boxes, but only after the student has demonstrated excellence in an area. For absentee problems, we reward with an "A" code for attendance if the student has been present five days in a row. There is a letter sent home from the principal after the card is filled, and the students really enjoy the letter. It does seem to have worked with some of our absentee problems.

Candi Nuzzolillo, Math Teacher
Gulf Middle School, Cape Coral, FL

At third grade I see little, if any, unnecessary absence from school. But my students do make such comments as, "I hope I'm not sick tomorrow because it's tournament day," or "Tuesday is special because my group gets to give its report."

I have trained my students to check with a team member regarding missed assignments when they are absent. Team members must each keep a record of what is expected of them and when work must be completed because they realize they are responsible for giving this information to absent members. If a student misses a teacher-directed lesson, team members just make a note for the student to see the teacher. This allows absent students to get missed work much faster than they would if they had to wait for the teacher to get to them, and is also a reminder to each member of the group of his or her own deadlines.

Phyllis McManus,
Third Grade Teacher
Hoagland Elementary School,
Hoagland, IN

The first solution is to bring all activity to a stop, get absolute quiet, and then whisper a reminder to students to speak softly. Students should be taught to stop talking immediately when the lights are flicked off for a moment, or a bell sounds, or some other signal is given. You may use the "zero noise signal" described earlier in this chapter.

If this does not work, you might try to make noise level a criterion for earning extra team points, as noted in the discussion of cooperative classroom management. However, you should do this as a last resort, for noise is more often just forgetfulness on the part of students than it is misbehavior.

4. Absences. Student absenteeism can be a major problem in a cooperative learning class, because students depend on one another to study together and to contribute points to the team. The solution, however, is relatively simple in classrooms where absenteeism is not extremely high. When students miss a tournament or a quiz, you may divide the team's score by the number of students present, to avoid penalizing the team for having an absent member.

When Student Team Learning is to be used in a class with very poor attendance, poor attenders should be distributed evenly among teams as fifth or sixth members, so that at least three or four students will be likely to show up on each team each day.

5. Ineffective use of team practice time. If students do not use their time in team practice effectively, you may impose some structure on the team practice sessions to be sure that they do.

One problem is that students may be used to doing their worksheets alone and thinking that they are finished when they get to the end, regardless of whether they or their teammates understand the material. This problem is dealt with primarily by providing only two worksheets per team so that students have to work together. You can also make (or have students make) flashcards with questions on one side and answers on the other. Have students drill each other in pairs or threes, putting items correctly answered in one pile and missed items in another. The students go through the missed pile until each flashcard has been correctly answered once, and then go through the entire set again until each student can get 100 percent on the questions in any order. This will work only if the answers are short. If the answers require figuring, as in the case of most mathematics problems, then students should work in pairs or threes, going through the items one at a time and checking answers after everyone has finished each item. If anyone misses a question, his or her teammates who got it right should explain what they did.

6. Too wide a range of performance levels. If you have this problem, first think about what you were doing before you began using cooperative learning. If you were doing whole-group instruction, you can do the same with cooperative learning, but you need to take time to work with low performers to help get them up to the level of the rest of the class. If you are teaching mathematics using math groups within the class, you may wish to use Team Assisted Individualization (TAI): if you are teaching reading and writing, try Cooperative Integrated Reading and Composition (CIRC). Both of these methods make student heterogeneity a strength rather than a problem.

RESOURCES FOR COOPERATIVE LEARNING

I. Research Reviews

SHARAN, S., and SHACHAR, H. (1988). *Language and learning in the cooperative classroom.* New York: Springer-Verlag.

SLAVIN, R. E. (1983). When does cooperative learning increase student achievement? *Psychological Bulletin, 94,* 429–445.

SLAVIN, R. E. (ed.) (1989). *School and classroom organization.* Hillsdale, NJ: Erlbaum.

SLAVIN, R. E., SHARAN, S., KAGAN, S., HERTZ-LAZAROWITZ, R., WEBB, C., and SCHMUCK, R. (eds.) (1985). *Learning to cooperate, cooperating to learn.* New York: Plenum.

II. Practical Guides

ARONSON, E., BLANEY, N., STEPHAN, C., SIKES, J., and SNAPP, M. (1978). *The Jigsaw Classroom.* Sage Publications, Inc., 275 Beverly Dr., Beverly Hills, CA 90212.

COHEN, E. (1986). *Designing Groupwork.* Teachers College Press, Columbia University, New York, NY 10027.

DISHON, D., and O'LEARY, P. W. (1984). *A Guidebook for Cooperative Learning.* Cooperation Unlimited, P.O. Box 68, Portage, MI 49081.

JOHNSON, D. W., and JOHNSON, R. T. (1986). *Learning together and alone* (2nd ed.). Prentice-Hall, Englewood Cliffs, NJ 07632.

JOHNSON, D. W., JOHNSON, R. T., HOLUBEC, E. J., and ROY, P. (1984). *Circles of learning.* ASCD, 125 N. West St., Alexandria, VA 22314.

KAGAN, S. (1989). *Cooperative learning resources for teachers.* Resources for Teachers, 27134A Paseo Espada #202, San Juan Capistrano, CA 92675

MADDEN, N. A., FARNISH, A. M., SLAVIN, R. E., and STEVENS, R. J. (1986). *Cooperative Integrated Reading and Composition: Teacher's manual for writing.* Johns Hopkins Team Learning Project, 3505 N. Charles St., Baltimore, MD 21218.

MADDEN, N. A., STEVENS, R. J., SLAVIN, R. E., and FARNISH, A. M. (1988). *Cooperative Integrated Reading and Composition: Teacher's manual for reading.* Johns Hopkins Team Learning Project, 3505 N. Charles St., Baltimore, MD 21218.

SLAVIN, R. E. (1986). *Using Student Team Learning* (3rd ed.). Johns Hopkins Team Learning Project, 3505 N. Charles St., Baltimore, MD 21218.

SLAVIN, R. E., LEAVEY, M. B., and MADDEN, N. A. (1988). *Team Accelerated Instruction–Mathematics.* Charlesbridge Publishing, 85 Main St., Watertown, MA 02172.

III. Curriculum Materials and Training

Curriculum materials and training for STAD, TGT, Jigsaw II, CIRC, and TAI are available from:

The Johns Hopkins Team Learning Project
Johns Hopkins University
3505 N. Charles St.
Baltimore, MD 21218
(301) 338-8249

1. STAD/TGT/Jigsaw. Inexpensive materials and training are available from the Johns Hopkins Team Learning Project. The materials include the following:

- teacher's manual
- filmstrip (twenty-minute overview of STAD and TGT)
- video tape of Edwin Newman interviewing Robert Slavin (other video tapes are in production)
- sets of curriculum materials for STAD and TGT:
    mathematics for each of grades 2–8
    consumer math (grades 9–10)
    metric education (grades 5–6)
    algebra I
    high school geometry
    language mechanics, grades 3–6
    language mechanics, grades 7–9
    life science, grades 7–9
    physical science, grades 7–9
    U.S. history, grades 7–10

2. CIRC. Materials and training for Cooperative Integrated Reading and Composition are also available from the Johns Hopkins Team Learning Project. Unlike STAD, TGT, and Jigsaw, CIRC is a complete approach to reading and writing in the upper elementary grades. Materials for CIRC—Reading include teacher's manuals, reading comprehension materials (grades 2–3 and 4–5), and "treasure hunt" packets, which replace traditional workbooks (see Chapter 5). These packets have been developed for a large number of widely used basal series. For a current list, contact the Johns Hopkins Team Learning Project.

Teacher's manuals and lessons for CIRC—Writing are also available from the Johns Hopkins Team Learning Project.

3. TAI—Math. Materials and training for Team Accelerated Instruction—Mathematics are available in two ways. They can be obtained through the Johns Hopkins Team Learning Project at the address previously given, or from their publisher:

Charlesbridge Publishing
85 Main St.
Watertown, MA 02172
1-800-225-3214

TAI materials replace traditional math texts, covering objectives from basic addition to an introduction to algebra. An introductory video tape on TAI is also available.

References

ALLEN, W. H., and VAN SICKLE, R. L. (1984). Learning teams and low achievers. *Social Education, 48,* 60–64.

ALLPORT, G. (1954). *The nature of prejudice.* Cambridge, MA. Addison-Wesley.

AMES, C., AMES, R., and FELKER, D. (1977). Effects of competitive reward structure and valence of outcome on children's achievement attributions. *Journal of Educational Psychology, 69,* 1–8.

AMES, G. J., and MURRAY, F. B. (1982). When two wrongs make a right: Promoting cognitive change by social conflict. *Developmental Psychology, 18,* 894–897.

ANDERSON, L. M., BRUBAKER, N. L., ALLEMAN-BROOKS, J., and DUFFY, G. G.' (1985). A qualitative study of seatwork in first-grade classrooms. *Elementary School Journal, 86* 123–140.

ARMSTRONG, B., JOHNSON, D. W., and BALOW, B. (1981). Effects of cooperative vs. individualistic learning experiences on interpersonal attraction between learning-disabled and normal-progress elementary school students. *Contemporary Educational Psychology, 6,* 102–109.

ARONSON, E., BLANEY, N., STEPHAN, C., SIKES, J., and SNAPP, M. (1978). *The Jigsaw classroom.* Beverly Hills, CA: Sage Publications, Inc.

ARTZT, A. F. (1983). The comparative effects of the student-team method of instruction and the traditional teacher-centered method of instruction upon student achievement, attitude, and social interaction in high school mathematics courses. Doctoral dissertation, New York University.

BAKER, L., and BROWN, A. L. (1984). Metacognitive skills and reading. In P. D. Pearson (ed.), *Handbook of reading research.* New York: Longman.

BALLARD, M., CORMAN, L., GOTTLIEB, J., and KAUFFMAN, M. (1977). Improving the social status of mainstreamed retarded children. *Journal of Educational Psychology, 69,* 605–611.

BECK, I., McKEOWN, M., McCASLIN, E., and BURKES, A. (1979). *Instructional dimensions that may affect reading comprehension: Examples from two commercial reading programs* (Technical Report No. 1979/20). Pittsburgh: University of Pittsburgh. Learning and Research and Development Center.

BELL, N., GROSSEN, M., and PERRET-CLERMONT, A-N. (1985). Socio-cognitive conflict and intellectual growth. In M. Berkowitz (ed.), *Peer conflict and psychological growth.* San Francisco: Jossey-Bass.

BEREITER, C., and SCARDAMALIA, M. (1982). From conversation to composition: The role of instruction in a developmental process. In R. Glaser (ed.), *Advances in instructional psychology.* Hillsdale, NJ: Erlbaum.

BLANEY, N. T., STEPHAN, S., ROSENFIELD, D., ARONSON, E., and SIKES, J. (1977). Interdependence in the classroom: A field study. *Journal of Educational Psychology, 69*(2), 121–128.

BRIDGE, C., and HIEBERT, E. (1985). A comparison of classroom writing practices, teachers' perceptions of their writing instruction, and textbook recommendations on writing practices. *Elementary School Journal, 2,* 155–172.

BRIDGEMAN, D. (1977). The influence of cooperative interdependent learning on role taking and moral reasoning: A theoretical and empirical field study with fifth grade students. Doctoral dissertation, University of California, Santa Cruz.

BROOKOVER, W., BEADY, C., FLOOD, P., SCHWEITZER, J., and WISENBAKER, J. (1979). *School social systems and student achievement.* New York: Praeger.

BROPHY, J., and GOOD, T. (1986). Teacher behavior and student achievement. In M. C. Wittrock (ed.), *Handbook of research on teaching* (3rd ed.) (pp. 328–375). New York: Macmillan.

BROWN, A., BRANSFORD, J., FERRARA, R., and CAMPIONE, J. (1983). Learning, remembering, and understanding. In J. Flavell and E. M. Markman (eds.), *Handbook of child psychology* (4th ed., Vol. 3). New York: John Wiley, pp. 515–629.

BROWN, A., and PALINSCAR, A. (1982). Inducing strategic learning from text by means of informed, self-controlled training. *Topics in Learning and Learning Disabilities, 2,* 1–17.

BRUININKS, V. (1978). Peer status and personality characteristics of learning disabled and non-disabled students. *Journal of Learning Disabilities, 11,* 29–34.

BRUININKS, V., RYNDERS, J., and GROSS, J. (1974). Social acceptance of mildly retarded pupils in resource rooms and regular classes. *American Journal of Mental Deficiency, 78,* 377–383.

BRYAN, T. (1974). Peer popularity of learning disabled children. *Journal of Learning Disabilities, 7,* 621–625.

BRYAN, T. (1976). Peer popularity of learning disabled students: A replication. *Journal of Learning Disabilities, 9,* 307–311.

BURNS, M. (1981, September). Groups of four: Solving the management problem. *Learning,* 46–51.

CALKINS, L. (1983). *Lessons from a child: On the teaching and learning of writing.* Exeter, NH: Heinemann.

CAVANAGH, B. R. (1984). Effects of interdependent group contingencies on the achievement of elementary school children. *Dissertation Abstracts, 46,* 1558.

COHEN, E. (1986). *Designing groupwork: Strategies for the heterogeneous classroom.* New York: Teachers College Press.

COLEMAN, J. (1961). *The adolescent society.* New York: Free Press.

COLEMAN, J., et al. (1966). *Equality of educational opportunity.* Washington, DC: U.S. Department of Health, Education and Welfare.

COOK, S. W. (1979). Social science and school desegregation: Did we mislead the Supreme Court? *Personality and Social Psychology Bulletin, 5,* 420–437.

COOPER, L., JOHNSON, D., JOHNSON, R., and WILDERSON, F. (1980). Effects of cooperative, competitive, and individualistic experiences on interpersonal attraction among heterogeneous peers. *Journal of Social Psychology, 111,* 243–252.

COOPERSMITH, S. (1967). *The antecedents of self-esteem.* San Francisco: W. H. Freeman & Company Publishers.

DAHL, P. (1979). An experimental program for teaching high speed word recognition and comprehension skills. In J. Button, T. Lovitt, and T. Rowland (eds.), *Communication Research in Learning Disabilities and Mental Retardation* (pp. 33–65). Baltimore: University Park Press.

DAMON, W. (1984). Peer education: The untapped potential. *Journal of Applied Developmental Psychology, 5,* 331–343.

DANSEREAU, D. F. (1985). Learning strategy research. In J. Segal, S. Chipman, and R. Glaser (eds.), *Thinking and learning skills: Relating instruction to basic research* (Vol. 1). Hillsdale, NJ: Erlbaum.

DANSEREAU, D. F. (1988). Cooperative learning strategies. In C. E. Weinstein, E. T. Goetz, and P.

A. Alexander (eds.), *Learning and study strategies: Issues in assessment, instruction, and evaluation* (pp. 103–102). New York: Academic Press.

DAVIDSON, N. (1985). Small-group learning and teaching in mathematics: A selective review of the research. In R. E. Slavin, S. Sharan, S. Kagan, R. Hertz-Lazarowitz, C. Webb, and R. Schmuck (eds.), *Learning to cooperate, cooperating to learn* (pp. 211–230). New York: Plenum.

DAY, J. (1980). Teaching summarization skills. Doctoral dissertation, University of Illinois, Urbana.

DE AVILA, E., and DUNCAN, S. (1980). *Finding Out/Descubrimiento*. Corte Madera, CA: Linguametrics Group.

DEUTSCH, M. (1949). A theory of cooperation and competition. *Human Relations, 2,* 129–152.

DEVIN-SHEEHAN, L., FELDMAN, R., and ALLEN, V. (1976). Research on children tutoring children: A critical review. *Review of Educational Research, 46*(3), 355–385.

DEVRIES, D., and EDWARDS, K. (1973). Learning games and student teams: Their effects on classroom process. *American Educational Research Journal, 10,* 307–318.

DEVRIES, D. L., EDWARDS, K. J., and SLAVIN, R. E. (1978). Biracial learning teams and race relations in the classroom: Four field experiments on Teams–Games–Tournament. *Journal of Educational Psychology, 70,* 356–362.

DEVRIES, D. L., EDWARDS, K. J., and WELLS, E. H. (1974). *Teams–Games–Tournament in the social studies classroom: Effects on academic achievement, student attitudes, cognitive beliefs, and classroom climate* (Report No. 173). Baltimore: Johns Hopkins University, Center for Social Organization of Schools.

DEVRIES, D. L., LUCASSE, P. R., and SHACKMAN, S. L. (1980). *Small group vs. individualized instruction: A field test of relative effectiveness* (Report No. 293). Baltimore: Johns Hopkins University, Center for Social Organization of Schools.

DEVRIES, D. L., and MESCON, I. T. (1975). *Teams–Games–Tournament: An effective task and reward structure in the elementary grades* (Report No. 189). Baltimore: Johns Hopkins University, Center for Social Organization of Schools.

DEVRIES, D. L., MESCON, I. T., and SHACKMAN, S. L. (1975a). *Teams–Games–Tournament (TGT) effects on reading skills in the elementary grades* (Report No. 200). Baltimore: Johns Hopkins University, Center for Social Organization of Schools.

DEVRIES, D. L., MESCON, I. T., and SHACKMAN, S. L. (1975b). *Teams–Games–Tournament in the elementary classroom: A replication* (Report No. 190). Baltimore: Johns Hopkins University, Center for Social Organization of Schools.

DEVRIES, D. L., and SLAVIN, R. E. (1978). Teams–Games–Tournament (TGT): Review of ten classroom experiments. *Journal of Research and Development in Education, 12,* 28–38.

DEWEY, J. (1970). *Experience and education.* New York: Collier.

DISHON, D., and O'LEARY, P. W. (1984). *A guidebook for cooperative learning.* Portage, MI: Cooperation Unlimited.

DUCETTE, J. (August, 1979). Locus of control and academic achievement. Paper presented at the annual meeting of the American Psychological Association, New York.

DUNN, L. M. (1968). Special education for the mentally retarded: Is it justified? *Exceptional Children, 35,* 5–22.

DURKIN, D. (1978–1979). What classroom observations reveal about reading comprehension instruction. *Reading Research Quarterly, 14,* 481–533.

DURKIN, D. (1981). Reading comprehension instruction in 5 basal reader series. *Reading Research Quarterly, 16,* 515–544.

EDWARDS, K. J., and DEVRIES, D. L. (1972). *Learning games and student teams: Their effects on student attitudes and achievement* (Report No. 147). Baltimore: Johns Hopkins University, Center for Social Organization of Schools.

EDWARDS, K. J., and DEVRIES, D. L. (1974). *The effects of Teams–Games–Tournament and two structural variations on classroom process, student attitudes, and student achievement* (Report No. 172). Baltimore: Johns Hopkins University, Center for Social Organization of Schools.

EDWARDS, K. J., DEVRIES, D. L., and SNYDER, J. P. (1972). Games and teams: A winning combination. *Simulation and Games, 3,* 247–269.

The effects of segregation and consequences of desegregation: A social science statement. Appendix to appellant's briefs: Brown vs. Board of Education of Topeka, Kansas (1953). *Minnesota Law Review, 37,* 427–439.

FITZGERALD, J., and SPIEGAL, D. (1983). Enhancing children's reading comprehension through instruction in narrative structures. *Journal of Reading Behavior, 14,* 1–181.

FLOWER, L., and HAYES, J. (1980). The dynamics of composing: Making plans and juggling constraints. In L. Gregg and E. Steinberg (eds.), *Cognitive processes in writing.* Hillsdale, NJ: Erlbaum.

FRANTZ, L. J. (1979). The effects of the student teams achievement approach in reading on peer attitudes. Master's thesis, Old Dominion University.

GEFFNER, R. (1978). The effects of interdependent learning on self-esteem, interethnic relations, and intra-ethnic attitudes of elementary school children: A field experiment. Doctoral dissertation, University of California, Santa Cruz.

GERARD, H. B., and MILLER, N. (1975). *School desegregation: A long-range study.* New York: Plenum.

GLASS, G., CAHEN, L., SMITH, M. L., and FILBY, N. (1982). *School class size.* Beverly Hills, CA: Sage Publications, Inc.

GLASS, G., McGAW, B., and SMITH, M. L. (1981). *Meta-analysis in social research.* Beverly Hills, CA: Sage Publications, Inc.

GONZALES, A. (August, 1979). Classroom cooperation and ethnic balance. Paper presented at the annual convention of the American Psychological Association, New York.

GONZALES, A. (1981). An approach to interdependent/cooperative bilingual education and measures related to social motives. Manuscript, California State University at Fresno.

GOOD, T., GROUWS, D., and EBMEIER, H. (1983). *Active mathematics teaching.* New York: Longman.

GOODMAN, H., GOTTLIEB, J., and HARRISON, R. H. (1972). Social acceptance of EMRs integrated into a non-graded elementary school. *American Journal of Mental Deficiency, 76,* 412–417.

GRAVES, D. (1978). *Balance the basics: Let them write.* New York: Ford Foundation.

GRAVES, D. (1983). *Writing: Teachers and children at work.* Exeter, NH: Heinemann.

GRAVES, N., and GRAVES, T. (1985). Creating a cooperative learning environment: An ecological approach. In R. E. Slavin, S. Sharan, S. Kagan, R. Hertz-Lazarowitz, C. Webb, and R. Schmuck (eds.), *Learning to Cooperate, Cooperating to Learn.* New York: Plenum.

GRAY, J., and MYERS, M. (1978). Bay Area writing project. *Phi Delta Kappan, 59,* 410–413.

GUSZAK, F. J. (1967). Teacher questioning and reading. *Reading Teacher, 21,* 27–34.

HAMBLIN, R. L., HATHAWAY, C., and WODARSKI, J. S. (1971). Group contingencies, peer tutoring, and accelerating academic achievement. In E. Ramp and W. Hopkins (eds.), *A new direction for education: Behavior analysis* (pp. 41–53. Lawrence: University of Kansas, Department of Human Development.

HANSELL, S., and SLAVIN, R. E. (1981). Cooperative learning and the structure of interracial friendships. *Sociology of Education, 54,* 98–106.

HANSEN, J. (1981). The effects of inference training and practice on young children's reading comprehension. *Reading Research Quarterly, 16,* 391–417.

HERTZ-LAZAROWITZ, R., SAPIR, C., and SHARAN, S. (1981). Academic and social effects of two cooperative learning methods in desegregated classrooms. Manuscript, Haifa University, Haifa, Israel.

HERTZ-LAZAROWITZ, R., SHARAN, S., and STEINBERG, R. (1980). Classroom learning styles and cooperative behavior of elementary school children. *Journal of Educational Psychology, 72,* 99–106.

HIDI, S., and ANDERSON, V. (1986). Producing written summaries: Task demands, cognitive operations, and implications for instruction. *Review of Educational Research, 56,* 473–493.

HIEBERT, E. (1983). An examination of ability groupings for reading instruction. *Reading Research Quarterly, 18,* 231–255.

HUBER, G. L., BOGATZKI, W., and WINTER, M. (1982). *Kooperation als Ziel schulischen Lehrens und Lehrens*. (Cooperation: Condition and Goal of Teaching and Learning in Classrooms). Tubingen, West Germany: Arbeitsbereich Padagogische Psychologie der Universitat Tubingen.

HULTEN, B. H., and DeVRIES, D. L. (1976). *Team competition and group practice: Effects on student achievement and attitudes* (Report No. 212). Baltimore: Johns Hopkins University, Center for Social Organization of Schools.

HUMPHREYS, B., JOHNSON, R., and JOHNSON, D. W. (1982). Effects of cooperative, competitive, and individualistic learning on students' achievement in science class. *Journal of Research in Science Teaching, 19,* 351–356.

IANO, R., AYERS, D., HELLER, H., McGETTIGAN, T., and WALKER, U. (1974). Sociometric status of retarded children in an integrative program. *Exceptional Children, 41,* 267–271.

JANKE, R. (1978, April). The Teams–Games–Tournament (TGT) method and the behavioral adjustment and academic achievement of emotionally impaired adolescents. Paper presented at the annual meeting of the American Educational Research Association, Toronto.

JOHNSON, D. W., and JOHNSON, R. T. (1974). Instructional structure: Cooperative, competitive or individualistic. *Review of Educational Research, 44,* 213–240.

JOHNSON, D. W., and JOHNSON, R. T. (1975). *Learning together and alone.* Englewood Cliffs, NJ: Prentice-Hall.

JOHNSON, D. W., and JOHNSON, R. T. (1979). Conflict in the classroom: Controversy and learning. *Review of Educational Research, 49,* 51–70.

JOHNSON, D. W., and JOHNSON, R. T. (1980). Integrating handicapped children into the mainstream. *Exceptional Children, 47,* 90–98.

JOHNSON, D. W., and JOHNSON, R. T. (1981a). Effects of cooperative and individualistic learning experiences on interethnic interaction. *Journal of Educational Psychology, 73,* 444–449.

JOHNSON, D. W., and JOHNSON, R. T. (1981b). The integration of the handicapped into the regular classroom: Effects of cooperative and individualistic instruction. *Contemporary Educational Psychology, 6,* 344–355.

JOHNSON, D. W., and JOHNSON, R. T. (1985). The internal dynamics of cooperative learning groups. In R. E. Slavin, S. Sharan, S. Kagan, R. Hertz-Lazarowitz, C. Webb, and R. Schmuck (eds.), *Learning to cooperate, cooperating to learn.* New York: Plenum.

JOHNSON, D. W., and JOHNSON, R. T. (1986). *Learning Together and Alone* (2nd ed.). Englewood Cliffs, NJ: Prentice-Hall.

JOHNSON, D. W., JOHNSON, R. T., BUCKMAN, L. A., and RICHARDS, P. (1986). The effect of prolonged implementation of cooperative learning on social support within the classroom. *Journal of Psychology, 119,* 405–411.

JOHNSON, D. W., JOHNSON, R. T., HOLUBEC, E. J., and ROY, P. (1984). *Circles of learning.* Alexandria, VA: Association for Supervision and Curriculum Development.

JOHNSON, D. W., JOHNSON, R. T., JOHNSON, J., and ANDERSON, D. (1976). The effects of cooperative vs. individualized instruction on student prosocial behavior, attitudes toward learning, and achievement. *Journal of Educational Psychology, 68,* 446–452.

JOHNSON, D. W., JOHNSON, R. T. and SCOTT, L. (1978). The effects of cooperative and individualized instruction on student attitudes and achievement. *Journal of Social Psychology, 104,* 207–216.

JOHNSON, D. W., and JOHNSON, W. (1972). The effects of attitude similarity, expectation of goal facilitation, and actual goal facilitation on interpersonal attraction. *Journal of Experimental Social Psychology, 8,* 197–206.

JOHNSON, D. W., MARUYAMA, G., JOHNSON, R., NELSON, D., and SKON, L. (1981). Effects of cooperative, competitive, and individualistic goal structures on achievement: A meta-analysis. *Psychological Bulletin, 89,* 47–62.

JOHNSON, G. O. (1950). A study of the social position of the mentally retarded child in the regular grades. *American Journal of Mental Deficiency, 55,* 60–89.

JOHNSON, L. C. (1985). The effects of the groups of four cooperative learning model on student problem-solving achievement in mathematics. Doctoral dissertation, University of Houston.

JOHNSON, L. C., and WAXMAN, H. C. (1985, March). Evaluating the effects of the "groups of four" program. Paper presented at the annual meeting of the American Educational Research Association, Chicago.

JOHNSON, R. T., and JOHNSON, D. W. (1981). Building friendships between handicapped and nonhandicapped students: Effects of cooperative and individualistic instruction. *American Educational Research Journal, 18,* 415–424.

JOHNSON, R. T., and JOHNSON, D. W. (1982). Effects of cooperative and competitive learning experiences on interpersonal attraction between handicapped and nonhandicapped students. *Journal of Social Psychology, 116,* 211–219.

JOHNSON, R. T., and JOHNSON, D. W. (1983). Effects of cooperative, competitive, and individualistic learning experiences on social development. *Exceptional Children, 49,* 323–330.

JOHNSON, R. T., and JOHNSON, D. W. (eds.) (1984). *Structuring cooperative learning: Lesson plans for teachers.* New Brighton, MN: Interaction Book Co.

JOHNSON, R. T., JOHNSON, D. W., SCOTT, L. E., and RAMOLAE, B. A. (1985). Effects of single-sex and mixed-sex cooperative interaction on science achievement and attitudes and cross-handicap and cross-sex relationships. *Journal of Research in Science Teaching, 22,* 207–220.

JOYCE, B., and WEIL, M. (1980). *Models of teaching.* Englewood Cliffs, NJ: Prentice-Hall.

KAGAN, S. (1989) *Cooperative learning resources for teachers.* San Juan Capistrano, CA: Resources for Teachers.

KAGAN, S., and MADSEN, M. C. (1972). Rivalry in Anglo American and Mexican American Children. *Journal of Personality and Social Psychology, 24,* 214–220.

KAGAN, S., ZAHN, G. L., WIDAMAN, K. F., SCHWARZWALD, J., and TYRELL, G. (1985). Classroom structural bias: Impact of cooperative and competitive classroom structures on cooperative and competitive individuals and groups. In R. E. Slavin, S. Sharan, S. Kagan, R. Hertz-Lazarowitz, C. Webb, and R. Schmuck (eds.), *Learning to cooperate, cooperating to learn.* New York: Plenum.

KARWEIT, N., and SLAVIN, R. E. (1981). Measurement and modeling choices and studies of time and learning. *American Educational Research Journal, 18,* 157–171.

KEPLER, K., and RANDALL, J. W. (1977). Individualization: Subversion of elementary schooling. *Elementary School Journal, 77,* 348–363.

KUHN, D. (1972). Mechanism of change in the development of cognitive structures. *Child Development, 43,* 833–844.

KUKLA, A. (1972). Foundations of an attributional theory of performance. *Psychological Review, 77,* 454–470.

LABERGE, D., and SAMUELS, S. J. (1974). Toward a theory of automatic information processing in reading. *Cognitive Psychology, 6,* 293–323.

LAZAROWITZ, R., BAIRD, H., BOWLDEN, V., and HERTZ-LAZAROWITZ, R. (1982). Academic achievements, learning environment, and self-esteem of high school students in biology taught in cooperative–investigative small groups. Manuscript, The Technion, Haifa, Israel.

LAZAROWITZ, R., BAIRD, J. H., HERTZ-LAZAROWITZ, R., and JENKINS, J. (1985). The effects of modified Jigsaw on achievement, classroom social climate, and self-esteem in high-school science classes. In R. E. Slavin, S. Sharan, S. Kagan, R. Hertz-Lazarowitz, C. Webb, and R. Schmuck (eds.), *Learning to cooperate, cooperating to learn.* New York: Plenum.

LEW, M., MESCH, D., JOHNSON, D. W., and JOHNSON, R. T. (1986). Positive interdependence, academic and collaborative-skills group contingencies, and isolated students. *American Educational Research Journal, 23,* 476–488.

LOTT, A. J. and LOTT, B. E. (1965). Group cohesiveness as interpersonal attraction: A review of relationships with antecedent and consequent variables. *Psychological Bulletin, 64,* 259–309.

LYMAN, F. (1981). The responsive classroom discussion. In A. S. Anderson (ed.), *Mainstreaming Digest.* College Park: University of Maryland, College of Education.

McCUTCHEN, D., and PERFETTI, C. (1983). Local coherence: Helping young writers manage a complex task. *Elementary School Journal, 84,* 71–75.

MADDEN, N. A., and SLAVIN, R. E. (1983a). Effects of cooperative learning on the social acceptance of mainstreamed academically handicapped students. *Journal of Special Education, 17,* 171–182.

MADDEN, N. A., and SLAVIN, R. E. (1983b). Mainstreaming students with mild academic handicaps: Academic and social outcomes. *Review of Educational Research, 53,* 519–569.

MADDEN, N. A., SLAVIN, R. E., and STEVENS, R. J. (1986). *Cooperative Integrated Reading and*

Comparison: Teacher's manual. Baltimore: Johns Hopkins University, Center for Research on Elementary and Middle Schools.

MEVARECH, Z. R. (1985a). The effects of cooperative mastery learning strategies on mathematics achievement. *Journal of Educational Research, 78,* 372–377.

MEVARECH, Z. R. (1985b, April). Cooperative mastery learning strategies. Paper presented at the annual meeting of the American Educational Research Association, Chicago.

MILLER, R. L. (1976). Individualized instruction in mathematics: A review of research. *Mathematics Teacher, 69,* 345–351.

MOSKOWITZ, J. M., MALVIN, J. H., SCHAEFFER, G. A., and SCHAPS, E. (1983). Evaluation of a cooperative learning strategy. *American Educational Research Journal, 20,* 687–696.

MOSKOWITZ, J. M., MALVIN, J. H., SCHAEFFER, G. A. and SCHAPS, E. (1985). Evaluation of Jigsaw, a cooperative learning technique. *Contemporary Educational Psychology, 10,* 104–112.

MUGNY, B., and DOISE, W. (1978). Socio-cognitive conflict and structuration of individual and collective performances. *European Journal of Social Psychology, 8,* 181–192.

MURRAY, F. B. (1982). Teaching through social conflict. *Contempory Educational Psychology, 7,* 257–271.

MYERS, M., and PARIS, S. (1978). Children's metacognitive knowledge about reading. *Journal of Educational Psychology, 70,* 680–690.

NEWMANN, F. M., and THOMPSON, J. (1987). *Effects of cooperative learning on achievement in secondary schools: A summary of research.* Madison: University of Wisconsin, National Center on Effective Secondary Schools.

OICKLE, E. (1980). A comparison of individual and team learning. Doctoral dissertation, University of Maryland.

OISHI, S. (1983). Effects of team assisted individualization in mathematics on cross-race interactions of elementary school children. Doctoral dissertation, University of Maryland.

OISHI, S., SLAVIN, R. E., and MADDEN, N. A. (1983, April). Effects of student teams and individualized instruction on cross-race and cross-sex friendships. Paper presented at the annual meeting of the American Educational Research Association, Montreal.

OKEBUKOLA, P. A. (1984). In search of a more effective interaction pattern in biology laboratories. *Journal of Biological Education, 18,* 305–308.

OKEBUKOLA, P. A. (1985). The relative effectiveness of cooperativeness and competitive interaction techniques in strengthening students' performance in science classes. *Science Education, 69,* 501–509.

OKEBUKOLA, P. A. (1986a). Impact of extended cooperative and competitive relationships on the performance of students in science. *Human Relations, 39,* 673–682.

OKEBUKOLA, P. A. (1986b). The influence of preferred learning styles on cooperative learning in science. *Science Education, 70,* 509–517.

OKEBUKOLA, P. A. (1986c). The problem of large classes in science: An experiment in co-operative learning. *European Journal of Science Education, 8,* 73–77.

PACE, A. J. (1981, April). Comprehension monitoring by elementary students: When does it occur? Paper presented at the annual meeting of the American Educational Research Association, Los Angeles.

PALINSCAR, A. S., and BROWN, A. L. (1984). Reciprocal teaching of comprehension monitoring activities. *Cognition and Instruction, 2,* 117–175.

PERFETTI, C. A. (1985). *Reading ability.* New York: Oxford University Press.

PERRAULT, R. (1982). An experimental comparison of cooperative learning to noncooperative learning and their effects on cognitive achievement in junior high industrial arts laboratories. Doctoral dissertation, University of Maryland.

PERRET-CLERMONT, A-N. (1980). *Social interaction and cognitive development in children.* London: Academic Press.

PIAGET, J. (1926). *The language and thought of the child.* New York: Harcourt, Brace.

RAPHAEL, T. E. (1980). The effects of metacognitive strategy awareness training on students' question answering behavior. Doctoral dissertation, University of Illinois, Urbana.

RICH, Y., AMIR, Y., and SLAVIN, R. E. (1986). *Instructional strategies for improving children's cross-ethnic relations*. Ramat Gan, Israel: Bar Ilan University, Institute for the Advancement of Social Integration in the Schools.

ROBERTSON, L. (1982). Integrated goal structuring in the elementary school: Cognitive growth in mathematics. Doctoral dissertation, Rutgers University.

RUCKER, C. N., HOWE, C. E., and SNIDER, B. (1969). The participation of retarded children in junior high academic and non-academic regular classes. *Exceptional Children, 26*, 617–623.

RYAN, E. (1982). Identifying and remediating failures in reading comprehension: Toward an instructional approach for poor comprehenders. In G. MacKinnon and T. Walker (eds.), *Advances in Reading Research* (Vol. 3). New York: Academic Press.

RYAN, F., and WHEELER, R. (1977). The effects of cooperative and competitive background experiences of students on the play of a simulation game. *Journal of Educational Research, 70*, 295–299.

SAMUELS, S. J. (1979). The method of repeated readings. *Reading Teacher, 32*, 403–408.

SCARDAMALIA, M., and BEREITER, C. (1986). Research on written composition. In M. C. Wittrock (ed.), *Handbook of research on teaching* (pp. 778–803). New York: Macmillan.

SCHMUCK, R. A., and SCHMUCK, P. A. (1983). *Group Processes in the Classroom*. Dubuque, IA: C. Brown.

SCHOEN, H. L. (1976). Self-paced mathematics instruction: How effective has it been? *Arithmetic Teacher, 23*, 90–96.

SCOTT, R., and MCPARTLAND, J. (1982). Desegregation as national policy: Correlates of racial attitudes. *American Educational Research Journal, 19*, 397–414.

SCRANTON, T., and RYCKMAN, D. (1979). Sociometric status of learning disabled children in an integrative program. *Journal of Learning Disabilities, 12*, 402–407.

SHARAN, S., HERTZ-LAZAROWITZ, R., and ACKERMAN, Z. (1980). Academic achievement of elementary school children in small group vs. whole class instruction. *Journal of Experimental Education, 48*, 125–129.

SHARAN, S., KUSSELL, P., HERTZ-LAZAROWITZ, R., BEJARANO, Y., RAVIV, S., and SHARAN, Y. (1984). *Cooperative learning in the classroom: Research in desegregated schools*. Hillsdale, NJ: Erlbaum.

SHARAN, S., and SHACHAR, C. (1988). *Language and learning in the cooperative classroom*. New York: Springer-Verlag.

SHARAN, S., and SHARAN, Y. (1976). *Small-group teaching*. Englewood Cliffs, NJ: Educational Technology Publications.

SHARAN, Y., and SHARAN, S. (Forthcoming). *Group Investigation: Expanding cooperative learning*.

SHATTUCK, M. (1946). Segregation vs. non-segregation of exceptional children. *Journal of Exceptional Children, 12*, 235–240.

SHERMAN, L. W., and THOMAS, M. (1986). Mathematics achievement in cooperative versus individualistic goal-structured high school classrooms. *Journal of Educational Research, 79*, 169–172.

SHERMAN, L. W., and ZIMMERMAN, D. (1986, November). Cooperative versus competitive reward-structured secondary science classroom achievement. Paper presented at the annual meeting of the School Science and Mathematics Association, Lexington, KY.

SHORT, E., and RYAN, E. (1982). Remediating poor readers' comprehension failures with a story grammar strategy. Paper presented at the annual meeting of the American Educational Research Association, New York.

SIPERSTEIN, G. N., BOPP, M. J., and BAK, J. J. (1978). Social status of learning disabled children. *Journal of Learning Disabilities, 11*, 98–102.

SLAVIN, R. E. (1975). Classroom reward structure: Effects on academic performance, social connectedness, and peer norms. Doctoral dissertation, John Hopkins University.

SLAVIN, R. E. (1977a). Classroom reward structure: An analytic and practical review. *Review of Educational Research, 47*, 633–650.

SLAVIN, R. E. (1977b). A student team approach to teaching adolescents with special emotional and behavioral needs. *Psychology in the Schools, 14* 1, 77–84.

SLAVIN, R. E. (1977c). *Student team learning techniques: Narrowing the achievement gap between the races* (Report No. 228). Baltimore: Johns Hopkins University, Center for Social Organization of Schools.

SLAVIN, R. E. (1978a). Student teams and achievement divisions. *Journal of Research and Development in Education, 12,* 39–49.

SLAVIN, R. E. (1978b). Student teams and comparison among equals: Effects on academic performance and student attitudes. *Journal of Educational Psychology, 70,* 532–538.

SLAVIN, R. E. (1979). Effects of biracial learning teams on cross-racial friendships. *Journal of Educational Psychology, 71,* 381–387.

SLAVIN, R. E. (1980a). Effects of individual learning expectations on student achievement. *Journal of Educational Psychology, 72,* 520–524.

SLAVIN, R. E. (1980b). Effects of student teams and peer tutoring on academic achievement and time on-task. *Journal of Experimental Education, 48,* 252–257.

SLAVIN, R. E. (1980c). Cooperative learning. *Review of Educational Research, 50,* 315–342.

SLAVIN, R. E. (1983a). *Cooperative learning.* New York: Longman.

SLAVIN, R. E. (1983b). When does cooperative learning increase student achievement? *Psychological Bulletin, 94,* 429–445.

SLAVIN, R. E. (1984a). Team assisted individualization: Cooperative learning and individualized instruction in the mainstreamed classroom. *Remedial and Special Education, 5*(6), 33–42.

SLAVIN, R. E. (1984b). Meta-analysis in education: How has it been used? *Educational Researcher, 13*(8), 6–15, 24–27.

SLAVIN, R. E. (1985a). Team-Assisted Individualization: Combining cooperative learning and individualized instruction in mathematics. In R. E. Slavin, S. Sharan, S. Kagan, R. Hertz-Lazarowitz, C. Webb, and R. Schmuck (eds.), *Learning to cooperate, cooperating to learn* (pp. 177–209). New York: Plenum.

SLAVIN, R. E. (1985b). Cooperative learning: Applying contact theory in desegregated schools. *Journal of Social Issues, 41*(3), 45–62.

SLAVIN, R. E. (1986a). *Using Student Team Learning* (3rd ed.). Baltimore: Johns Hopkins University, Center for Research on Elementary and Middle Schools.

SLAVIN, R. E. (1986b). Best-evidence synthesis: An alternative to meta-analytic and traditional reviews. *Educational Researcher, 15*(9), 5–11.

SLAVIN, R. E. (1987a). Mastery learning reconsidered. *Review of Educational Research, 57,* 175–213.

SLAVIN, R. E. (1987b). Cooperative learning: Where behavioral and humanistic approaches to classroom motivation meet. *Elementary School Journal, 88,* 29–37.

SLAVIN, R. E. (1987c). Ability grouping and student achievement in elementary schools: A best-evidence synthesis. *Review of Educational Research, 57,* 293–336.

SLAVIN, R. E. (1989). Cooperative learning and student achievement. In R. E. Slavin (ed.), *School and classroom organization.* Hillsdale, NJ: Erlbaum.

SLAVIN, R. E. (in press). Cooperative learning and achievement: Six theoretical perspectives. In C. Ames and M. L. Maehr (eds.), *Advances in motivation and achievement.* Greenwich, CT: JAI Press.

SLAVIN, R. E., DEVRIES, D. L., and HULTEN, B. H. (1975). *Individual vs. team competition: The interpersonal consequences of academic performance* (Report No. 188). Baltimore: John Hopkins University, Center for Social Organization of Schools.

SLAVIN, R. E., and KARWEIT, N. (1981). Cognitive and affective outcomes of an intensive student team learning experience. *Journal of Experimental Education, 50,* 29–35.

SLAVIN, R. E., and KARWEIT, N. L. (1984). Mastery learning and student teams: A factorial experiment in urban general mathematics classes. *American Educational Research Journal, 21,* 725–736.

SLAVIN, R. E., and KARWEIT, N. L. (1985). Effects of whole-class, ability grouped, and individualized instruction on mathematics achievement. *American Educational Research Journal, 22,* 351–367.

SLAVIN, R. E., LEAVEY, M., and MADDEN, N. A. (1984). Combining cooperative learning and individualized instruction: Effects on student mathematics achievement, attitudes, and behaviors. *Elementary School Journal, 84,* 409–422.

SLAVIN, R. E., LEAVEY, M. B., and MADDEN, N. A. (1986). *Team Accelerated Instruction: Mathematics.* Watertown, MA: Charlesbridge.

SLAVIN, R. E., and MADDEN, N. A. (1979). School practices that improve race relations. *American Educational Research Journal, 16*(2), 169–180.

SLAVIN, R. E., MADDEN, N. A., and LEAVEY, M. (1984). Effects of Team Assisted Individualization on the mathematics achievement of academically handicapped students and nonhandicapped students. *Journal of Educational Psychology, 76,* 813–819.

SLAVIN, R. E., and OICKLE, E. (1981). Effects of cooperative learning teams on student achievement and race relations: Treatment by race interactions. *Sociology of Education, 54,* 174–180.

SLAVIN, R. E., STEVENS, R. J., and MADDEN, N. A. (1988). Accommodating student diversity in reading and writing instruction: A cooperative learning approach. *Remedial and Special Education, 9,* 60–66.

SMITH, K. A., JOHNSON, D. W., and JOHNSON, R. T. (1981). Can conflict be constructive? Controversy versus concurrence seeking in learning groups. *Journal of Educational Psychology, 73,* 651–663.

SOLOMON, D., WATSON, M., SCHAPS, E., BATTISTICH, V., and SOLOMON, J. (in press). Cooperative learning as part of a comprehensive classroom program designed to promote prosocial development. In S. Sharan (ed.), *Recent research on cooperative learning.* New York: Praeger.

STEIN, N. L. and GLENN, C. G. (1979). An analysis of story comprehension in elementary school children. In R. Freedle (ed.), *New directions in discourse processing* (Vol. 2, pp. 53–120). Norwood, NJ: Ablex.

STENDLER, C., DAMRIN, D., and HAINES, A. C. (1951). Studies in cooperation and competition: I. The effects of working for group and individual rewards on the social climate of children's groups. *Journal of Genetic Psychology, 79,* 173–197.

STEVENS, R. J., MADDEN, N. A., SLAVIN, R. E., and FARNISH, A. M. (1987). Cooperative Integrated Reading and Composition: Two field experiments. *Reading Research Quarterly, 22,* 433–454.

STEVENS, R. J., SLAVIN, R. E., FARNISH, A. M., and MADDEN, N. A. (April, 1988). *Effects of cooperative learning and direct instruction in reading comprehension strategies on main idea identification.* Paper presented at the Annual Conference of the American Educational Research Association, New Orleans.

TALMAGE, H., PASCARELLA, E. T., and FORD, S. (1984). The influence of cooperative learning strategies on teacher practices, student perceptions of the learning environment, and academic achievement. *American Educational Research Journal, 21,* 163–179.

THOMAS, E. J. (1957). Effects of facilitative role interdependence on group functioning. *Human Relations, 10,* 347–366.

THURLOW, M., GRODEN, J., YSSELDYKE, J., and ALGOZZINE, R. (1984). Student reading during class: The lost activity in reading instruction. *Journal of Educational Research, 77,* 267–272.

TOMBLIN, E. A., and DAVIS, B. R. (1985). *Technical report of the evaluation of the race/human relations program: A study of cooperative learning environment strategies.* San Diego: San Diego Public Schools.

VAN OUDENHOVEN, J. P., VAN BERKUM, G., and SWEN-KOOPMANS, T. (1987). Effect of cooperation and shared feedback on spelling achievement. *Journal of Educational Psychology, 79,* 92–94.

VAN OUDENHOVEN, J. P., WIERSMA, B., and VAN YPEREN, N. (1987). Effects of cooperation and feedback by fellow pupils on spelling achievement. *European Journal of Psychology of Education, 2,* 83–91.

VEDDER, P. H. (1985). *Cooperative learning: A study on processes and effects of cooperation between primary school children.* The Hague: Stichting Voor Onderzoek Van Het Onderwijs.

VROOM, V. H. (1969). Industrial social psychology. In G. Lindzey and E. Aronson (eds.), *The handbook of social psychology* (Vol. 5, 2nd ed.). Reading, MA: Addison-Wesley.

VYGOTSKY, L. S. (1978). *Mind in Society* (ed. M. Cole, V. John-Steiner, S. Scribner, and E. Souberman). Cambridge, MA: Harvard University Press.

WADSWORTH, B. J. (1984). *Piaget's theory of cognitive and affective development* (3rd ed.). New York: Longman.

WEBB, N. (1985). Student interaction and learning in small groups: A research summary. In R. E. Slavin, S. Sharan, S. Kagan, R. Hertz-Lazarowitz, C. Webb, and R. Schmuck (eds.), *Learning to cooperate, cooperating to learn* (pp. 147–172). New York: Plenum.

WEIGEL, R. H., WISER, P. L., and COOK, S. W. (1975). Impact of cooperative learning experiences on cross-ethnic relations and attitudes. *Journal of Social Issues, 31*(1), 219–245.

WEINER, B. (1979). A theory of motivation for some classroom experiences. *Journal of Educational Psychology, 71,* 3–25.

WEINER, B., and KUKLA, A. (1970). An attributional analysis of achievement motivation. *Journal of Personality and Social Psychology, 15,* 1–20.

WEINSTEIN, C. E. (1982). Training students to use elaboration learning strategies. *Contemporary Educational Psychology, 7,* 301–311.

WHEELER, R., and RYAN, F. L. (1973). Effects of cooperative and competitive classroom environments on the attitudes and achievement of elementary school students engaged in social studies inquiry activities. *Journal of Educational Psychology, 65,* 402–407.

WITTROCK, M. C. (1978). The cognitive movement in instruction. *Educational Psychologist, 13,* 15–29.

YAGER, S., JOHNSON, D. W., and JOHNSON, R. T. (1985). Oral discussion, group-to-individual transfer, and achievement in cooperative learning groups. *Journal of Educational Psychology, 77,* 60–66.

YAGER, S., JOHNSON, R. T., JOHNSON, D. W., and SNIDER, B. (1986). The impact of group processing on achievement in cooperative learning. *Journal of Social Psychology, 126,* 389–397.

ZIEGLER, S. (1981). The effectiveness of cooperative learning teams for increasing cross-ethnic friendship: Additional evidence. *Human Organization, 40,* 264–268.

APPENDIX 1. EXAMPLES OF STAD/TGT WORKSHEETS, GAME SHEETS, AND QUIZZES

LIFE SCIENCE UNIT: LIFE PROCESSES
WORKSHEET: FOOD MAKING, PHOTOSYNTHESIS

Objective: III.5.2 a. Students will identify the steps in the food-making process.

                                       b. Students will compare the light and dark phases of photosynthesis.

Instructions: This worksheet will help you prepare for the Photosynthesis Game/Quiz. Study the diagram on the next page carefully to assist you in answering each item. For items 1–24, choose the correct answer from the choices provided. For items 25–30, write the word or formula that completes the summary of photosynthesis.

Vocabulary: ATP
chlorophyll
dark phase
energy
glucose
light phase
photosynthesis

WORKSHEET: III.5.2 PHOTOSYNTHESIS

**SUMMARY
OF
PHOTOSYNTHESIS**

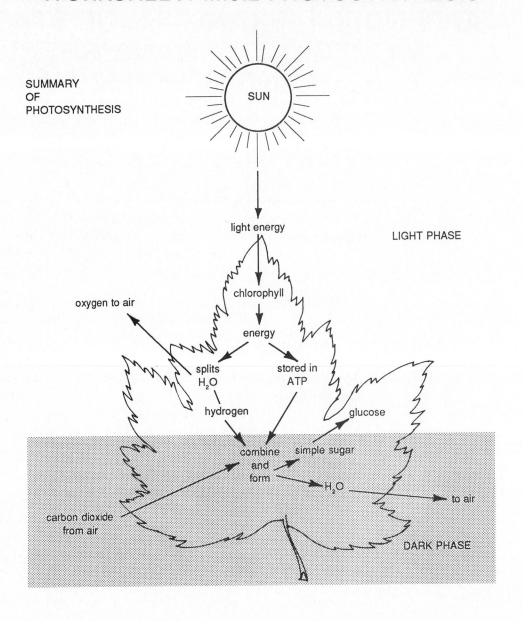

SUN

light energy

LIGHT PHASE

chlorophyll

energy

oxygen to air

splits
H_2O

stored in
ATP

hydrogen

glucose

combine
and
form

simple sugar

H_2O

carbon dioxide
from air

to air

DARK PHASE

WORKSHEET: III.5.2 PHOTOSYNTHESIS

The organ of the plant in which photosynthesis most often takes place is the a. stem b. root c. leaf 1	Plants need which of the following to carry on photosynthesis? a. O_2, CO_2, chlorophyll b. H_2O, CO_2, light energy, chlorophyll c. H_2O, O_2, light energy, sugar 2	The energy stored in plants comes from a. soil b. air c. sunlight 3
The first phase of photosynthesis is sometimes called the a. light phase b. dark phase c. chlorophyll phase 4	The oxygen released during photosynthesis comes from the a. chlorophyll b. carbon dioxide c. water 5	Photosynthesis takes place in the _____ of a plant cell. a. cell wall b. cytoplasm c. chloroplast 6
The energy from the sun is stored in a chemical compound called a. ATP b. CO_2 c. H_2O 7	The second stage of photosynthesis is called the a. light phase b. dark phase c. chlorophyll phase 8	The phase of photosynthesis requiring chlorophyll is the a. light phase b. dark phase c. chlorophyll phase 9
Hydrogen combines with carbon dioxide to make a. starch b. simple sugar c. glucose 10	The energy for the second stage of photosynthesis is stored in a. ATP b. sunlight c. hydrogen 11	Water is released to the air during the a. light phase b. dark phase c. chlorophyll phase 12
Animals depend on green plants for a. oxygen and carbon dioxide b. carbon dioxide and food c. food and oxygen 13	The final products of photosynthesis are a. glucose, O_2, and H_2O vapor b. simple sugar and water c. oxygen and simple sugar 14	Water molecules are split a. in the dark phase b. in the light phase c. in the chlorophyll phase 15

Plants grown in darkness for a time do not develop a. stomata b. roots c. chlorophyll 16	During the light phase of photosynthesis, light energy is converted into a. water b. chloroplast c. chemical energy 17	Using the energy from ATP, hydrogen and carbon dioxide combine during the a. light phase b. dark phase c. chlorophyll phase 18
A substance that is necessary for photosynthesis and is given off as a result of photosynthesis is a. oxygen b. carbon dioxide c. water 19	A final product of photosynthesis released to the atmosphere during the light phase is a. hydrogen b. oxygen c. carbon dioxide 20	The state of photosynthesis that does not require light as a source of energy is the a. chlorophyll phase b. light phase c. dark phase 21
The green compound found in green plants which uses the energy of the sun to split the water molecule is a. chloroplast b. carbon dioxide c. chlorophyll 22	The two final products of photosynthesis produced during the dark phase are a. hydrogen and carbon dioxide b. glucose and water c. oxygen and glucose 23	The source of energy for the dark phase is a. sunlight b. ATP c. chlorophyll 24

Items 25–30: Summarize the entire process of photosynthesis in words.

Green plants containing   chlorophyll + _____ + _____ + _____

                                                     (25)   (26)   (27)

produce   _____ + _____ + _____

                        (28)   (29)   (30)

WORKSHEET ANSWERS:
III.5.2 PHOTOSYNTHESIS

1. (c) leaf
2. (b) H_2O, CO_2, light energy, chlorophyll
3. (c) sunlight
4. (a) light phase
5. (c) water
6. (c) chloroplast
7. (a) ATP
8. (b) dark phase
9. (a) light phase
10. (b) simple sugar
11. (a) ATP
12. (b) dark phase
13. (c) food and oxygen
14. (a) glucose, O_2, and H_2O vapor
15. (b) in the light phase
16. (c) chlorophyll
17. (c) chemical energy
18. (b) dark phase
19. (c) water
20. (b) oxygen
21. (c) dark phase
22. (c) chlorophyll
23. (b) glucose and water
24. (b) ATP
25. carbon dioxide ⎫
26. water   ⎬ any order
27. light energy ⎭
28. glucose ⎫
29. oxygen ⎬ any order
30. water   ⎭

GAME/QUIZ: III.5.2 PHOTOSYNTHESIS

Water is released to the air during the a. light phase b. dark phase c. chlorophyll phase 1	Plants need which of the following to carry on photosynthesis? a. O_2, CO_2, H_2O, chlorophyll b. H_2O, CO_2, light energy, chlorophyll c. H_2O, sugar, O_2, light energy 2	A final product of photosynthesis released to the atmosphere during the light phase is a. hydrogen b. oxygen c. carbon dioxide 3
The first phase of photosynthesis is sometimes called the a. light phase b. dark phase c. chlorophyll phase 4	The oxygen released during photosynthesis comes from the a. chlorophyll b. CO_2 (carbon dioxide) c. water 5	During the light phase of photosynthesis, light energy is converted into a. water b. chloroplast c. chemical energy 6
Animals depend on green plants for a. oxygen and carbon dioxide b. carbon dioxide and food c. food and oxygen 7	The stage of photosynthesis that does not require light as a source of energy is the a. chlorophyll phase b. light phase c. dark phase 8	The phase of photosynthesis requiring chlorophyll is the a. light phase b. dark phase c. chlorophyll phase 9
Hydrogen combines with carbon dioxide to make a. starch b. simple sugar c. glucose 10	The energy for the second stage of photosynthesis is stored in a. ATP b. sunlight c. hydrogen 11	The source of energy for the dark phase is a. sunlight b. ATP c. chlorophyll 12
A substance that is necessary for photosynthesis and is given off as a result of photosynthesis is a. oxygen b. carbon dioxide c. water 13	The final products of photosynthesis are a. glucose, H_2O vapor, and O_2 b. simple sugar and water c. oxygen and simple sugar 14	Water molecules are split a. in the dark phase b. in the light phase c. in the chlorophyll phase 15

GAME/QUIZ ANSWERS: III.5.2 PHOTOSYNTHESIS

1. (b) dark phase
2. (b) H_2O, CO_2, light energy, chlorophyll
3. (b) oxygen
4. (a) light phase
5. (c) water
6. (c) chemical energy
7. (c) food and oxygen
8. (c) dark phase
9. (a) light phase
10. (b) simple sugar
11. (a) ATP
12. (b) ATP
13. (c) water
14. (a) glucose, H_2O vapor, and O_2
15. (b) in the light phase

STUDENT TEAM LEARNING
SUBJECT: MATHEMATICS
WORKSHEET: W-16: PERCENT

Topics: fractions
decimals and percents
percent of a number

Fill in the blank:

1. $\frac{5}{8}$ = _____%
2. .233 = _____%
3. $4\frac{7}{8}$ = _____%
4. $\frac{3}{1000}$ = _____%
5. $\frac{16}{25}$ = _____%

Fill in the blank:

16. 24 = _____% of 96
17. 6 = 48% of _____
18. _____ = 125% of 86
19. .5 = _____% of 20
20. 15 = .2% of _____

Write as a mixed
number or fraction
in lowest terms:

6. 28%
7. 105%
8. .72%
9. $2\frac{1}{5}$%
10. 7.5%

Fill in the blank:

21. _____ = .2% of 2.5
22. 12 = _____% of 3
23. 5.76 = 6% of _____
24. _____ = 140% of 60
25. 3.5 = _____% of 40

Write as a decimal:

11. 342%
12. $6\frac{1}{2}$%
13. $27\frac{1}{9}$%
14. 4.63%
15. $\frac{1}{8}$%

---

26. John borrowed $175 from the bank at an interest rate of 10% per year. What is the *total* amount John would owe the bank if he paid the money back 18 months later?

27. Sally studied her history lesson for 15 minutes, did math problems for 20 minutes, and spent $1\frac{1}{2}$ hours writing her English composition. What percentage of time did she spend on her math problems?

28. If it cost the jewelry store $15 to make a ring, and they sold the ring for $30, their profit would be what percent of their costs?

29. 2 tablespoons of peanut butter contain 9 grams of protein. This equals 15% of your body's recommended daily allowance of protein. How many grams of protein does your body need daily?

30. 2 tablespoons of peanut butter also contain .8% of your body's recommended daily allowance of vitamin A. How many tablespoons of peanut butter would you have to eat to give your body its total recommended daily allowance of vitamin A?

WORKSHEET ANSWERS:
SUBJECT: MATHEMATICS
W-16: PERCENT

1. 62.5%
2. 23.3%
3. 487.5%
4. .3%
5. 64%
6. $7/25$
7. $1 1/20$
8. $9/1250$
9. $11/500$
10. $3/40$
11. 3.42
12. .065
13. $.27\overline{11}$
14. .0463
15. .00125
16. 25%
17. 12.5
18. 107.5
19. 2.5%
20. 7500

21. .005
22. 400%
23. 96
24. 84
25. $8 3/4$% or 8.75%
26. $201.25
27. 16%
28. 100%
29. 60 grams
30. 250 tablespoons

STUDENT TEAM LEARNING
SUBJECT: MATHEMATICS
GAME/QUIZ: W-16: PERCENT

Fill in the blank:

1. $^7/_{25}$ = _____%
2. 7.293 = _____%
3. $3^5/_{16}$ = _____%
4. $^1/_{250}$ = _____%
5. $2^2/_{125}$ = _____%

Fill in the blank:

16. 2.2 = _____% of 50
17. 3 = .5% of _____
18. _____ = 250% of 42
19. 280 = _____% of 70
20. 21 = 25% of _____

Write as a mixed number or fraction in lowest terms:

6. 320%
7. .25%
8. $30^2/_5$%
9. 480%
10. 6.5%

Fill in the blank:

21. _____ = 170% of 6
22. .4 = _____% of 20
23. .6 = .5% of _____
24. _____ = .2% of 70
25. 7 = _____% of 8

Write as a decimal:

11. .35%
12. 428%
13. 32.7%
14. $3^1/_4$%
15. $20^5/_8$%

26. It costs $4 to manufacture a pair of gloves. At the store, the gloves are sold for $11. What is the percent of profit made compared with the manufacturing cost?

27. One serving of Cheerios contains 3.9 grams of protein. The recommended daily allowance of protein is 60 grams. Therefore, one serving of Cheerios contains what percent of the recommended daily allowance of protein?

28. A Martian weighing 19 pounds on Mars would weight 50 pounds on Earth. The weight on Mars is what percent of the weight on Earth?

29. David borrowed $180 from the bank and agreed to pay 10% interest per year. When it was time to pay the bank back, he owed a total amount of $225. David borrowed the money for how many years?

30. Susan bought a radio priced at $28. The sales tax was 7% of the price. What was the total amount Susan had to pay for the radio?

GAME/QUIZ ANSWERS:
SUBJECT: MATHEMATICS
W-16 PERCENT

1. 28%
2. 729.3%
3. 331.25%
4. .4%
5. 201.6%
6. $3\frac{1}{5}$
7. $\frac{1}{400}$
8. $\frac{38}{125}$
9. $4\frac{4}{5}$
10. $\frac{13}{200}$
11. .0035
12. 4.28
13. .327
14. .0325
15. .20625
16. 4.4%
17. 600
18. 105
19. 400%
20. 84
21. 10.2
22. 2%
23. 120
24. .14
25. 87.5%
26. 175%
27. 6.5%
28. 38%
29. 2.5 years
30. $29.96

STUDENT TEAM LEARNING SUBJECT: INTERMEDIATE LANGUAGE ARTS WORKSHEET: OBJECTIVE XIII: COMPOUND SENTENCES

Topics: Form compound sentences from two independent clauses using coordinating and correlative conjunctions or by using a semicolon.
Identify the correct use of coordinating and correlative conjunctions in compound sentences.
Correctly punctuate compound sentences.

Introduction: This worksheet will help prepare you for the *Compound Sentences* Game/Quiz.

1. A compound sentence consists of two or more simple sentences joined together.
2. They are joined either with coordinating conjunctions or with correlative conjunctions.
3. Coordinating conjunctions used in compound sentences are: and, but, or, nor, for, yet
    Example: Terri loves to go swimming, but she doesn't like to go to swimming class.
4. Correlative conjunctions are always used in pairs. The most common correlative conjunctions used in compound sentences are *either–or* and *neither–nor*.
    Example: Either you take back what you said, or I will not stay here tonight.
5. A compound sentence can also be formed without a conjunction by using a semicolon.
    Example: One of my favorite sports is hockey. Another is baseball.

    One of my favorite sports is hockey; another is baseball.

Instructions: Correctly punctuate the following compound sentences.

1. I studied all day but I failed the test.
2. Provide an example from you own experience or provide one from your textbook.
3. It rained all day and it thundered all night.
4. Sally understood the problem but she raised her hand to ask a question.
5. He cleans and she cooks.
6. Either Mr. Jones was not trying hard enough or he was having bad luck.
7. Every time I took the test I failed but I kept taking it.
8. My uncle gave me advice about fishing but I did not listen to him.
9. Elm Street is lined with maples and Maple Street is lined with elms.
10. Alice worked hard in school for she was eager to learn.

Instructions: Correctly combine the simple sentences into a compound sentence by using a semicolon.

11. We had to leave Fluffy at home.
    Grandma doesn't like cats.

12. I feel sorry for Jill.
     She doesn't have a pet.
13. It wasn't an old movie I saw.
     It was a television special.
14. I didn't say a word about the party.
     It was supposed to be a surprise.
15. The builder had to begin again.
     The owner had changed his mind about the style of the house.

Instructions: Correctly combine the simple sentences into a compound sentence, using the coordinate or correlative conjunction indicated.

16. I studied very hard for the test.
     I didn't do as well as I had hoped.   (but)
17. Jack drove fast on the way to the airport.
     He wanted to be on time to meet Ellen.   (for)
18. David goes to California each winter.
     Harriet flies to Bermuda.   (and)
19. Bill and Frank weren't home that night.
     They had both gone to sleep.   (either . . . or)
20. I may not like Jimmy very much.
     I am sorry he is not feeling well.   (but)

Instructions: Choose the conjunction which correctly completes the sentence.

21. He says he wants to help you, _____ he is not sincere.   (and, but)
22. Either the store on the corner was closed on Sunday, _____ the owner was out to lunch.   (nor, or)
23. He took the test again, _____ he failed it the first time.   (for, yet)
24. Alice wrote the letter yesterday _____ she mailed it today.   (nor, and)
25. Either Sally works downtown _____ she goes to school there.   (for, or)

Instructions: Decide whether the conjunctions in the following sentences are coordinate or correlative.

26. I have never played the tuba, nor do I wish to.
27. You buy the candy and I'll buy the soda.
28. Either the winning team played very well, or the losing team played very badly.
29. Neither did the Americans want to sign the treaty, nor did the British.
30. I ate the fruit and he ate the vegetables.

WORKSHEET ANSWERS
SUBJECT: INTERMEDIATE
LANGUAGE ARTS
OBJECTIVE XIII: COMPOUND SENTENCES

1. I studied all day, but I failed the test.
2. Provide an example from your own experience, or provide one from your textbook.
3. It rained all day and it thundered all night.
4. Sally understood the problem, but she raised her hand to ask a question.
5. He cleans and she cooks.
6. Either Mr.Jones was not trying hard enough, or he was having bad luck.
7. Every time I took the test I failed, but I kept taking it.
8. My uncle gave me advice about fishing, but I did not listen to him.
9. Elm Street is lined with maples, and Maple Street is lined with elms.
10. Alice worked hard in school, for she was eager to learn.
11. We had to leave Fluffy at home; Grandma doesn't like cats.
12. I feel sorry for Jill; she doesn't have a pet.
13. It wasn't an old movie I saw; it was a television special.
14. I didn't say a word about the party; it was supposed to be a surprise.
15. The builder had to begin again; the owner had changed his mind about the style of the house.
16. I studied very hard for the test, but I didn't do as well as I had hoped.
17. Jack drove fast on the way to the airport, for he wanted to be on time to meet Ellen.
18. David goes to California each winter, and Harriet flies to Bermuda.
19. Either Bill and Frank weren't home that night, or they had both gone to sleep.
20. I may not like Jimmy very much, but I am sorry he is not feeling well.
21. but
22. or
23. for
24. and
25. or
26. coordinate
27. coordinate
28. correlative
29. correlative
30. coordinate

STUDENT TEAM LEARNING
SUBJECT: INTERMEDIATE
LANGUAGE ARTS
GAME/QUIZ: OBJECTIVE XIII:
COMPOUND SENTENCES

Instructions: Correctly punctuate the following compound sentences.

1. He likes catsup on hamburgers but on hot dogs he likes mustard.
2. Jimmy lives in the country and he plays in the woods.
3. Either the lightbulb burned out or the switch is not working.
4. Neither did the girls play basketball nor did they go hiking.
5. To get exercise, Dorothy plays tennis for an hour or she swims for two hours.
6. I have studied the problem for two days yet I have not come up with a solution.
7. Either there will be food at the picnic or there will be a trip to McDonald's at lunchtime.
8. Donna arrived early for she didn't want to miss the opening ceremonies.
9. Mr. Goldsmith tried the front door but it was locked.
10. Eddie will not work after school nor will he work on weekends.

Instructions: Correctly combine the simple sentences into a compound sentence by using a semicolon.

11. Roy liked the spotted dog best.
    It reminded him of Spooky.
12. Martha passed the test.
    She did not miss a single question.
13. Don't be afraid of the dog.
    His bark is worse than his bite.
14. It wasn't a flying saucer that you saw.
    It was a shooting star.
15. I prefer the red candy.
    It tastes sweeter.

Instructions: Correctly combine the simple sentences into a compound sentence using the coordinate or correlative conjunction indicated.

16. Billy never goes to the movies.
    Donald goes every week.   (but)
17. David opened the door on his way out.
    It was never closed.   (either . . . or)
18. He followed the map exactly.
    He got lost.   (yet)
19. Tommy's uncle caught the fish.
    Tommy cleaned and cooked them.   (and)
20. We waited for a long time.
    The bus was late.   (for)

Instructions: Choose the conjunction which correctly completes the sentence.

21. He wanted to work all day _____ he got sick.   (and, but)
22. Either he never sent the money, _____ the letter was lost in transit.   (yet, or)
23. Julie wrote the letter late at night _____ she mailed it the next morning.   (or, and)
24. Either the movie wasn't funny, _____ I was not in the mood for humor.   (or, and)
25. Darrell practiced every day, _____ he wanted to make the team.   (for, yet)

Instructions: Decide whether the conjunctions in the following sentences are coordinate or correlative.

26. Steve will never be rich, nor will he be famous.
27. Either the Smiths will come over tonight, or the Joneses will invite us over.
28. I must cut the lawn or I will be punished.
29. No one came to the wedding, but hundreds of people showed up for the reception.
30. Neither of the victims reported the accident, nor did they wait for the police.

GAME/QUIZ ANSWERS
SUBJECT: INTERMEDIATE
LANGUAGE ARTS
OBJECTIVE XIII: COMPOUND
SENTENCES

1.   He likes catsup on hamburgers, but on hot dogs he likes mustard.
2.   Jimmy lives in the country and he plays in the woods.
3.   Either the lightbulb burned out, or the switch is not working.
4.   Neither did the girls play basketball, nor did they go hiking.
5.   To get exercise, Dorothy plays tennis for an hour or she swims for two hours.
6.   I have studied the problem for two days, yet I have not come up with a solution.
7.   Either there will be food at the picnic, or there will be a trip to McDonald's at lunchtime.
8.   Donna arrived early, for she didn't want to miss the opening ceremonies.
9.   Mr. Goldsmith tried the front door, but it was locked.
10. Eddie will not work after school, nor will he work on weekends.
11. Roy liked the spotted dog best; it reminded him of Spooky.
12. Martha passed the test; she did not miss a single question.
13. Don't be afraid of the dog; his bark is worse than his bite.
14. It wasn't a flying saucer that you saw; it was a shooting star.
15. I prefer the red candy; it tastes sweeter.
16. Billy never goes to the movies, but Donald goes every week.
17. Either David opened the door on his way out, or it was never closed.
18. He followed the map exactly, yet he got lost.
19. Tommy's uncle caught the fish, and Tommy cleaned and cooked them.
20. We waited for a long time, for the bus was late.
21. but
22. or
23. and
24. or
25. for
26. coordinate
27. correlative
28. coordinate
29. coordinate
30. correlative

APPENDIX 2

TEAM SUMMARY SHEET

TEAM NAME _____

Team Members	1	2	3	4	5	6	7	8	9	10	11	12	13	14
Total Team Score														
Team Average*														
Team Award														

*Team average = total team score ÷ number of team members.

APPENDIX 3

QUIZ SCORE SHEET (STAD AND JIGSAW II)

Student	Date: Quiz: Base Score	Quiz Score	Improvement Points	Date: Quiz: Base Score	Quiz Score	Improvement Points	Date: Quiz: Base Score	Quiz Score	Improvement Points

APPENDIX 4

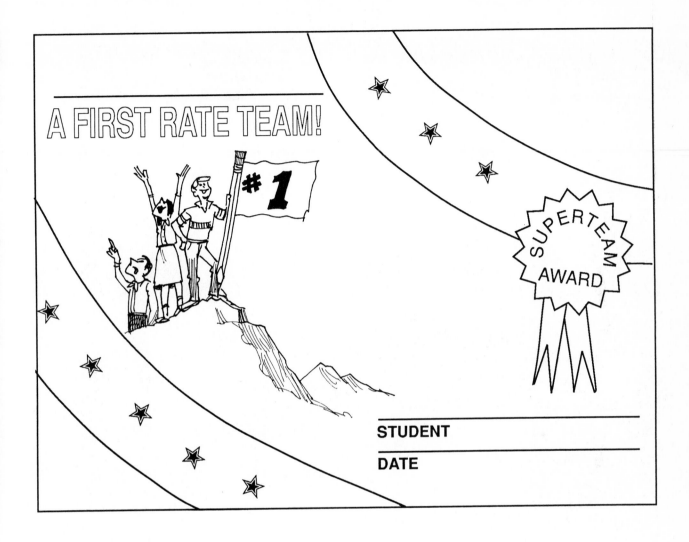

A GREET TEAM

Team

did a GREAT JOB this week

Date

A GREAT TEAM!

TEAM

did a GREAT JOB this week

DATE

A GREAT TEAM!

TEAM

did a GREAT JOB this week

DATE

APPENDIX 5

TOURNAMENT TABLE ASSIGNMENT SHEET (TGT)

Tournament Number:

Student	Team	1	2	3	4	5	6	7	8	9	10	11	12	13

APPENDIX 6

TABLE # _____   GAME SCORE SHEET (TGT)   ROUND # _____

Player	Team	Game 1	Game 2	Game 3	Day's Total	Tournament Points

TABLE # _____   GAME SCORE SHEET (TGT)   ROUND # _____

Player	Team	Game 1	Game 2	Game 3	Day's Total	Tournament Points

TABLE # _____   GAME SCORE SHEET (TGT)   ROUND # _____

Player	Team	Game 1	Game 2	Game 3	Day's Total	Tournament Points

TABLE # _____   GAME SCORE SHEET (TGT)   ROUND # _____

Player	Team	Game 1	Game 2	Game 3	Day's Total	Tournament Points

APPENDIX 7. EXAMPLE OF A JIGSAW II UNIT

STUDENT TEAM LEARNING
SUBJECT: UNITED STATES HISTORY
EXPERT SHEET: THE CHALLENGES AND RESPONSIBILITIES OF WORLD POWER

1. What was the Cold War and how did it begin?
2. How successful was the United States in preventing the spread of communism?
3. Why did the Korean War break out and how was it settled?
4. Describe the civil rights movement and what Martin Luther King, Jr., is famous for.

For discussion: Do you think U.S. policy toward the Soviets following World War II was right, or should we have done things differently? What do you think American policy should be toward the Soviets today? Should we depend more on military strength, negotiation, or both?

STUDENT TEAM LEARNING
SUBJECT: UNITED STATES HISTORY
QUIZ: THE CHALLENGES AND
RESPONSIBILITIES OF WORLD POWER

1. After World War II, the two most powerful nations in the world were:
    a. the Soviet Union and Germany.
    b. the U.S. and the Soviet Union.
    c. the Soviet Union and Japan.
    d. Great Britain and the U.S.
2. The Cold War began because:
    a. the United States began to turn against Communist governments.
    b. the Germans tried to rearm.
    c. Winston Churchill introduced the concept of the "iron curtain."
    d. the Soviet Union took control of Eastern Europe and threatened other countries.
3. A satellite country is one which:
    a. enters into a treaty with several others.
    b. has a space exploration program.
    c. is small, and controlled or influenced by a larger country.
    d. is formed by a violent revolution.
4. The Berlin blockade:
    a. was set up by the U.S. to drive the Soviets out of that city.
    b. was set up by the Soviets to drive other nations out of that city.
    c. was successful in keeping the necessities of life away from Berliners.
    d. has never been lifted.
5. Why was NATO formed?
    a. To strengthen the Soviet Union and her satellites.
    b. To help lessen Communist pressure on Western European nations.
    c. To write a peace treaty with Germany.
    d. To establish a larger world peace organization, the United Nations.
6. The revolution in China ended with:
    a. the establishment of Taiwan as a Communist nation.
    b. a huge victory for non-Communists.
    c. the Soviet-backed Communists defeating the Nationalists.
    d. China being divided among several larger nations.
7. The Korean War began when:
    a. the U.S. sent troops to Korea.
    b. South Koreans invaded the North.
    c. Chinese troops attacked American soldiers.
    d. North Koreans invaded the South.
8. Aid for the South Koreans in their fight against North Korean communism:
    a. was provided by the United States, as well as other U.N. countries.
    b. was never sent.
    c. was sent by the Soviet Union and its satellites.
    d. was provided by the Chinese.

9. As a result of the Korean War:
   a. communism in Southeast Asia retreated.
   b. South Korea began to decline economically.
   c. the Korean border remained where it was originally.
   d. the U.S. occupied large areas of China.

10. Martin Luther King, Jr., was:
    a. a great fighter for the rights of black people.
    b. a leader of the civil rights movement.
    c. a leader of demonstrations for black equality who was assassinated.
    d. all of the above.

11. The civil rights movement sought to achieve:
    a. better working conditions in the factories for blacks.
    b. social, political, and educational equality for blacks.
    c. a level of violence that would let the whites know the power of the blacks.
    d. equality for all women and especially their right to vote.

12. Martin Luther King, Jr., succeeded in all his goals for equal rights except:
    a. economic equality for women and minorities.
    b. desegregation in public facilities and schools.
    c. the right of blacks to vote freely, without fear of injury.
    d. spreading the word about human rights and the meaning of freedom to many people.

STUDENT TEAM LEARNING SUBJECT: UNITED STATES HISTORY QUIZ ANSWERS: THE CHALLENGES AND RESPONSIBILITIES OF WORLD POWER

1. b
2. d
3. c
4. b
5. b
6. c
7. d
8. a
9. c
10. d
11. b
12. a

Index